THE MASTER DIRECTOR

Gurudev

THE MASTER DIRECTOR

A JOURNEY THROUGH
POLITICS, DOUBT & DEVOTION
WITH A HIMALAYAN MASTER

THOMAS K. SHOR

City Lion Press Edition

This book was originally
published by HarperCollins in 2014
Cover design: Arijit Ganguly

ISBN: 9780999291832

I dedicate this book
to the Master Director himself,
without whom this story would not be.

Other Books by Thomas K. Shor:

(see page 297 for details)

Prose:

A STEP AWAY FROM PARADISE:
THE TRUE STORY OF A TIBETAN LAMA'S JOURNEY
TO A LAND OF IMMORTALITY
(Penguin 2011 & City Lion Press 2017)

INTO THE HANDS OF THE UNKNOWN
AN INDIAN SOJOURN WITH A HARVARD RENUNCIANT
BEING PART II OF *WINDBLOWN CLOUDS*
(Escape Media Publishers 2003, Pilgrims Publishers 2013
City Lion Press 2019)

THE MONK AND THE SLY CHICKPEA
TRAVELS ON CORFU
BEING PART I OF *WINDBLOWN CLOUDS*
(Escape Media Publishers 2003, City Lion Press 2019)

LEOPARD IN THE CITY
AN URBAN FABLE
(City Lion Press 2018)

Photography Books:

SCULPTURE GARDEN OF THE GODS
ANIMATED LANDSCAPE PHOTOGRAPHY FROM
THE GREEK ISLAND OF IKARIA
(City Lion Press 2018)

GANGES LAMENT
BLACK AND WHITE PHOTOGRAPHIC PORTRAITS
FROM THE SACRED INDIAN CITY OF VARANASI
(City Lion Press 2018)

CONTENTS

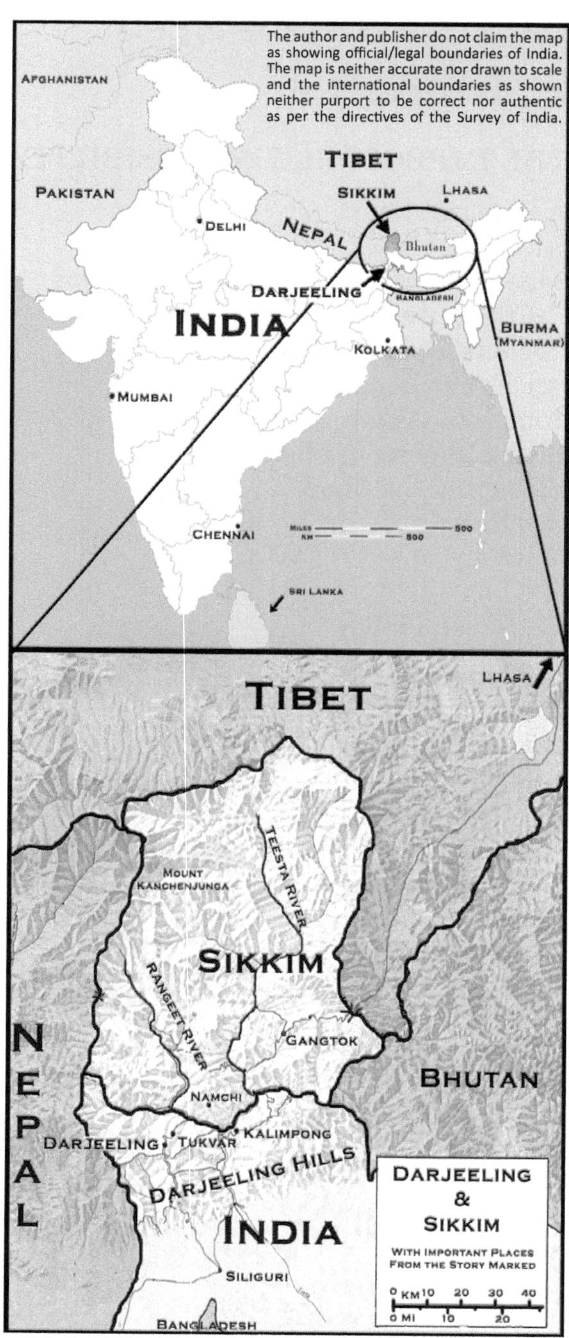

Map of Darjeeling and Sikkim, showing the main places where the story takes place

PROLOGUE

THE GREAT ESCAPE

This sign for a mobile phone company in the rubble of Darjeeling took on new meaning during my final days there

It is a scene of mass exodus. Jeeps stuffed beyond capacity, buses with their roofs heavily laden with suitcases, boxes and men, and flatbed trucks packed with frightened people clog the narrow road south out of Darjeeling, trying to reach the safety of the north Indian plains.

I'm right in the middle of it, hanging onto the back of a jeep, trying to buck the flow and actually enter the city. We turn a corner and there, inching across the road like a phantom of the past, belching rhythmic jets of white steam and clouds of black coal smoke, is Darjeeling's British-era narrow gauge 'toy' train, also leaving town. Its tracks run along the twisting road and cross it often, as if the colonial past is still entwined with the present. It adds another layer of chaos to the madness. In Darjeeling, the past seems always to be impacting the present, usually impeding the way.

With the way blocked, the drivers cut their engines to save fuel, which is in short supply. I let my gaze go beyond the passing tumult and I am struck, as always, by the beauty of the place. Darjeeling, a hill station in India's eastern Himalayas, was built by the British upon a mountain ridge that ends abruptly at its northern end where the land drops thousands of feet through steep-sloped tea gardens to the river at the bottom, marking the border with Sikkim. From Darjeeling, Sikkim appears as a series of wooded ridges rising to the razor-sharp heights of the Kanchenjunga Massif—a mass of snow peaks dominated by the powerful presence of the third highest mountain on the planet, Mount Kanchenjunga. Darjeeling's northern horizon is a sharp jagged line of shining snow peaks marking the border with Tibet. There is peace in Darjeeling, but it seems always just beyond reach.

I jump off the jeep when I reach the market. I shoulder my way through the crowd and start climbing to the centre of town. I'm after my bag, which I've left with a friend. There are only four hours left until the eight-hour break in the siege ends and it all starts up again. No one can say how long it will last. For the past two weeks, everything has been ordered closed: a shopkeeper caught selling as much as a potato would have been beaten and his shop torched. Till now, fleeing has been impossible since vehicles have been prohibited from plying the roads. Some have tried to defy the ban by putting a cross of red tape on their windshields and claiming they are ambulances, but the goons who patrol the roads have caught on and started beating the drivers. Supplies have run dangerously low.

This is not what I came to Darjeeling for. It was the spring of 2001, and I had come at the new year with the expectation of staying for some time and slowly immersing myself in the place. I hoped a writing project would emerge from it. My interest was Himalayan culture, especially its spiritual traditions. I wasn't interested in the politics, which I knew was dark. But it seems you can't escape politics in the Darjeeling Hills. In Darjeeling, you have to go down before you can go up. This is the second time I've had to flee. The first time, about six weeks ago, I fled immediately when the troubles began. When I heard it was quiet again I returned, but it turned out it was only a lull.

What I call a siege is really a bandh, or a strike, called by Subash Ghising, the political leader of Darjeeling, who recently survived a brutal assassination attempt. Some say the attack has left him in a disturbed state of mind. Like a madman putting a gun to his own children's heads to get what he wants, he has ordered everything—from government offices, post offices, banks, shops, schools, tea gardens, transportation, restaurants, hotels, and whatever else you can think of throughout the Darjeeling Hills—closed, and has proceeded to starve his own 'constituency' to assert his demand, which he claims is to pressure the government to catch his would-be assassins. No one believes his motives: they say he is taking the opportunity to pressure the government into rounding up those who oppose him and throw them in jail, which he has them doing. Ghising announced only yesterday that there will be a relaxation of the strike today from 8 a.m. till 4 p.m. so that those who want to get out can do so, and those who don't can stock up on food and provisions for the ongoing siege.

Schools, for which Darjeeling is famous, including the British-era boarding schools, have been closed and now the outstation pupils have been ordered to leave. Students in school ties and jackets with insignias of Saint Paul's and Saint Joseph's, Mount Hermon and Loreto College, are all pushing down the hill towards the jeep stand, weighed down by huge duffel bags and suitcases.

Tourists who were ignorant enough to blunder into Darjeeling before the siege began have spent the past two weeks huddled in their hotel rooms. They are fleeing too, the young Westerners with their backpacks and the Indians with huge suitcases and porters to carry them. Everyone fears being left behind with no way out of a situation that is turning increasingly violent. The road is clogged with escaping vehicles, their horns blaring. People are throwing themselves at the drivers, who are exacting exorbitant fares.

While all these visitors to Darjeeling—the 'Queen of the Hills' as it is popularly known—are like a tide rolling down the town's steep roads, the citizens of Darjeeling are rapidly emptying the market of every sack of rice and scrap of food, every candle and drop of cooking fuel left in town. People are paying increasingly exorbitant prices for the remaining scraps. As the porters drop the tourists and students at the jeep stand, they are then hired to carry goods against the tide of those fleeing, back up the hill to people's houses. With hardly a day's reserve of money or food under the best of circumstances, the two-week bandh has brought many porters to the brink of starvation.

Though I decided to weather the storm this time, within days I regretted my decision and decided to escape again. But by then the roads were closed and there was no way out. A few days ago the mood in Darjeeling turned especially ugly after a homemade bomb went off next to the courthouse. So I took refuge in a Tibetan Buddhist monastery just on the outskirts. It was peaceful there, but still I couldn't leave. Food was running low, and I knew I'd become a burden. Last night, a tinny loudspeaker strapped to a jeep driving past the monastery's gate informed us of today's temporary relaxation of the bandh. Now I am pushing against all those escaping, so that I can retrieve my bag and join the exodus, if there are any vehicles left.

I grab my bag and make my way back towards the market, walking a knife-edge, knowing I am approaching a major fork in the road. I could go south with the exodus for the safety of the north Indian plains. This would be prudent, and it is what I did last time. But if I flee the mountains again, I will probably give up the entire enterprise and never return. I also contemplate going north to Sikkim, the formerly independent Tibetan Buddhist Himalayan kingdom. The only problem is that Sikkim, now a part of India, is ringed on three sides by a horseshoe of high snow peaks at the edge of the Tibetan Plateau. The passes have been closed since the 1962 border war between India and China. The only roads in or out of Sikkim are from the south and go through the Darjeeling Hills. Therefore, when Darjeeling is closed, supplies to Sikkim are cut off as well, and there is no way out. During the last strike, the army was forced to evacuate tourists from Sikkim by helicopter.

At the bottom of Nehru Road, a young guy in a black T-shirt and reflecting sunglasses stands beside what must be the last unoccupied vehicle in town, a beat-up Maruti van. It's as if he's been waiting for me. He sees my bags and asks if I want a ride. 'Siliguri? Sikkim? I take you.'

As I said, there are only two options, up or down.

I hear my voice say, 'Sikkim.'

At the edge of town, there is chaos at the petrol station as vehicles crowd around the pumps, trying to get petrol before it runs dry. There are so many vehicles that they spill onto the road, clogging it. Since we need petrol to get to the border, we have no choice but to nose our way into that tight knot of vehicles. Drivers are abandoning their vehicles and elbowing their way to the two available pumps with cans, water bottles—anything that will hold liquid.

Three hours later I am dumped at the bridge that marks the border with Sikkim. I walk across the bridge, which is strewn with colourful Tibetan prayer flags, and pass beneath the Tibetan-style gateway into Sikkim. It is difficult at first to realize that I am back in a land of peace. It is also a land of spectacular natural beauty.

PART I

THE IMPECCABLE IMPOSSIBILITY

1

INTO THE IMPERIAL COURT

I am led into the presence of the man the entire village has been filling my ears about, telling me he isn't really a human being but a god. He is clad in the burgundy robes of a Tibetan lama and his large head is shaved, its shape reminiscent not so much of a god, but of a Hollywood alien. The smile on his face is at once friendly, intense, and infectious. In the few hours I've been in this tea-pluckers' village on the slopes of Sikkim's sacred Tendong Hill, I have heard stories of his divine childhood, his miracles, and his ability to be in two places at the same time. Let me introduce myself. My name is Thomas and, like the Thomas of the Bible, I am a doubter.

They call him Gurudev, and he motions for me to sit on the little couch opposite him. It is a bedroom done up especially for his visit, the other furniture having been taken out. Flowers are strewn all around and the bed is adorned like a throne, a woven Tibetan rug spread over it. The walls are made of planks and there are gaps between them, chinks open to the night.

A barefoot woman, dressed in a green sari with the end draped over her head, enters the room, a look of rapture upon her face. She is carrying Gurudev's tea, the cup held at the level of her forehead as a sign of respect. After offering it to him, she backs out of the room with palms pressed together and head bowed, as if he were a king. People are massed outside, peering in through the open door, observing Gurudev's every move. And though the night is cool and it has been raining, his attendant, a young man with large glasses named Dawa, is fanning him with a piece of cardboard.

Gurudev is regarding me silently, the smile on his face so self-assured, the choreography of the scene around him so perfect, that I begin to wonder whether I *have* just entered the court of a king. Yet something seems absurd, if not an illusion altogether, for the fan is made of cardboard and not peacock feathers, as would befit a potentate; his throne is but a rug on a bed; his subjects are tea pluckers gathered from the surrounding wood-plank houses. The word 'surreal' surfaces in my mind.

Dawa often put a piece of leaf on the bridge of his nose to steady his glasses

Gurudev has a look of sheer delight on his face as he reaches for a cloth sack. Dawa puts down the piece of cardboard he has been fanning him with and holds the sack open. Gurudev reaches into the sack and takes out an ornate ceremonial lamp made of copper and brass, which he hands to me. It is suddenly a solemn moment.

I look to Dawa for guidance. He motions that I am to receive it. So I lean forward and, with bowed head, receive the lamp. A murmur arises from the people crowded at the door.

Dawa can see my confusion. 'Take it home,' he whispers. 'It is a present.'

Gurudev reaches into his bag again and takes out a block of Tibetan tea pressed into the shape of a bell. He holds it out to me. Again, I lean forward and receive it in what I hope is the culturally appropriate manner. In this part of the world, if one has to hand something to someone or to receive, one does so with the right hand. One places one's left fingertips gently on one's right forearm.

When I look up, he is holding out a handful of the juniper needles used as incense. I take them and stuff them in my shirt pocket. Then he hands me a bar of scented soap. A moment later he hands me a bottle of germicidal liquid, two metal tea strainers, a plastic soap container, a bag of rice, two handfuls of brown Tibetan rock salt, a bag of table salt, a handful of litchi nuts, an apple, and a hat.

He goes on to open a cloth sack filled with rocks that he has picked up somewhere along the road, and gives me one. All this is done with the utmost of courtly ceremony, heads bowed, palms pressed. It is as if these are holy relics, gifts offered to an emissary of a distant land. While he has been giving these things to me, the people at the door have quietly come in and taken their seats on the floor, trying to get as close to him as possible, their eyes gazing intently at everything he does as if at any moment a miracle might occur or a mystery be revealed. With over thirty people watching, he reaches into the folds of his robes and takes out a wad of money. With a finger to his lips, he hands it to me and indicates that I should pocket it discreetly.

Someone produces two bamboo baskets and fills them with my presents. I had wandered into this village on foot. Am I now supposed to start walking in the mountains with baskets containing blocks of rock salt and stones?

The woman with the tea returns, her head bowed, another cup held at the level of her forehead. She presents it to me as if it were a bejewelled crown on a velvet pillow. I take the cup and Gurudev lifts his. He has been waiting for mine to arrive. He takes a sip, looks me in the eye, winks, and bursts out laughing.

Gurudev breaks a piece of a flowering branch from a vase on the low table before him. He holds it up and, with Dawa interpreting, tells me how it cures headaches and brings down a fever. He breaks off a sprig and holds it out to me. As I take the dripping sprig, he motions that I am to put it in my shirt pocket. So I stuff it in with the juniper needles. He explains the medicinal qualities of a few other flowers. Soon, my pockets are all bulging and soggy with medicinal herbs.

Gurudev puts his hand on Dawa's shoulder and pulls him closer. With their heads bent close together in a conspiratorial way, their hands covering their mouths for privacy, Gurudev gives Dawa instructions. As he does so, Dawa looks at me, his eyes sparkling. Then, Dawa dashes from the room and runs out of the house barefoot, without a jacket, into the rainy night. He returns drenched some minutes later, holding a flowering plant, mud dripping from its ball of roots. It was for this that Gurudev had sent him into the night. Dawa has the most delightful smile as a puddle forms beneath him, his glasses fogged and dripping. He gives the plant to Gurudev. Gurudev speaks,

The woman who brought me tea

and Dawa interprets: 'He is saying if you cut yourself, you can use this plant to stop the bleeding.' Gurudev takes a leaf, crushes it between his fingers, rubs it on an imaginary cut and wags his head to emphasize its potency. He tells me what it's called and then gestures for me to write it down, which I do in my pocket notebook. He is pleased I have a notebook; and from that time onward, he often indicates that I write something down—the name of a plant or a place, a date, a word in Nepali or a Buddhist term. It is as if he already knows I am a writer, and knows—even before I know it myself—that I will be writing about him and should start keeping notes.

The entire time, an impossible number of people are entering the room with gifts for Gurudev—ceremonial scarves, sacks of rice, envelopes containing money, a stack of wooden bowls, washing powder, a tightly bound bundle of hand towels—things exactly as varied, incongruous, and random as the things Gurudev had given me. They lay them on the low table before him and bow, some touching their foreheads to the table's edge.

An old man comes in and prostrates himself on the wooden floor before Gurudev with tremendous fervour. Gurudev yawns in an almost exaggerated manner, raises a great ball of phlegm with a horrendous, gurgling sound and spits it into a white plastic bucket that has been put beside him expressly for the purpose. The man gets to his feet and proceeds to prostrate himself two more times. As he does so, Gurudev lets his gaze pass over the heads of the people packed together on the floor and looks into my eyes with an intense and intimate look, at once ironic and above it all, edging on bemusement. It is as if he is taking me into his confidence, offering me a glimpse behind the role he is playing. I have the distinct impression he is inviting me to witness the show with detachment—as he apparently must, in the face of such devotion.

Before stepping into this room, I had never been in the presence of someone shown such a royal respect. We can all imagine what it might be like for, say, the queen of England or for the Pope or maybe some African dictator. But we don't meet these people, certainly not up close, and have tea with them. I feel deeply honoured to be granted the intimacy he seems to be offering.

A young man in black dungarees comes in. His hair is falling over his eyes and he is wearing a tricoloured T-shirt with an image of Bob Marley superimposed on a cannabis leaf. He bows before Gurudev in a perfunctory way. Gurudev grabs him by the shirt and wraps a ceremonial scarf around his head as if it were a bandanna. He picks up a large red flower, tucks it into the scarf over his right temple, and laughs as if somebody's tickled his belly. The laughter soon spreads through the room. He sends the young man out for a large clay bowl of water, which the man then places on the floor in front of Gurudev's throne. A mound of flowers has accumulated on either side of Gurudev, and now he throws them into the water one by one, delighted each time one goes 'plop'. He reminds me of a baby playing in its bath. I look around, and the room is full of looks of enchantment and wonder.

Gurudev breaks into song. Everyone starts clapping and making room as the man with the Bob Marley T-shirt stands up and does a traditional Nepali dance. Thick incense wafts in from the other room where Tibetan Buddhist monks are chanting, blowing horns, banging drums, and crashing cymbals like long rolls of thunder. The rain is pounding the corrugated metal roof and cascading down the windows in thick furrows. The village is enshrouded in the thickest cloud, accentuating my feeling that I have entered a world whose coordinates cannot be found on any map.

When the song is over, at some signal I don't see, everybody gets up to leave, bowing, touching their heads to the edge of Gurudev's bed and backing out of the room so as not to turn their backs to him. I too get up to leave, but Dawa indicates for me to stay. When everyone else has left, Dawa closes the door. It is just Dawa, Gurudev and I in the room. Gurudev speaks in Nepali to Dawa, and Dawa interprets. 'He is saying that you have come very far to get here. There are so many foreigners, and millions of Americans. He is asking how is it that you out of all of them have come to this village this night and to this very house.'

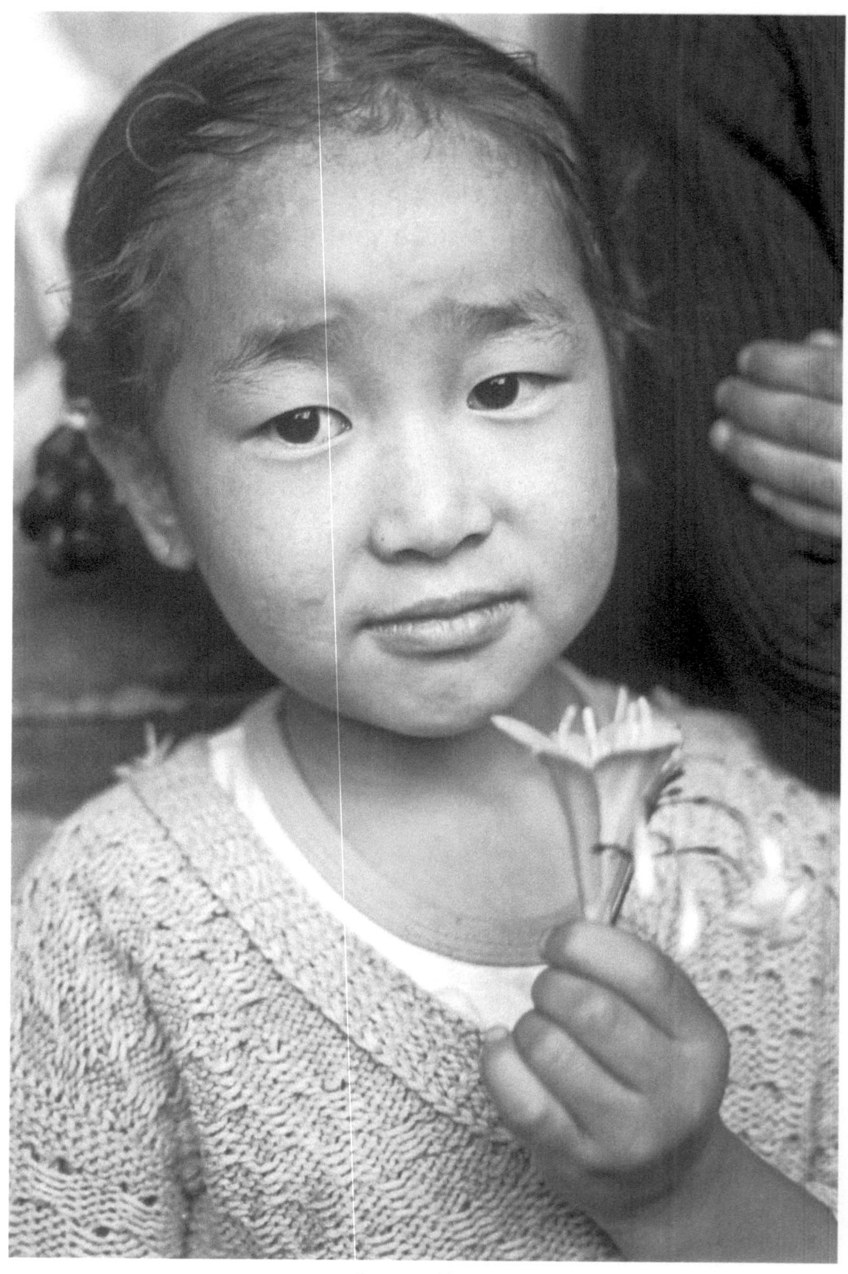

Flower offering

2

HOTEL STAY PUT

How to explain my improbable presence in that tea pluckers' house on a cloud-enshrouded Himalayan slope? For sure, it was a long road from my suburban Boston beginnings. Though born into a loving, close family, I had always known that I didn't belong to the world into which I was born. Perhaps the fact that at a very young age I had a fascination for astronomy and preferred to look beyond the earth's atmosphere to those wondrous heavenly bodies—along with the fact that I stuttered—tells it all. While feeling out of place in my world as a child, I accepted it as fact as an adult and set out to find a place more resonant. My trajectory has been constant. As an adult, I've travelled and lived in many places.

Yet how to answer Gurudev's question? The Buddha taught that there is no single, independent cause for anything, that everything is linked together in a vast net. And, as with everything else, there are the immediate causes and there are those that are more distant, even in time—yet are of no less importance. Heraclitus said that character is destiny. The whole is reflected in every part. Every step, every fork in the road, every situation we've been in and every decision we've made determines what is to come.

My journey to India began with surrender. It was 3 a.m. and I was being driven through the slums surrounding

Mumbai's international airport after a flight so long, travelling across so many time zones, that I had seen the moon rise twice from the same seat. Though I had been to India before, one's arrival in India can be a jolt. And I was being driven by a man I was beginning to suspect was not, in fact, the man from Hotel Stay Put. If the ride were to end at Hotel Stay Put, or with my throat cut in a back alley, there was little I could do now. To the opportunistic thugs who descend on India's international airports, unsuspecting tourists arriving from overseas must seem like fatted pigs ready for slaughter, ripe for ensnaring in their nefarious scams.

Having passed through immigration and customs, I had stopped at the government tourist information stall. The young guy behind the counter looked out of place. Wearing dark glasses despite the late hour and the low-wattage neon lights, a greasy black jacket with an insignia for the United States Army, and bright yellow plastic slippers, he looked like one of the thugs waiting outside the airport rather than the government's man mandated to protect tourists from them.

When I asked if he could confirm the hotel reservation I had made via a crackly transcontinental phone line with a man who spoke no English, he convinced me that Hotel Stay Put was closer to the airport, was a better hotel for a better price, and it would send a man around to drive me there for no extra charge. Although fully aware that his advice was hardly neutral since a booking meant he would get a kickback, I decided to go with his advice. He called the hotel and told me to wait—their driver would come for me.

The hotel must have been just round the corner, for it seemed but a moment later that there was a knock on the frosted-glass window on the back wall of the tourist information stall, which must have opened to the parking lot. The clerk opened the window and spoke to a man there in the darkness. Then, as the man poked his head in through the window, he said, 'This is your driver. Go to the front exit and he will be waiting for you there.'

I braced myself as I approached that door where the restricted space of the airport met the Indian subcontinent, where—despite the hour—a throng of taxi drivers, touts, expectant relatives, beggars, people holding placards with names scrawled on them, petty thieves, con artists, curious onlookers and what seemed half the population of Mumbai clawed at each other as if they believed that by placing themselves at the front of that crowd they would be first in line for the only life raft on a sinking ship.

Hugging my bags and alert to hands in my pockets, I girded myself for my passage to India, which was heralded by a buzz of activity akin to when a bee from one hive lands at the entrance to another. And pressing through that door, every bit as tight as the birth canal, a chorus arose: 'Taxi—taxi!' 'Hotel, good price,' 'Change money, very-good-rate.' It was then I realized that in my jet-lag stupor I hadn't taken note of what the driver looked like. Fending off all those who would sell me something, take me somewhere, or engage me in their schemes, I passed through the knot at the door.

A young man approached me with a look akin to recognition.

'Hotel Stay Put?' I asked.

'Hotel Stay Put. Yes, I drive you there.'

I followed him out of the building and across the wide road, away from the other taxis and under a row of palms whose shredded fronds were silhouetted against the orange petrochemical glow of the Mumbai night. We crossed an empty lot and I realized my tactical error. *I* had given *him* the name of the hotel, and now I'd never know whether he was in fact the man from the hotel. He looked for all the world like a cut-throat tout.

When we arrived at his car, not only was it parked in darkness and lacked the hotel's name on the door, but it was also a dented old wreck. Three young guys smoking cigarettes tumbled out of the car when we arrived. One of them, a barefoot man in a ripped brown T-shirt that had once been white, opened the trunk for my bags. I indicated that I would carry them with me. Then he held the back door open with a gap-toothed grin. I threw my bags in and sat down next to them, the door shutting behind me. Instinctively, I looked for the inside door handles, but they had been removed. I rolled the window down, but its track was broken and it would only go halfway. 'Let me out,' I said. 'I want to sit in front.' By this time the driver was in his seat and the motor was running. 'Front seat no good,' he said, and he demonstrated how the seat was loose on its moorings. I think the guy with the ripped T-shirt had wanted to sit in front. But I held firm and, after a considerable exchange between the two in the local language, during which I made clear that I would raise a stink, his friend pulled the handle from the outside with the benevolent look of a jailor releasing an inmate before the end of his sentence. I got in the front, sickly sweet smoke wafting over me from a stick of incense that burned before a plastic statue glued to the dashboard; it was the dancing Shiva, lord of creation and destruction.

The streets were deserted but for figures sleeping under dirty strips of cloth that looked like well-used burial shrouds. We turned onto a road, one side of which had a long trench dug into it. A line of dark-skinned men in dirty loincloths with picks and shovels were digging through the Mumbai night, their muscles glistening in the dull glow of hissing gas lights. It looked as if they were doing the night shift in hell.

We turned again, this time into an alley through which it was highly improbable that an airport hotel would lie. Hotel

Stay Put. I tried not to think of sinister implications. A pack of mangy mongrel dogs tried first to block our way and then to bite holes in our tyres. Failing that, they fell behind, yapping at the back fender, escorting us through their territory.

Given my state of exhaustion, it was easy to surrender.

My plan was to get over my jet lag in Mumbai and then continue on to Delhi. From Delhi I would take a train across the country to West Bengal, then a jeep into the foothills of the eastern Himalayas and go up to Darjeeling. While my choice of Darjeeling was not arbitrary, I knew little about the place except that it was heavily influenced by Himalayan Buddhist culture. Somehow, a writing project would result.

That was my plan. Yet I was acutely aware of the power of the unforeseen. No matter how much we plan, we do not know the outcome of events. Don't they say we should meet our fate with equanimity? I tried to remember that as we turned a corner into another and even darker alley. At the end of the alley the car stopped. The driver got out. We were at Hotel Stay Put.

3

PILGRIMAGE IN SEARCH OF THE PRESENT MOMENT

My journey in Sikkim was equally marked by a sense of surrender. When I was dumped at the border after escaping from Darjeeling, I left the bulk of my belongings at a hotel in the Sikkimese capital, Gangtok, and simply started wandering. With neither a map nor much more than a change of clothes, I set forth into the wooded foothills of Mount Kanchenjunga with the express aim of having no aim. Setting out purposefully to have no purpose, I went on a sort of pilgrimage to nowhere. The mountains were beautiful and high, the people kind and gentle. Sikkim was an excellent place to make such an experiment in present living.

I walked in the spirit of Edmond Spencer. I had come to India for the first time twenty years earlier at the age of twenty-two with Ed, who taught me a lot about walking. Seventy years old at the time, he was an ex-Harvard professor who had given up everything in the West years earlier for a life of walking through India as a wandering ascetic. Within an hour of meeting him on a Greek ferry, during which time he had asked me probing questions as if he were plumbing my depths, he had turned to me and said, 'I think you should come with me to India.' And so it was that my first trip to India was at the invitation of this powerful and brilliant renunciant from New Jersey. I wrote about my journey with him in my first book, *Windblown Clouds*. Even though our ways were ultimately different, he had instilled something in me. He left his indelible mark. It was with a nod to Ed Spencer, who had died in the intervening years, that upon arrival in Sikkim I simply set out on foot without knowing where my next meal would come from or where I would sleep that night.

To set out with a very light pack, just one change of clothes and no destination is a little like stepping off the face of the earth. The first time it can be scary, like plunging into deep waters. When you find that it is the nature of water to buoy you, you can learn to delight in it. Once you let go, you are governed by pure chance and you are then open to the experience of unprecedented good fortune.

As a seeker with nothing to seek, a traveller without destination, my wish was simply to fully experience the present moment, which never becomes the future and never was the past. From the start, each moment unfolded into a beautiful vignette—be it a smile on a face or a tight little thunderhead rushing up a valley just as I discovered a small cave in which I could take shelter, as if the mountains themselves were providing me refuge and upholding me. Later, a cloud was clinging to a mountainside with a waterfall flowing through it. The cloud simply rose into the diamond-blue sky and disappeared, leaving the cascading water glistening. By opening to the moment, the moment simply unfolded, and everything took on the quality of that passing cloud.

From Darjeeling, Mount Kanchenjunga rose pristine and white in the distance as if emerging out of the sky itself, since the intervening lower mountains and valleys of Sikkim were lost in a blue haze indistinguishable from the sky. From

Darjeeling, the mountain appeared to rise out of the sky itself, entirely transcendent.

Mount Kanchenjunga from the town of Darjeeling

Now that I was in Sikkim, not only was I in the land that had been lost in that haze but I was also in the land that actually ascended to such tremendous heights. Mount Kanchenjunga dominated the landscape, a huge silent presence piercing the sky. It stood above these wooded mountains dotted with villages, terraced fields of grain and corn, and innumerable cascading streams. I was overcome with a sense of imminence. From here, the land rose naturally to heights beyond the reach of other places.

Few can hope to experience the simplicity of the unfolding Now all the time. All we can hope for are glimpses. There have always been those rare individuals who have lived continuously and effortlessly in the present moment. They tend to make enigmatic statements about how the truth is simpler than we can imagine with our complicating minds. They point out that to fully realize the condition we're already in—riding the wave of the continuously unfolding present moment—is really very simple; it is in fact far simpler than upholding the artifices of Past and Future. They employ paradox to trick the mind out of its habituated ruts.

Some sit in meditation and let the reality of the present moment surface. Others, like the Sufis, engage in ecstatic dance. And yet others imbibe mind-altering drugs. Another way of coming fully to the experience of the unfettered Now, which I find quite effective, is to wander without design. It is a radical, practical and concrete way of letting go of both the past and the future.

On a conventional pilgrimage the pilgrim feels some lack that needs fulfilling by going to a holy place or by encountering a holy man. On such a pilgrimage, the pilgrim marks his progress step by step, and then he arrives. The pilgrimage I set out on, in search of the present moment, was different. I realized that there was no way off the razor's edge; the present moment continuously unfolds, and one is always right *there*.

Buddhists do a circuit of the holy places of the Buddha—his place of birth, enlightenment, where he first taught, and where he died. Tibetans go to Mount Kailash. Hindus go to Varanasi and Vrindaban. Muslims go to Mecca. Christians go to Lourdes, St. Peters and Fátima. Innumerable tribal peoples go to a sacred mountain, a large rock or a river.

A pilgrimage in search of the present moment is a pilgrimage for awareness. To borrow a spatial analogy, we're already there. Only we aren't aware of it. When we're not aware of it, we think there's something we lack, something we have to *do*. We think in terms of mathematics. We think we have to add or subtract something from the present moment to be happy. But nothing can be taken from, or added to, what is.

As I walked, I made this pilgrimage my meditation. I passed through a forest, asking myself when was the last time I did something in the future. Say I decide to do something tomorrow afternoon; I have to wait until tomorrow afternoon becomes the present moment. And I've never done anything in the past. Even though I had spent six months planning my trip to India and arrived a month ago, when I got there it was also the present moment. How to deny this basic truth? I came upon a huge outcropping of rock from which I watched an eagle soar. When is the last time an eagle fell out of the sky because he realized he was flying in a medium that was invisible?

On my first night out, the monks at a Tibetan monastery extended their hospitality to me. The next morning I walked through a small market town and then took a road that passed through a forest of pine trees. On the other side of the forest, I reached a clearing—a village of woodcutters. Schoolchildren swarmed around with broad, toothy smiles at the sight of me. Beyond the village, the road clung to the side of a mountain and turned a corner over a 2,000-foot drop. It was a landscape on a grand scale, too vast to echo my exuberant shouts of joy. I was on the road and happy, with no idea where I was going. Without an expectation in my head, without a notion, I was free!

As I continued walking, I passed a small village straddling a ridge. Beyond the village, I came upon a slab of rock on the side of the road. Painted on it was a sign informing me that I was at the sacred Tendong Hill.

This is what was written on the implausible sign:

SIKKIM FOREST DEPARTMENT WELCOME TO ECODEVELOPMENT TENDONG NATURE RESERVE A MYSTIC HOLY TABOO HILLS AND TOP PLACES OF SPIRITUAL REFRESHMENT ABODE OF NATURE'S BOUNTY TREASURIES OF LIFE BIOLOGICAL HARBORIUM, DYNAMIC LANDSCAPES, MAGNIFICENT SCENERY AND QUALITIES OF REMOTENESS AND WILDERNESS A PERFECT DESTINATION AND SOLACE TO NATURALISTS, RAMBLERS, PILGRIMS, ADVENTURERS, TREKKERS, VACATIONERS, TOURISTS AND PUBLIC

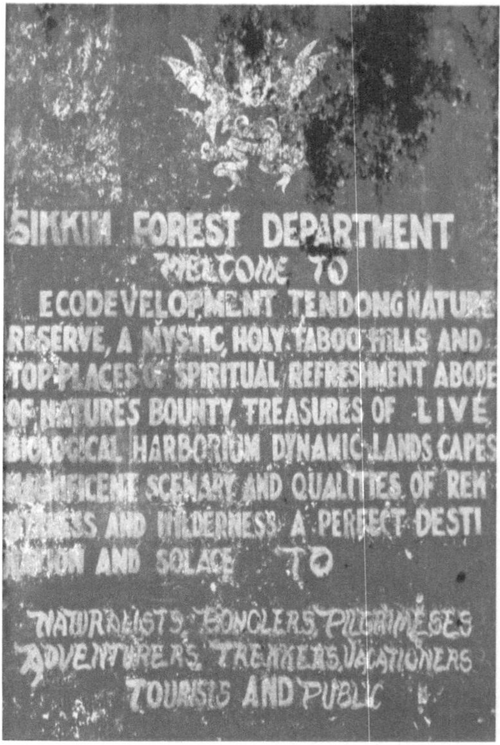

The sign

The road forked here and went round this 'mystic holy taboo hill,' and even though I was an aimless wanderer, I had to choose which way to go. I went left on a winding road that passed through a forest of ancient trees, which were hung with moss and vines and full of orchids. Then I came upon a young Tibetan Buddhist monk dressed in burgundy robes, walking with a village man who was leading a long-haired black goat with a bell around its neck. The man with the goat asked if I was going to Timi.

'Is this the road to Timi?' I asked.

'Yes it is,' he said.

'Then I'm going to Timi.'

'You are lucky,' he said. 'This monk is also going there. He speaks no English, but if you follow him, he will take you. By road it is far, but he is taking a shortcut straight down the mountain.' And though 'shortcut' loses its meaning when you have no destination—begging the question of shortcut to *where*—I agreed to follow him.

As if on cue, the monk plunged off the side of the road on a footpath I hadn't seen that angled down the side of the mountain. Barely did I have time to thank the man with the goat when the last fold of the monk's robes disappeared round the first bend of the path. I scampered after him down the path that wound through thick jungle, skirting cascading waterfalls and huge outcroppings of rock. He looked back only once or twice, more out of curiosity, it seemed, than out of concern for whether I was still there. Perhaps his friend hadn't had the chance to inform him that he was to be my guide. I think he was wondering why I was following him.

We came to the edge of cultivated fields. The monk left the path and started snaking between fields of vegetables, potatoes, and corn. I followed him. An old woman was using a heavy stick to break the clods of earth left behind by a wooden plough pulled by a team of oxen. She put her stick down and straightened herself, her thick gray braid falling to the small of her back. Her grandson, a toddler who had been sitting on the earth playing with a stone, got up and stood beside her. They pressed their palms together and inclined their heads as the monk passed. Beyond the fields was a village, and beyond that a hillside rising in tea bushes. While most of the hills of Darjeeling were long ago denuded of trees to create tea gardens, Timi is the only tea garden in Sikkim.

I followed the monk into the village, unsure if I should keep following him. We were passing through people's yards now, ducking beneath drying clothes, scattering chickens along the packed dirt paths. He stopped in front of a wood-slat house and went inside.

I was standing there awkwardly, wondering what to do, when a man came out of the house.

'Is there a town of Timi somewhere down there?' I asked, pointing vaguely further down the mountain's steep slope. 'Somewhere where I could maybe stay the night?'

The man's face lit up with a smile that was at once mischievous and full of delight.

'You are lucky today,' he said. 'You don't know how lucky. You can stay here, in our house. You are lucky because Gurudev is coming!'

'Who?'

'Gurudev,' he replied. 'Is it possible you haven't heard of him? He is a living master, a teacher, our guru. He's a Tibetan lama, a rinpoche, a famous reincarnation. He is coming this evening and staying in this very house. And now, so will you.'

He took me by the elbow. 'You cannot possibly know your luck!' he repeated. 'Come, come—you must be tired and hungry.'

I was brought into the house with a great surge of excitement, put on a bed in the middle of the living room, and handed a cup of tea and a plate of biscuits. It was a big room, the main room of the house. The monk I had followed joined three other young monks who were already busy preparing for Gurudev's arrival by making *torma*, ritual objects fashioned from coloured dough. Through the back door I could see huge cauldrons of food hanging over wood fires.

'You cannot possibly know your luck!'

There was an almost electric buzz as the entire village converged on the house.

As day turned to evening, excitement built. Darkness

fell, and with it came heavy rain. Tension grew as the rain falling on the sheet-metal roof, with a deafening roar, cascaded into the ever-growing muddy torrent flowing by the house. Roads would be washed out. Every noise in the night, every cracking of a branch in the gusting wind, brought a knot of people to the door. They peered hopefully into the cloud this mountain slope was enshrouded in for the distant glow of the jeep's bobbing headlights.

Then he arrived. So many people pressed forward that I couldn't even see him enter. They whisked him into an adjoining room. It was after some time that his attendant came out and announced that the lama would see me.

And thus it is that I find myself in that room, sitting before him, explaining my pilgrimage in search of the present moment, how I have been walking with the specific aim of having no aim, no destination, and it is in this way—purely by chance—and on my second day in Sikkim, that I happen on this house. As Dawa interprets my words, I watch Gurudev closely. He is like a child, the delight he feels registering on his face without artifice.

Gurudev searches for English words. He bursts out laughing. 'No destination,' he says. 'No looking—finding!' He runs his hand over the stubble on his shaved head and hands me a mango.

Gurudev with a lamb

4

MASTER OF DISGUISES

Master of Disguises

They put me in the room next to Gurudev's that first night, and while I lie there on the cotton mattress awaiting sleep I can hear through the thin wood-slat walls everything that happens in the room of the living god. With Gurudev in the house, there is no mistaking it. He punctuates the silence with a variety of abrupt and loud noises heard throughout the house.

Some are vocal, like his sudden calls of 'Hooooe!' They seem to come at random intervals, and their purpose is as unknown and mysterious as the grunts of an exotic animal that one might capture and put up for the night. Perhaps, like an animal's call, they merely proclaim and affirm his existence. Other noises he makes are not vocal, though no less loud and abrupt. They are produced by the regurgitation of huge balls of phlegm, which he then expels with an exaggerated sound into a plastic bucket, which responds with a loud and resonate thud. I can barely hear him whispering with his attendant one minute, then shouting out an order the next. And, lest the shouted order should echo too long in anyone's mind, he invariably follows that with a bout of laughter. Then another 'Hooooe!'

The juxtaposition of sounds emanating from his room is strange, exotic, and somehow comforting. I cannot help but toy with the idea that next door *is* a man of another order, discovered in this tea pluckers' village as if a meteorite had fallen on the earth. Wouldn't these tea pluckers, with their simple mix of Hindu and Buddhist folk religion, worship in their own way a star found in their midst? Why should their beliefs colour what was actually found? It would be easy to dismiss Gurudev on the evidence of his disciples who, in the short time I'd been there, had told me far too many stories of his divine miracles. Yet I've had this strange feeling from the start that he is inviting me to see through the game he is playing and to perceive what lies beyond, as if he manufactures the illusion around him in order to dispel it—and by doing so, gives a profound teaching about the nature of reality.

I lie there in the darkened room with my eyes closed, listening. The walls are so thin that it is as if we are all sleeping in one big room. Behind another wall, the four young monks finish their evening chants, unroll mats on the floor, and become quiet as they lie down to sleep.

In Gurudev's room, I hear Dawa settle down to sleep too. It is only when I hear Gurudev's rhythmic breathing that I lose consciousness of that hillside village and fall into the deep sleep that comes after a long day of trekking.

The morning is announced not by the rising sun, but by Gurudev performing his ablutions in the predawn. He rinses his mouth with water and spits it with gusto into what must be a plastic washbasin. The monks in the next room receive their tea, which they slurp loudly, after which they start chanting and clashing cymbals. There is an eager patter of bare feet on the wooden floors, and then I hear soft voices in Gurudev's room. The dawn announces itself through fine strips of light between the walls' wooden planks through which also come the sounds of crowd gathering outside, punctuated by excited children's voices. A little girl holding a flower opens the outer door of my room, gasps as she sees me lying there, and quickly closes the door again. They have to pass through my room on the way to Gurudev's. Then comes the sound of people pressing against that outside door, as if the pressure of their wish to see Gurudev might force it open.

The door to Gurudev's room opens and Dawa calls me in. Gurudev is sitting cross-legged on his bed and has me sit on the couch. Before him is a low table upon which are numerous bowls of water, rice, fruits, and incense. The woman of the house comes in with a cup of tea for Gurudev held above her forehead and places it before him. He dips the tip of his ring finger in and sprinkles some drops into the air for the gods. The outer door to my bedroom opens and the people rush in. Since they haven't yet been given permission to enter Gurudev's room, they mass at the door to his room. Each is holding a flower and has a huge smile, watching closely every move he makes.

Soon, I am also offered a cup of tea. The door is then closed and I am alone with Gurudev. We drink tea in silence. His presence is immense; the atmosphere practically hums, as if in the proximity of an electrical transformer. Who is this man?

Dawa comes in with a bowl of biscuits for Gurudev. Gurudev takes one, then has Dawa hand me the bowl. As Dawa offers me the biscuits, he has a huge smile. He explains in an excited whisper that since the biscuits have been given to Gurudev, they are blessed. Now that Gurudev is giving them to me, Dawa wants me to understand that I am receiving a tremendous blessing.

Then he interprets for Gurudev. 'Gurudev is saying that he will be in this village for three days, and he is inviting you to stay.' Then he adds in a softer voice, 'You *must* say yes!'

It takes little to convince me to stay. It is rather like having a ringside seat at the greatest show on earth, there as the

The author with Gurudev at Timi

personal guest of the ringmaster himself. A constant stream of people converges on the house. People from farther and farther away, some even as far as Gangtok, are getting wind of Gurudev's presence here.

There is a constant ebb and flow of people in Gurudev's room. One minute it is packed with people, the next moment it is empty, though I never quite understand why. Then a few people are allowed back in and the door is closed. Suddenly, the door will swing open again and, within seconds, an impossible number of people will be squeezed in on the floor. Often, I am allowed to stay when everyone else is asked to leave. The flow of people in and out of the room is orchestrated by Gurudev, and his ways seem as mysterious to everyone else as they do to me. He has complete command of both the script and actors. Every time Dawa ushers me into Gurudev's presence he whispers, with a twinkle in his eye, 'You're so *lucky*!'

Later on my journey, I will meet a man who had first heard of Gurudev twenty years before. He had always wanted to meet Gurudev but had been unable, no matter how he tried, even to catch a glimpse of him: circumstances always conspired to make it impossible.

I never could have set out to meet Gurudev; if it had been my aim to search such a one out, I would have been unable to draw close.

I have the distinct impression that although Gurudev is the constant centre of the whirl that surrounds him and though others take his role seriously, he stands at the centre weaving his spell, the only one aware that it is all only a show. And although he looks at me sometimes over the heads of the others as if inviting me into his confidence, I hardly feel up to the task; despite my best intentions, I find myself falling in and out of his spell. Yet what is he really doing? He is constantly being offered presents—vegetables and sacks of rice, money, bars of soap for washing clothes, and other strangely incongruous things—and he hands those presents out again, transformed by the blessing of having passed through his hands. He is like a vast transforming vortex for people's energies.

That afternoon, they clear Gurudev's room so that he can take a nap. Some time later, I am sitting outside speaking with a retired schoolteacher in a tweed jacket holding a small bouquet of flowers for Gurudev. He had walked three hours to reach the village when he'd heard Gurudev had come. He is telling me stories of Gurudev's childhood, how he was born in 1944 and is presently fifty-six years of age; how, when he was a child, he was put in jail for releasing all the cows and sheep of his village; and how he used to go up to Darjeeling riding backwards on a donkey.

Gurudev, as a child

I am talking with the schoolteacher when Dawa comes and whispers in my ear, 'Get ready, we'll be leaving soon.' To go where, I don't know, but he has the usual twinkle in his eye as if to say, 'Your luck continues!' The young monks come out of the house blowing horns and holding metal buckets billowing with clouds of incense. Everybody lines up on the path leading to the waiting jeep; there must be eighty people there. Then Gurudev appears at the door.

There is a collective intake of breath and the pressing together of palms, as if everyone has just been afforded a vision of a god. The way Gurudev stands at the threshold, his chest proudly pushed out as an attendant arranges the folds of his robes over his shoulder before he sets forth, I sense that he is consciously acting, though no one else can see it. They are all under his spell. I feel myself standing outside it, observing; yet he comports himself with such aplomb that I suddenly have to wonder whether a human being actually *could* have the ability to manifest the divine in his person. Perhaps it is only the eyes of the one looking that would have to be transformed.

Gurudev starts walking between the double line of devotees. When he gets to me, he smiles. Putting his hand on my shoulder, he draws me close and has me walk with him through the adoring throng to the waiting vehicle. He affords me, for those few steps, a glimpse of what it looks like from his perspective.

They place Gurudev on the front seat, which has a handwoven Tibetan rug on it. There is a yellow towel tied over the headrest. The back door opens and I am ushered inside. Dawa jumps in next to me, then two others squeeze in. Someone opens the jeep's rear gate and four more people jump in.

By now the crowd is gathered outside Gurudev's window, and as the driver starts the engine they bow deeply at the passing of their master, guru, and incarnate god.

We head down the bumpy dirt road, splashing through the puddles from last night's rain, and pass through the low tea bushes. Gurudev turns around and looks at us with utter delight; like a child he is happy in the moment, just to be moving.

Dawa tells me Gurudev didn't always travel in a vehicle. He used to go on foot from place to place, sometimes alone, sometimes with devotees, and they would walk for weeks at a time, passing—as he does now—a night, sometimes three, at people's homes throughout Darjeeling and Sikkim. The delight Gurudev takes in simply moving mirrors what I have been feeling on my pilgrimage in search of the present moment.

We follow the switchback road up through the tea garden and then enter a forest with a clearing, where some people are selling vegetables on the side of the road. We stop and Dawa jumps out and goes to Gurudev's open window. Gurudev instructs Dawa what to buy. A young man gets out from the back and helps Dawa with the bundles of spinach, green-topped carrots, and armfuls of huge squash. Those squeezed in the back are now packed in with enough vegetables to open a small stall.

We ascend through another series of hairpin turns until we come upon a family walking on the side of the road. Gurudev tells the driver to stop. When they see it's Gurudev, even the toddler strapped with a blanket to his mother's back puts his palms together and lifts his hands to his forehead as they approach Gurudev's window. Soon we are all conveying bundles of vegetables up to Gurudev, who hands them to the villagers through his open window. These simple gifts are received as blessed, having come directly from the hands of so realized and holy a man. It is beautiful to see the expressions of love and devotion on the faces of the villagers, who are glowing with delight at our sudden appearance and their good fortune of having been at the right time at the right place.

A little later, two old men are talking on the side of the road. We stop. They have no idea who we are. They throw us puzzled looks, wondering what we want. Gurudev calls them to his window. They see that he is a lama and there is the respect they all know for the lamas. So they come over. Gurudev

A ninety-eight-year-old woman seeking Gurudev's blessing

hands them each an apple, a small bundle of carrots, and some money. They receive these things with heads bowed—and they do look poor, as if they could truly use both the food and the money. By the looks on their faces as they watch us drive off, their hands laden with gifts, you can see that these two old men have just experienced a strange little miracle.

At first I thought we were going somewhere, but it becomes clear that we are on a journey to nowhere in particular, and that travelling with Gurudev is less to actually go somewhere and more for what happens along the way. For we never get very far before he suddenly tells the driver to stop and has Dawa scramble up a steep bank to break off a branch from a particular bush. Then Gurudev explains that if you have a cut, this one prevents infection; another, with red flowers, is effective against diabetes. The sides of the road are his pharmacopoeia. Invariably, he gives me a branch of the plant in question. My hands are always full, my pockets bulging.

Dawa, doing his master's bidding

One time, we stop where some urchins in rags are selling tiny tomatoes by the side of a deserted stretch of mountain road. We all get out of the jeep. Gurudev waves his hand over the pyramid of sorry-looking tomatoes and tells the kids he'll buy them all, even the burlap sack the pyramid rests on. To these children, it is a miracle. Judging by the condition of the tomatoes, they had probably been sitting on that lonely stretch for days without a sale.

Later, we stop in a village. Dawa takes the sack of tomatoes out of the back, and we all follow Gurudev to the front door of a house, where we are greeted by an ancient Tibetan woman and her entire family. We are led into the back and into their shrine room, where Gurudev's picture is dominant. Gurudev gives the tomatoes to the family. He takes his seat, cross-legged on a big bed decked out with a rug. The family members prostrate themselves before him one by one. They present him with ceremonial scarves. Then each takes his or her place on the floor. Soon word gets out that Gurudev is there and a constant stream of people enters the room, presenting him with scarves and flowers, and prostrating themselves before him.

At one point there is a man sitting in front; I think he is a schoolteacher. He is slightly better dressed than the others, and he has a pen in his shirt pocket that he keeps fingering, as if to make sure it is still there. Gurudev notices this and asks if he can look at the pen. The man immediately takes it from his pocket. By the way he cradles it in his hand to present to Gurudev, it is clear that this is a prized possession. Gurudev examines it with an almost exaggerated attention.

'Where did you get this fine pen?' he asks.

'Oh, Siliguri!' he exclaims when told.

'So far away. How much did it cost?' and he raises his eyebrows at the expense. 'May I have this pen,' he asks.

'Of course, Gurudev,' the man says, 'I would be most honoured if you would have the pen.'

And he means it. Gurudev holds the pen between his

thumb and forefinger and, without missing a beat, leans forward and gives it away to another man sitting before him. He straightens himself out and for a moment he is still, like stone. Then he turns his attention to someone else in the room. The entire episode, a teaching in non-attachment, is completely spontaneous on Gurudev's part.

A woman comes in with her teenage son, who has a high fever. The boy sits on the floor in a heat-induced stupor as his mother describes his malady to Gurudev. Gurudev asks the woman of the house whether she has a particular herb, which she does. So she gets it and Gurudev takes a pinch, puts it on a little piece of newspaper, blows on it, recites a mantra, wraps it up, and hands it to the mother. He explains in what manner it is to be mixed with hot water and given to her child.

Then he turns to me. 'So much of health is in the mind,' he says. 'Don't think too much. If you think too much, you'll get sick. If someone tells you that you are sick, don't take it too seriously, don't think about it too much—it can affect your health,' and he bursts out laughing.

We are driving back to the village, the sun sinking behind jagged stone peaks, when Gurudev starts singing Nepali songs. He has a way of singing a popular song, often a love song, then changing the words through rhyme in such a way that the song is in a constant process of transformation; and he does it in such a funny way that a few times I am afraid the driver's laughter is going to make him miss a tight twist in the mountain road.

Being in the presence of such a free soul, I can't help but sing myself. So I sing and get everybody to sing the last line of a poem by the visionary poet William Blake, a poem that was put to music by the madman poet of the Beats, Allen Ginsberg. The line, repeated endlessly, goes: 'And all the hills echoed, and all the hills echoed, and all the hills echoed, and all the hills echoed.' And though it is night-time and the windows are closed against the chill, our song reaches the cliffs on the edge of who knows where, and echos! I tell you, it echoes. Our song sung in that jeep, with the crazy lama at our lead, with windows closed—our song echoes to the furthest reaches.

And then we turn a corner. In the headlight's glare appears a sixty-foot-tall boulder on the side of the road, left, no doubt, by a rogue—and long-forgotten—glacier. The boulder is split in half, the gap being just wide enough to squeeze through. Gurudev, playing well his role of Master Director, has the driver stop. He commands us all to get out and pass through the crack while he watches. We jump out and squeeze through the narrow crack in the huge boulder, the mosses growing on the boulder streaking our clothes green. Then we jump back into the jeep and ride on.

We are twisting along a forested road when, out of the blue, Tharbu, a young lama who is riding with us, leans forward. He thrusts his face a few inches in front of mine, raises a finger towards the heavens, and with a look of utter delight and wonderment exclaims, 'Life is a flower!'

I shoot back, 'Then what's death?'

Without missing a beat, he says, rather matter-of-factly, 'Death is death.' His face lights up. He has the formula: 'Life is a flower—and death is death!'

What better summing up of the whole shebang can there be? Life *is* a flower, ever unfolding. And death? Who can say? Even this Buddhist lama, who performs the rituals to aid the departed soul through the *bardo* regions between death and rebirth, who recites the *Tibetan Book of the Dead* over the deceased, would speculate no further than to say death is what it is: death is death.

Tharbu

5

LITERAL BELIEFS AND METAPHYSICAL TRUTHS

From the moment I step into Gurudev's movie, there is a struggle going on within me as I try to figure out who this man called Gurudev is and what he wants with me.

I feel myself being inexorably drawn to him. Have I stumbled upon my teacher, in that more formal, Indian, sense? Though I have had contact with other spiritual teachers and people with deep spiritual understanding, some of whom I've grown quite close to, being a disciple is something I've always believed myself incapable of. It has never seemed desirable to sit under someone else's tree. It would seem contrary to the very nature of my pilgrimage, at whose core is the experience of that which is unmediated. One could, of course, feel that way until one's teacher appears. Could Gurudev be playing the part of a nectar-filled flower, with me as the bee? Is the nectar designed to trap the bee?

If I were to listen only to his followers, I would flee. They never tire of filling my ears with fantastic stories of his miraculous childhood and deeds, his ability to know everything that anyone is thinking. To his followers, these are not metaphorical truths. They speak literally when they tell me he isn't a human being but a god. The literal belief in metaphorical and metaphysical truths not only grates on my nerves; it is, I believe, dangerous, whether expressed by a Bible-thumping fundamentalist or a starry-eyed follower of a realized being. Knowing that I am and will always be incapable of such exuberance, I realize that I am fundamentally different from everyone else who surrounds him. I try to judge Gurudev by my experience of him, not by the show.

In a way, it *is* all a big show, with one man playing God, the others playing life in the presence of a god. But I suppose you could say my faith had gone through the wringer of the American experience of throwing off our kings when we rid ourselves of the British colonial yoke. I feel a visceral repulsion at seeing one man treated like royalty, having others enter his presence bowing and back out bowing, never showing their backs to him. I didn't realize how ingrained this American prejudice was in me until confronted with behaviour so strange to me. It is at the borders, when confronted by something alien, that we know who we are.

Master of Ceremonies

Ever vigilant against what I conceive as mumbo-jumbo, I am convinced of the fundamental equality of all people, that our divinity—the ratio of the human to the divine—is equal in all of us. While there are people worthy of great veneration and may even be 'God-realized', that doesn't make them superhuman or a 'god'. This makes them more fully human. They show us what we all could be.

No stories of divine childhood or miracles are needed to convince me of someone's greatness. I consider my mind open, but ultimately my beliefs are based not on faith but on experience. I've had experiences of things that are clearly beyond what can be explained by science. I am not afraid of accepting conclusions based on these experiences. But I must taste for myself. Someone's description of salt or sugar—or even nectar—does me no good.

And what do I taste? What do I feel in Gurudev's presence? I feel drawn to him, mainly by his extraordinary quality of being a fully childlike adult. He is playing an incredible game, allowing—and even demanding—the respect due a god, yet he barks out an order one moment, and laughs the next. Then he sits, eyes half closed, with an angelic smile. Moods cross his face like clouds flitting across a summer sky, like the emotions that flash across the face of a baby, who cries one minute, eyes bursting with tears, those same tears turned into tears of mirth before rolling down its cheeks. Though I don't want to judge him by the continuously swirling circus, the love the people express by bowing low before him also moves me greatly. Although I want to believe as the others do that before us is a being of another order, my name is Thomas and I am a doubter. The Buddha admonished his followers not to take his word for the truth he proclaimed; he exhorted them to experience for themselves. I believe the Buddha would have agreed with my attitude.

I find myself observing Gurudev more closely than I have ever observed a human being before. He is such an enigma that everything he does seems a cipher to a vast mystery. His teaching seems embedded in his actions.

One gets the impression with Gurudev that he is above it all, playing with reality. In India, there is a term for this: maya-lila, the Dance of Illusion. They even say the difference between the sage and the ordinary person is that while both are taking part in this play called Life, it is the sage who knows it is but a play, and he an actor on a stage. While he may be playing a serious role, by virtue of his detachment he is free. The sage knows that everything is ultimately empty. He embraces with no discomfort the paradox of life being of ultimate—and ultimately of no—importance.

I often wonder how seriously Gurudev takes his role. But every time I get nervous that he is serious—and his part *is* serious, that of a living god—he does something that shows he sees right through what a moment before he performed with the solemnity of the Pope performing Mass. He often follows his most serious expression as a lama with a moment of consummate absurdity. I sometimes see in him a certain playful detachment. As the saying goes, if one were truly detached, one could probably move mountains.

The Master Director on his throne

At times, I have the distinct impression that he has called me into his sphere of play, that it was more than mere chance that led me to him. Something is going on, but what it is I don't know.

Other times, I sit back and observe him from a cool distance. I can see right through his act, the way he plays with the devotees' need to have someone to bow low before, to have in their midst a living god, a fully realized being. This leads me to speculate about his motives and ask myself what might have happened to him as a child that he has such an exaggerated need of an adoring following.

Sometimes he puts on a look of utter boredom at the line of people who come, full of expectation, to make him an offering of a flower or some fruit and to bow low before him. He yawns conspicuously, flips through old magazines, raises a great ball of phlegm with a horrendous sound, and spits it into the bucket by his side. This seems choreographed to underline his greatness among the devotees. We don't expect a god to take an interest in our petty selves.

The more I see people bow low before him, the more I feel like holding onto my dignity and holding my head high before him. I make the conscious decision to take him as an equal and observe from that perspective—strange as it is to have to say it, human to human. And sometimes it happens that he enters a room and everybody presses their palms, bows their heads, and looks at the ground. I just stand, watching him enter the room as I'd watch anybody enter a room, with my head high, not defiant, but looking right into Gurudev's eyes and greeting him.

What do I have to lose? He seems to be the receptacle for people's expectations. I have none. The moment I set out without an aim, neither knowing nor caring where my feet would take me nor where I'd lay my head at night, I both freed myself and insured that I would fall into no one's trap. I came to Timi with a little bag, without much more than a change of clothes. Despite the gifts he gave me, which I can't possibly carry and will give away, I will leave with nothing more—perhaps a story.

Sometimes I feel as if I am between energy states, observing the scene around Gurudev from two vastly different perspectives. One moment I'm the cool observer, as if looking through the show, and then something happens. My perspective shifts. Maybe it is the atmosphere, all the fanfare, the lines of people coming to get his blessing, the love in *their* eyes. And something about him.

❖ ❖

We are sitting alone in the room, Dawa, Gurudev, and I. We are silent. Gurudev gazes at me and I am struck by the tremendous love in his eyes. It is an all-giving love, that which we would expect from a saint. Its power seems based in its being impersonal. It comes with the knowledge that it encompasses whatever it encounters. Love itself is shining through, before it splits into love *of* or *for* anything in particular. I can glimpse the width and depth of his being, but cannot begin to fathom it.

His childlike adherence to the present moment endears him greatly to me. Jesus said that unless you become like a little child you cannot enter the Kingdom of Heaven. Gurudev is playful, like a child, collecting stones and giving them out as holy relics.

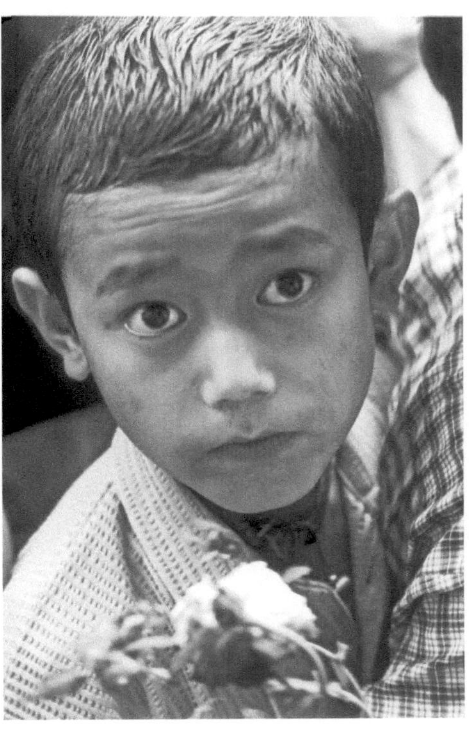

6

THE BRANCH THAT BENDS LOW

The third and last day of Gurudev's visit to the village is the big day. People descend on the village from all sides for his blessing. Huge pots of food are prepared, and everywhere is a buzz of excitement. The culmination is a puja, or ritual, performed by Gurudev and the lamas, replete with chanting from ancient Tibetan texts, clashing cymbals, long brass horns, and clouds of incense. Hundreds press forward to receive Gurudev's blessing. He stops the ritual many times to have Dawa interpret for me his explanation of what is happening. Despite my attempted detachment, I feel honoured that he takes the trouble.

Gurudev is a powerful leader of ritual, his sonorous voice seemingly partaking in and expressing the formative energies of the universe itself. Yet having created an atmosphere of sanctity, he then interjects his well-developed sense of the absurd. He culminates the ritual by leading the huge crowd through a remnant of the British colonial past still part of the Indian school curriculum, the English nursery rhyme 'Baa, Baa, Black Sheep':

'Baa, baa, black sheep,
Have you any wool?
Yes, sir, yes sir,

Three bags full.
One for my master,
One for my dame,
One for the little boy who lives down the lane.'

When the puja is over, the monks lead a procession to the waiting jeep. They are blowing long Alpine horns, crashing cymbals, and sending clouds of incense before him to ward off malevolent spirits. Gurudev is going to Tukvar, his home village, a three-hour drive away in a tea garden below Darjeeling, just south of the Sikkim border. Great piles of aromatic pine branches are burning, producing huge clouds of auspicious, sweet smoke.

As with everything surrounding this man, the choreography is perfect. He arrives at the vehicle, which is surrounded by a large knot of villagers, who part to let him through. Dawa opens the door for him. Though Gurudev whispers something in Dawa's ear, he is looking at me. Once again, in his eyes I see tremendous love. Then Dawa comes over to me with that twinkle in his eye. He cups his hand to my ear and says, 'Gurudev is inviting you to come with us to Tukvar!' Dawa is excited for my invitation—or, as he would call it, my continued good fortune.

The very thought of crossing the border into Darjeeling brings a tight knot to my stomach.

Maybe I have experienced Sikkim as such a peaceful union of mountain, cloud, village, and aimless wandering because Darjeeling had been so darkly violent. One can neither deny history nor the present moment. There is no light without darkness. I've heard things have quieted down in Darjeeling, but it doesn't matter. As I stand there, Gurudev's eyes upon me, I hesitate also because of the struggle Gurudev has caused within me. He alternately attracts and repulses me like the poles of a very strong magnet.

Setting off in search of nothing special—you could even say The Nothing Special—suited me well because of my ingrained sense that no intermediary is needed to experience the Highest. Organized religion has always been dubious for me at best, fascinating and containing kernels of truth, yet fundamentally flawed by grand concepts that needlessly complicate the simplicity of what is, which is then worshipped as dogma. What greater travesty could there be than a church locked up tight, as if the priests have lured God in there and now lock him in so they can retain their monopoly.

On the one hand, I have the feeling that Gurudev might just be what he purports to be, or what others believe him to be: a spiritual master. Yet the circus around him, the very devotion the others show him, their insistent stories of miracles he has performed, never cease to bother me. As does his allowing others to treat him like a god.

A few times over the past days I've tried to ask Gurudev about this, to challenge him on the dichotomies. But always when I was about to put a tough question to him, he'd suddenly get up or clear the room—as if what his followers say is true and he is privy to our innermost thoughts. It seems part of his way of controlling every situation. In fact, sometimes I have the feeling by the situations he creates, and by the way he places me in them, that he *wants* these reactions to arise within me; he wants to create within me an inner fire.

Gurudev stands before the open door of his jeep, holding me in those guru eyes of his, and I stand frozen before him, caught between poles, unable to decide whether or not to go with him. A woman steps from the crowd and, in a great show of devotional passion, prostrates herself in the dirt before him. This precipitates a rash of people who all start prostrating themselves before him in the dirt. He visibly swells with the attention, literally puffing out his belly, and placing his palm on their heads as if he were the Pope.

My reaction is ingrained and instantaneous. How can a man of truth act this way? If he truly experiences the unicity and believes we are all sparks of the divine, how can he allow others to treat him like a god? How can he bask in it? If his aim is to impress me, it isn't working. It makes me firmly decide to grab my pack and continue on my pilgrimage without a backward glance.

As he reaches down to place his open palm on the head of an old man bowing deeply before him—both of them enveloped in the dust raised by those prostrating themselves—Gurudev turns to me and speaks. Dawa interprets: 'He is saying the branch laden with fruit naturally bends low.' What can that statement, so eloquently put, about the natural humility of the man of wisdom, possibly have to do with this show of grovelling and arrogance I am witnessing?

Dawa had relayed Gurudev's invitation with such earnestness; it is with a look of disbelief that he hears me decline the offer. He conveys my answer to Gurudev.

To Gurudev, it suddenly seems like nothing. It is something I've noticed in him, a strict adherence to the present moment that precludes even the possibility of disappointment. He makes a move to take his seat. Dawa rushes forward to help him—as if he can't simply sit in a vehicle without help, as if he were a rare and precious vessel. Once he sits, Dawa arranges Gurudev's robes on his shoulder and smoothes the fabric out as if he were about to be transformed into a stone sculpture, and the robes had to be just right for all time. He shuts the door. Gurudev opens the window. He whispers something in Dawa's ear and Dawa tells me Gurudev will be back in Sikkim in two weeks' time, for a three-day puja for world peace in the town of Namchi. Gurudev is inviting me to attend.

The driver starts the engine. There is an electric excitement in the air at the passing of this god incarnate. The monks are blowing horns and crashing cymbals. Clouds of sweet smoke billow.

Then he calls Dawa over again; they cover their mouths in private conversation. Dawa calls another man over, a driver. The three of them speak and then the man runs to his vehicle, a van parked a short way off.

Dawa is beaming with joy. He opens the door behind Gurudev. 'Jump in!' he exclaims. 'Gurudev wants to prolong your time together. You can ride with us as far as the border with Darjeeling. This van will follow us and bring you back.'

My rejection has been met with an act of love.

As we approach the bridge over the Rangeet River, which marks the border between Sikkim and the Darjeeling Hills, Dawa tells me that it isn't too late to change my mind and come with them over the border. 'I think you don't yet understand the reality of who Gurudev really is,' he says. 'He is offering you a tremendous opportunity, which anybody else would jump at—no matter what the cost.'

Again, I decline the offer, and though I don't give my reasons, I do have them.

7

THE ATTEMPTED ASSASSINATION

View of the Darjeeling market from my balcony

Why was I reluctant to return to Darjeeling with Gurudev? To answer that we must go back to Darjeeling, to when I first arrived and took a room with a balcony overlooking the heart of the market. It is the dead of night, my room is pitch black and I suddenly find myself sitting upright in bed, sheets wrapped around my legs, clammy with sweat. A nightmare is echoing through me, the tips of my fingers still tingling from the rush of adrenaline. It takes an uneasy moment for me to realize I'm in my hotel room in Darjeeling. I've been living here now for about three weeks. I dreamt that I was standing on the sidelines of an American football game in which the players were not human beings, but bulls. They were charging up the field with the ball. The teams clashed in front of me and spilled over the sidelines. I had to scramble so as not to be trampled upon.

I fall back on my pillow, freeing my legs from the knotted sheets. My heart is still pounding; there is a throbbing in my ears. Then I hear something outside my window, many voices together, rising and falling as if carried by the wind. I wrap a blanket around myself against the cold and step out onto my balcony.

For a city of over 100,000 people, Darjeeling is surprisingly dark at night. It is also usually silent except for the occasional dog. But tonight the dogs all across town are howling, barking, and yapping, fighting amongst themselves, both given licence from and mirroring the loud voices of men, as yet hidden from view, filling the air with their distant chant. My balcony is high, and the way is steep down into the heart of this Himalayan city. I can see right into the centre of the market. But there is nobody to be seen. The voices come from afar, from the far side of the market, growing louder and softer, disappearing and coming back again louder than before as the procession moves through the streets and comes closer. At first I think it is a religious procession. I can just make out the flickering shadows cast by torches. As it grows louder, the tone becomes more distinct.

Two bare street lights illuminate a widening of the road in the centre of the market. It is the one point of light in the otherwise dark city. And into this light march the people I have been hearing—four, five, and six abreast; they march into this illuminated space as if onto a distant stage. Because of the sudden clear line of sight, their voices become more distinct too. If I knew Nepali I could have understood the words, but the tone is easily read; I feel it directly in my gut.

This is no religious procession.

It is anger, and it is raw. And more than the anger of individuals, it is the anger of the mob, a call and response, one voice shouting a slogan while the rest—their fists raised, some clutching impromptu torches made of cloth-tipped sticks smudging the air with smoke—roar an angry refrain. The dogs of the city are howling like an angry wound. I feel a gulf open beneath me, and my heart falls into it.

They pass through the market, leaving the small patch of illumination empty. Their dark rhythmic chant rises and falls with the wind and the configuration of intervening buildings as they mount the hill from the market, heading towards the ridge where I stand on my balcony. The neighbourhood dogs greet them with a fierce and angry din.

Suddenly, the chant becomes distinct. They turn the corner and start up the narrow alley that runs behind the hotel and beneath my balcony, their voices echoing sharply off the buildings. How uncanny that, of all the narrow alleys up the ridge, they chose the one over which I was perched. The tall buildings of the narrow alley dance with the shadows cast by their cloth-tipped torches. The acrid smoke of kerosene bites my nose.

I pull back into the shadows in order not to be seen. Then I peer over the edge. There must be fifty of them. As they pass I can suddenly understand what they're chanting. The one in front, brandishing a curved sword glinting in the torches' flickering flames, is calling out in English: 'We want Gorkhaland!' To which the others respond angrily—brandishing knives, sticks, and torches, their voices resounding—'Gorkhaland! Gorkhaland!'

'We want Gorkhaland!'

'Gorkhaland! Gorkhaland!'

And thus they pass beneath my balcony and fade into the night.

❖ ❖

Next morning I awake to brilliant sunshine. I head down the stairs to the hotel lobby. It is a rather fancy hotel that would be beyond my means, especially for an extended stay, during the tourist season. It being January, I was able to negotiate a weekly price for my room on the upper floor, with a private balcony offering a fine view of the city and the snow-capped mountains of Sikkim. At first I was surprised by the manager's agreeing to my first offered price, but I can now understand why he jumped at my offer: I've been the hotel's only guest the entire time I've been here. There must be a dozen employees, mostly young Nepali men, boys really—who treat each other like brothers and have an innocence about them—and a few older women who dust the corridors and polish the marble floors. No matter how many times I tell them to remain seated when I walk into the lobby, and to continue watching TV or sipping one of their endless cups of sweet milky tea, they insist on jumping to attention and even opening the door for me. They even did this recently, when the Bengali manager, a fastidious rotund man whom no one really likes, was in Kolkata with his family taking his winter holiday.

I enter the lobby and immediately notice two things that are different. First, the manager is standing by the front desk. He is surrounded by half a dozen of the boys. He must have returned the evening before. Not only did the staff prefer it when he was away, but I did too. Because I was the sole guest, his job was intolerably boring, a fact that impacted on me every time I passed through the lobby. He would catch me and chew my ear off with whatever was on his mind, and it would take me an inordinate amount of time to squeeze out a polite exit. He longed to be back in Kolkata with his wife and two children but was trapped in Darjeeling by his job. He was so happy when he left on his little holiday.

The second thing I notice is that though my room had been bathed in sunshine, the lobby is dark. It takes me a moment to realize why: the rolling metal shutters are down over the hotel's glass doors.

'What's going on?' I ask.

The boys had been in a tight knot around the manager, who was reading from the newspaper. They step back. I can sense something seriously wrong.

'Didn't you hear?' the manager says. 'Subash Ghising has been shot. He was coming back from meetings with government officials in Delhi late yesterday afternoon. His heavily armed convoy was attacked in a tight ravine with AK-47s and grenades.'

I had read in the papers that Ghising, the supreme leader of the Darjeeling Hills, had been threatened by opposition forces to leave or pay the ultimate price.

'Was he killed?' I ask.

'There was a half-hour firefight,' the manager says, 'and there were deaths on both sides. But somehow Ghising managed to survive with seven pieces of shrapnel in his head.' He flutters the newspaper. '*The Statesman* here says the shrapnel *couldn't* penetrate his skull. I'm not surprised. I always thought his skull was thick. Now we know it. Anyway, he is in hospital in Siliguri. If he dies …' Unable to make himself finish the sentence, he looks down at his feet and studies the laces in his shoes. When he looks up I see horror in his eyes.

'If he dies,' he says, controlling his voice, 'the situation will become grave.'

I look from one face to another. I recall the angry mob of the night before, now obviously a spontaneous reaction to the news of the attack hitting the streets. The fear registered in the lines of worry, the long, almost trembling expressions, leave no doubt about the gravity of the situation.

For the second time in a few hours, I feel a gulf open beneath me.

I look nervously at the slits of light coming in through the closed metal shutters. I can hear the sound of agitation outside at the passing of what must be a mob of young men.

'What's going to happen now?' I ask.

'God only knows,' he says, 'but for now it means there's a bandh.'

'What's that?'

'It means a strike, but that English word doesn't quite fit. Siege would come closer to the reality. It means that Ghising's men are flexing their muscles to show they're still in control; they've called for the Hills to be closed.'

'Closed?'

'Everything. It means if a shopkeeper is caught selling as much as a gram of salt, he'll be pulled from his shop, beaten, and his shop ransacked or torched.'

'By whom?'

'By Ghising's goons, who'll be roaming the streets with *kukris* (they're the big Nepali knives), just looking for trouble. They'll undoubtedly be settling old scores. They're angry, you can be sure. Their leader has been attacked, and they'll be looking for revenge, even though no one knows yet who the assailants were. And it isn't only shops that are closed, but absolutely everything—restaurants, banks, post offices, government offices, even the army and police won't dare ply the streets.' The manager eyes the shuttered doors. 'Even hotels must remain closed, though don't worry, you can stay. We can't very well kick you out, can we? Where would you go? It is a sorry state of affairs in these hills. We have these bandhs all the time. But this one will be different. This is the first time someone attacked Ghising. This time it'll be worse.'

'Maybe I should leave,' I say.

'How?'

The answer seems obvious: 'Take a jeep,' I say. 'Go down to Siliguri.'

'I'm afraid you do not understand,' the manager says, now speaking slower as if that will aid my understanding. 'Everything being closed includes the roads. Any vehicle caught on the road will be stopped. The mob will pull the driver out and he'll be beaten to a pulp, if not killed, and his vehicle will be turned into a fireball. The only vehicles you'll see plying the roads will be those of party members, and you'll know it from the huge green flag of Gorkhaland they'll be sporting.'

'You mean there's no way out of the Hills?'

'No way out,' he says. Throwing up his hands, he continues, 'I'm stuck here as well; we're all in the same boat. And just to think, I came back only yesterday. If I had come only a few hours later, I would have been stuck *out* of the Hills. I could have returned to my family in Kolkata to ride this one out. There's no telling how long this will last.

'Don't you remember,' the manager goes on, with a bitter look on his face, 'before I left on my holiday you told me you're here to write about this place. You were always wanting to know about the Buddhism and whatever other ideas you came here with. Don't think I didn't notice when you tried to redirect our conversations when I told you about Ghising, and about what is really happening here. Now is your chance to know this place, for what it is. This is what you wanted, isn't it—to know this place?' He is really agitated now, not at me but at the situation. 'Now you can see the Queen of the Hills in all her glory.'

What he said about my wanting to redirect conversations that turned to local politics was true. When I had arrived in Darjeeling a few weeks earlier, my head was just about as much in the clouds as the city itself, which was more often than not immersed in fog. Having travelled halfway around the world to reach Darjeeling, I had expected a mountainous land with a jagged northern horizon of snow-capped peaks bordering Tibet. I had read that there were many Tibetan monasteries in Darjeeling, and that it was a part of India that was culturally akin to that land beyond the peaks, a place where ancient spiritual traditions lived on, now in diaspora in this particular part of India. Like many, I was drawn to the East by an existential dissatisfaction with the West, its hollow insistence on rationality and the repeatable laws of science. I wanted to discover what the people of the highest mountains in the world had to teach.

What might have set me apart was that I was there not only to experience, but to write about what I experienced. So perhaps it was with a more serious intent, a gaze that sought to record, that I took a jeep up into those mountains in India's eastern Himalayas and first arrived at the Queen of the Hills, the hill station of Darjeeling.

I had noticed and duly noted that when I left Siliguri, the last town on the north Indian plains, and the nose of my jeep suddenly pointed towards the heavens and we entered the Darjeeling Hills—which rise abruptly and without warning from the flat table of land that stretches southward for hundreds of miles—that there was not only a sudden and drastic change in the landscape, but also in the people. Eyes shifted to a Mongolian cast. Hindu temples were largely replaced by Tibetan Buddhist temples and monasteries. Colourful prayer flags were strung across the bridges, fluttering in the breeze, sending out their prayers for the happiness of all sentient beings.

Expecting an extended stay, I set myself the task of systematically getting to know the place. During my first days I walked from one end of the ridge upon which the city is built to the other. I descended the steep roads and alleyways into the market and explored the edges of the city, where the tea gardens began, and where forests of tall pines covered the steep terrain. And to the north, as expected, the jagged peaks of ice and snow cut into the heavens like teeth, like a portent of the heights and mysteries that could be uncovered in such a place. And when those peaks were covered in cloud, it quickened the imagination all the more, just knowing that those clouds were hiding in their secret heights the mysterious land of Tibet.

During those first days, I was struck by the peaceful, gentle quality of the people and the way in which people of such diverse backgrounds lived in apparent harmony. It was not unusual to hear cymbals and horns from the Tibetan monasteries merging over the city with the mosques' call to prayer and the conch shells being blown at Hindu temples. It was my luck that I came in January, when Darjeeling's 7,500-foot altitude ensures that the city is cold and the clouds in which the city is regularly submerged bring a dampness that sends tourists south to the plains. Touristed places generally reveal themselves and are friendlier when tourists are absent—and Darjeeling was no exception. I was met everywhere with pressed palms, genuine smiles, and greetings of namaste. Though I was so new to the place that I knew neither its history nor its ethnic mix, I was struck by the peace that permeated Darjeeling.

The first inkling of my naiveté surfaced the moment I opened my mouth and started speaking with people, though I was slow to accept it. While I kept trying to point conversations upward, in the direction of spirituality and what I considered the high Himalayan culture, when people figured out my interest was more than that of a passing tourist and that I was a writer, there was, much to my chagrin, a certain intensity with which they wanted to speak about the political situation, what they termed the 'Agitation' and the 'Troubles'. The way they both wanted to speak of these matters and the obvious reluctance they had to do so, which I sensed was out of fear, made clear the dark nature of local politics and made me try to avoid the subject all the more in my futile attempt to point conversations towards matters more to my expectation and liking. Finally, I realized that if my aim was to come to know these hills I would have to educate myself.

It seemed I had to go down before I could go up.

So I transformed my initial resistance into a stance of active inquiry. Instead of trying to change the subject when people started speaking of these dark matters, I started asking questions. And even though everyone wanted to speak about it, almost without exception they would say nothing openly against the movement, the ruling party, or its leader, Subash Ghising—until they were confident I would not

Poster of Ghising's party, the Gorkha National Liberation Front (GNLF)

betray them. Their fears seemed based on a well-founded fear of violence. The fact that I was a sympathetic outsider often made people open up to me in a way they wouldn't with one of their neighbours.

In the days leading up to this fateful Sunday when I awoke to the changed reality of Darjeeling, I educated myself about the history of Darjeeling, which I recorded in my notebook in the following fashion:

A Brief History of Sikkim and the Darjeeling Hills

Once upon a time, there was no border between Sikkim and Darjeeling. It was one land inhabited by the Lepchas, a gentle people who worshipped nature—the river that gave them water and fish, the tree that gave them wood, shade, and nuts, the mountain upon whose slopes they lived. They called their land Mayel Lyang, the Land of Hidden Treasures. They called themselves the Mutunchi-Rongkup, which means Mother's Beloved Children. They believed their first ancestors arose from the pristine snows of Mount Kanchenjunga and that their language was the oldest on the earth, and was therefore the language spoken in the Garden of Eden.

Since Paradise divided ceases to be paradise, things changed when the Tibetans, who were fighting amongst themselves, came south over the Himalayan passes sometime before 1642. This is the date generally used for the founding of the Tibetan Buddhist kingdom known as Sikkim, situated in the Lepchas' traditional land. Tibetan Buddhism supplanted the Lepchas' worship of nature. The Lepchas, who didn't even have a word for war, left the most fertile land and moved up the mountainsides or into the ravines without a struggle. In fact, the Lepchas' own name for themselves is the Rongpa, or 'Ravine Dwellers'.

In the mid-eighteenth century in the mountains west of the kingdom of Sikkim, a Gorkha king named Prithwi Narayan

Shah was waging bloody wars of conquest. He and his heirs consolidated their rule over what is now known as Nepal, and moved well into what are now the Indian Himalayas to the west. And in the east there were numerous wars between the Nepalis, Sikkimese, and Bhutanese—the exact timings and nature of which are still being worked out by historians.

What we do know is that British India gained control of the ridge upon which they would build the city of Darjeeling in 1835. They acquired the rest of the surrounding mountains south of the present Sikkim (the Darjeeling Hills) in 1850. The city of Darjeeling, at 7,500 feet, was conceived first as a sanatorium and refuge where British colonials unaccustomed to the climate—especially those living in Calcutta (now known as Kolkata), the capital of British India a few hundred miles directly south of the Darjeeling Hills—could go to escape the malarial heat. The British soon found that the surrounding hills (they would be called mountains anywhere else on the planet) were well suited to the cultivation of tea. They brought Nepalis in as labourers to clear the virgin forests and to plant and pluck the tea. It did not take long for the Nepalis to far outnumber the Lepchas, Tibetans, and British. As sure as the name Darjeeling became synonymous with tea, the lingua franca of Darjeeling became Nepali.

Fast forward now to 1947 and Indian independence from Britain. Darjeeling, though predominantly Nepali, was part of British India and remained with independent India as part of the state of West Bengal, which is administered out of Kolkata. Sikkim, which was an independent kingdom before Indian independence, remained an independent kingdom under Indian suzerainty until an internal democratic movement directed against the monarchy caused the king to invite the Indian Army in to help restore order. This move resulted in the ouster of the king and India's annexation of Sikkim as its twenty-second state in 1975.

The cultural shift that one cannot help but notice upon leaving the north Indian plains and entering the Darjeeling Hills has its political side as well, which has had a tendency to grow violent. The Nepalis of Darjeeling don't much like being administered by Bengalis, a people they have very little to do with culturally, and whose language they neither read, nor write, nor speak. It doesn't help that when Nepalis go south to Bengal they often do so to fill menial, low-caste jobs of night guards, gardeners, and servants. When Bengalis travel up to Darjeeling to escape the heat and to holiday in the Queen of the Hills, they still tend to treat the Nepalis as servants, and this attitude permeates their political domination over the region from the state capital of Kolkata. All of this has spurred a separatist movement among the Nepalis of the Darjeeling Hills. While they are not trying to break away from India, as is the case with some of the other separatist movements in India (especially in the far east of the country), they are calling to break away from West Bengal and to form a separate state within the Indian Union, which they would call Gorkhaland.

The Gorkhaland movement began non-violently. Then one of the leaders, Subash Ghising, broke with the others and said that to achieve a separate state it was necessary to pick up arms. As is often the case with violent wings of popular movements, especially ones that have a strong leader willing to utilize violence against his own people, Ghising's movement gained strength and the Gorkhaland movement reached its bloody climax in the mid-1980s, when there were clashes and many people were killed. There was no family that was unaffected. Everybody had a brother or sister, parent, uncle, or cousin who was killed. The state and Central governments sent in their troops, who committed many atrocities of extrajudicial killings, torture, and disappearances. But perhaps more terror was instigated by the separatists themselves, who would break down doors in the middle of the night to take away those they suspected of not being sufficiently behind the movement or having collaborated with the other side. Often people were taken away just to settle an old score. Many of these people were hacked to pieces with the native *kukri* (the Nepali machete) and thrown into the river. Some, including a journalist and the director of a school, were beheaded by the exponents of Gorkhaland and had their heads impaled on sticks and exhibited on the main street of Kalimpong, the Darjeeling Hills' second-largest town, to serve as an example of what happens to people not sufficiently committed to the cause.

On 27 July 1986, government troops fired into a crowd of men, women, and children in Kalimpong, killing at least nineteen by most accounts. This led to a frenzy of violence on both sides. To get out of the impasse, Subash Ghising and the state and Central governments arrived at a compromise to the call for separate statehood. A legislative body called the Darjeeling Gorkha Hill Council or DGHC was created in 1988 to administer many of the state functions. Its representatives were to be elected from the various districts of the Darjeeling Hills and were to meet in Darjeeling. Subash Ghising was given the chairmanship of the DGHC. It seemed part of the deal. It was a post he was to hold through many a questionable election.

By most accounts, it is the people in the movement who have left the longest shadow of terror. And clearly, it is with the very real threat of violence that Subash Ghising rules the Hills. Most people I speak with about the political situation first tell me that they are all behind the Gorkhaland movement and think Ghising is a great leader. But it doesn't take long for them to take me into their confidence, often with a glance over their shoulders, and tell me in a hushed tone that he is actually a ruthless dictator. Nobody dares criticize either Ghising or the movement publicly. Yet when you scratch the surface, everybody is living in fear. It has become clear to me that the society in the Darjeeling Hills is deeply traumatized and fractured.

Now it is a dozen or so years since Ghising took control. Even those who backed him at the beginning are growing dissatisfied with the state of affairs. Or perhaps it would be more accurate to say they are growing dissatisfied with feeling dissatisfied with the state of affairs. An example: long before local issues were taken up by the DGHC, the water system in Darjeeling was hopelessly inadequate. The British had designed the water system in the 1800s for a city with a fraction of the present population. Now, many people in Darjeeling have no water whatsoever. They either have to buy it from improvised tanker trucks—flatbeds with metal barrels strapped on the back filled with water collected from various streams and waterfalls in the surrounding mountains—or they find leaks in the few municipal pipes (which tend to bypass the homes of the poor) and collect their water in plastic tubs. Before, blame could easily be placed on the Bengalis in Kolkata. Now, increasing dissatisfaction is directed at their very own DGHC in Darjeeling, which receives money from the government for waterworks, money that never seems to be used for that purpose. It is a similar story for just about every other sector of the infrastructure, the crumbling roads, etc. Yet this dissatisfaction is a private affair. Few dare voice dissent. In Darjeeling, the most powerful political tool is fear.

The picture that has emerged from the many people I have spoken with is deeply contradictory, yet consistent. Many hold Subash Ghising in an almost mystical awe. They tell me, some of them literally misty-eyed, that he is the one who gave the Nepalis of India their identity. From the way they speak, it is clear that he is a charismatic leader. Yet the same people then go on to bitterly complain of his corruption and how he has at his command a band of young thugs who don't stop short of murder to secure their leader's position. I have no way of knowing whether these stories are true or not, though I can say that most people in Darjeeling believe them to be. Many stories about Ghising include *kukris* and people hacked to pieces in broad daylight.

Shortly before my arrival here in Darjeeling, one of Ghising's former deputies who had broken with him went into hiding and then came out publicly to denounce Ghising, saying he had sold out the fight for Gorkhaland. Since Ghising was in power in the present system, his argument ran, Ghising was secretly working with the state and Central governments to oppose the fight for separate statehood in exchange for the government turning

> a blind eye to his siphoning off government funds for his personal gain. His argument had merit: since Ghising has flouted so many laws and so many government funds have gone missing, if the state or Central governments wanted him out, they would clearly have legal grounds. Saying he will lead the fight for separate statehood, and that violence is the only path, this former deputy has given Ghising and the entire council of the DGHC a month to resign or risk death.

As I stand in that darkened hotel lobby, hearing the angry voices through the rolled-down metal shutters, I am stunned to realize that even as I was collecting this information, I had the detachment of one learning history. I never thought I'd be caught in the middle of it.

'How long will this last?' I ask the manager.

'Who can say? In the late 1980s they had a forty-day bandh. The same length as your Biblical flood. After a few days people started running out of food. Remember, there is no way in *or* out. There is no way for food to get to the market. There *is* no market. After a few weeks people attacked one another for food. No one can say how long this one will last. First we must see what happens to Mr Ghising.'

'This means we cannot even go outside?'

'Not me!' he retorts. 'I'm a Bengali. This whole thing is about the Nepalis' fight against the Bengalis, isn't it, to break away from West Bengal? If I show my face out there, I might not make it back. And the others,' he says referring to the local workers at the hotel, who are all Nepali, 'they'd better be careful. You never know what side they might be caught up in. But you are a foreigner. Nobody will touch a foreigner. You can certainly go out.'

I respond with a stunned silence.

'Would you like to go out?' he asks, solicitously.

It seems a tricky question.

'You're sure it's all right?'

'Quite certain. The only thing is that you'll have to leave through the basement door. When you want to come back in ring the buzzer twice, then once. That's the signal; then we'll unlock the basement for you.'

One of the boys leads me to the basement and through a little pantry with boxes of tiny shrivelled potatoes and old onions. 'This is all the extra food we have,' he says. 'Hope this bandh doesn't last too long.'

Beyond the pantry is a door made of roughly welded metal bars, directly behind which is a wooden door. He unlocks both doors for me. I climb the narrow concrete stairs to the street. The boy cautiously climbs halfway up the stairs, just far enough to point out the buzzer to the right of the metal shutters. I hear the boy lock both the doors from the inside, and I am alone on the street.

I scurry down to Nehru Road, the main shopping road, and everything is eerily quiet. The world as I knew it has come to an end, and a new world has begun—a world of shops battened down as if expecting a storm, a world of fear and uncertainty. Ghising has been attacked. This is new territory.

At the bottom of Nehru Road I see a tight knot of young guys heading down into the market. They have a menacing air. A jeep goes by with a huge Gorkhaland flag waving off a stick, a green flag with the *kukri* on it. The jeep is filled with men from Ghising's party. Noticeably absent are the policemen in the booth at the bottom of Nehru Road.

I walk up to the Chowrasta, the city's main square on top of the ridge, and watch columns of smoke rising from the market as Ghising's men burn vehicles owned by members of the opposition parties. There is a deeply disturbing uncertainty. The city is stunned by violence.

The Ghorka flag

Darjeeling in the aftermath of the assassination attempt on Subash Ghising

That night I wrap myself in a blanket and sit out on my balcony. I peer down into the market. Again it is dark; again the city is silent but for the dogs, who take the darkness as their own to howl to the high heavens, voicing what we are all feeling. And there are voices, too, in the night, angry voices of mobs rising up on the ill winds from the market like poisonous vapours, sounds of breaking glass, of fists on car roofs.

In the morning something very strange happens: I walk out of the hotel through the basement door and it seems normal to do so. I go down to Nehru Road and everything is locked down and there seems nothing strange in it. The only store open is the pharmacy. Pharmacies are sometimes allowed to open during bandhs, but only to sell medicine. I go in, open my daypack, and put it on the counter. I wait until no one can overhear me whisper, 'Do you have milk powder?'

The clerk indicates with a slight wink of his right eye that he does. He scans the room to make certain no one is looking before reaching under the counter and slipping a bag of milk powder directly into my open bag. I pay him and leave with a glance over my shoulder. The only other commerce on Nehru Road is the guy selling newspapers. He is in his usual place, doing a brisk business. I learn that apart from party vehicles, milk trucks and the jeep with the daily newspapers are the only other vehicles allowed to ply the roads. One can surmise that the party has the local journalists in their pocket—probably held there with fear—and use the papers to promulgate their version of events. About the milk truck I am less certain. Could the party have a soft spot for the Holy Cow and her full udders? I buy a copy of *The Statesman*, the Kolkata paper, and continue up to the Chowrasta, reading as I walk. I read that since Sikkim is completely cut off by the Darjeeling bandh, the army is taking people out of its capital, Gangtok, by helicopter.

'Thomas!' I hear my name called out. It is Annette, an Australian woman who has been living in Darjeeling for some months, volunteering at a school for disabled children and at Mother Teresa's outpost there. I mention to her how odd it is that the strange new reality becomes so quickly normal. She knows exactly what I mean.

'I lived in Cyprus during the war,' she says. 'At first, when the bombs started falling out of the sky and hitting neighbouring villages, everybody was frightened and ran for cover. But it was surprising how quickly we all adjusted. Within a few days it seemed normal to hear the bombs blast and to hear of the dead and wounded, to hear the sirens wail. I think it is because the reality of war is so punishingly huge and there is nothing we can do in the face of it. There is nothing you *can* do, but adjust.'

The next day I discover that the rooftop restaurant of a nearby hotel is open. As far as I know it is the only restaurant open in town. It is a concession the party makes to the tourists, in recognition of the fact that tourists neither take sides in the struggle for Gorkhaland nor have any alternative source of food. I am surprised there are so many foreign tourists in town. There must be over a dozen of us. Though there is a tacit understanding that it can remain open, the metal shutters over the doors of this hotel remain down. There is an external staircase encased in bars. The door is not locked. You enter quietly and go up when no one is watching. Day by day the menu gets thinner and thinner, until there isn't much more than potatoes, cooked in a variety of increasingly uninteresting ways.

One morning the buzz amongst the foreigners is that the Indian military will begin armed convoys to evacuate tourists, both foreign and Indian, as well as businessmen and students who happen to be stuck there. On the Chowrasta there is a pony stand where, under normal circumstances, tourists can hire a pony for a few rupees. The tourists have been joking about stealing ponies to make their escape. Some have grown nervous and wonder whether we should all contact our embassies. Others wonder whether their families at home are reading about the Siege of Darjeeling, which of course they aren't. When I go back to my hotel, men in military fatigues are on the embankment opposite, patrolling with rifles. Everybody is in an uneasy holding pattern, waiting for something to change, either towards normalcy or outright violence. Daytime feels safe enough. The Indian tourists stuck in town start strolling around with their children. Local children take advantage of the empty streets to play cricket and badminton. There descends on the centre of Darjeeling an uneasy calm, though one hears stories of violence in the tea gardens and among people involved in politics. I don't venture into the market. Someone said they were walking down there and heard gunshots. The noises I hear from there at night set my nerves on edge. Under such circumstances one takes one's cue from the locals, who retreat into their houses well before nightfall.

When I go for an early dinner at the rooftop restaurant that night, some of the tourists are on their way with their luggage to the police station to wait for the military convoy out. They are instructed to get to the police station, which is in the middle of the market, before nightfall. They are told they will have to wait there until 2 or 3 a.m. It isn't until that hour that the police consider it safe enough to head for the plains. That way, the convoy will be less likely to meet people along the way. The convoy will, after all, be breaking the bandh. As one official in the police department puts it, 'At 3 a.m. it's too cold outside and everybody's sleeping.'

I do not fancy such a journey. I know I am safe in my hotel room at night and will awaken safe in the morning. Such a convoy, travelling the very route on which Ghising was attacked, seems dubious at best.

That night I sit again on my balcony wrapped in a blanket. I see the buses for those fleeing, heading to the police station in the market. I hear angry voices, people banging on the sides of the buses. I hear broken glass. And in the headlights' glare I see the mob of angry young men trying to block them. I sleep very uneasily that night.

The convoy makes it safely. I read about it in the paper the next morning, which describes the 'tourists huddling in the police station for safety'. The next night there is another convoy. Over 500 are evacuated in those two nights. Then they announce the third night will be the last time the army will help people out; it is the last chance to escape Darjeeling.

I had met a Danish family who had been living in Bhutan for three years with Danida, the Danish government aid organization. Hans, the husband, does agricultural work. His brother has just come from Copenhagen for a visit and they are taking a week's holiday to drive to Darjeeling and Sikkim. As luck would have it, they came up from the plains about an hour before Ghising's convoy. They arrived in Darjeeling just about the time Ghising was ambushed. So Hans, his wife, brother, and his three young children—a baby, a four-year-old son and an eight-year-old daughter—are stranded in Darjeeling. They offer to take me when they flee.

I go with Hans to the police station in the afternoon of the final convoy. In the chief of police's office we are joined by a woman leading a group of college kids from all over the world, who are in Darjeeling to learn how to become Christian missionaries. They also want to flee that night. The police inform us that it won't be a proper convoy since all the bus drivers willing to risk a convoy have already left, and there aren't many military vehicles available either. So it will be a looser collection of vehicles. The missionaries will have to find drivers willing to risk the journey. He warns them that it will be expensive. He wants them there by sunset. Since we have our own vehicle, he will send two army jeeps to the Danes' hotel at 8 p.m. to escort us down to the police station to await departure. Hans is nervous because of his children. He asks whether the police chief thinks it will be safe. 'It would probably be best if you aren't the first in the convoy, nor the last. Wait for the vehicles to start out, and join somewhere in the middle.'

The leader of the missionaries stands up. 'Make us first in the convoy,' she says. 'We have a whole host of angels with us!'

By 8 p.m. we have the jeep packed and ready. Two army jeeps arrive with close to twenty soldiers. Each soldier is armed with a big rifle. One sits in the passenger seat of our vehicle with his rifle sticking out of the open window. With one jeep in front of us and one behind, we drive without incident down to the police station. The moment we arrive and turn into the compound, our army escort leaves.

We are approached by the man who is obviously in charge, and he tells us the convoy is called off. 'It is too dangerous,' he tells us. 'A tourist vehicle was attacked today on the road to Siliguri. It took the army's intervention to get them out. Go back to your hotel.'

Hans tells him that is fine, but where is our army escort?

'Don't worry,' the man tells us. 'Just drive back to your hotel. Nothing will happen to you.'

Hans grows red in the face. 'How can you say this? My children are in the car. Fifteen minutes ago you thought it dangerous enough to have twenty armed men in two army jeeps escort us down here! You *cannot* send us back without an escort.'

'I am only the head of transportation,' the man says with the stony tone of a bureaucrat, 'I am not involved in security. There is no one here who can help you. They have all gone home.'

We demand, plead, and cajole; in the end he offers to escort us himself. We have no choice but to agree. So with the head of transportation sitting in front, we drive out of the police station compound and into the market. We reach the widening of the road that I have been looking down into every night from my balcony where the angry mob gathers, the place from which all those angry night sounds emanate. Hans noses the vehicle into the mob, people glaring and parting as we inch our way forward. To the side, a man is standing on the roof of a van, addressing the assembled crowd, gesticulating wildly. Our escort tells Hans to stop. Then he opens the door and jumps out. 'Stay here,' he says, 'I'll be right back. I must see what's going on.' We lock the doors quickly as close to a hundred men make a circle around us. It is a moment diplomats describe as 'fluid'. It seems an eternity until the head of transportation returns. But he does, and we drive without incident back to the hotel.

Early the next morning it is announced that the bandh will be open for eight hours from 8 a.m. till 4 p.m.—for transportation only. It will allow people who have to leave to leave, and those who live in Darjeeling and are stuck on the plains to return. Hans and I walk down to the police station early to get the story from them. On the way we see a shop open, selling vegetables. The temporary lifting of the bandh is only for transportation and it doesn't include shops. In the crazy reality of Darjeeling at that time, an open shop is a potential flashpoint of violence. We jog past it.

The police arrange an army jeep to take us back to the hotel and to escort our vehicle back to the police station so that we can enter the exodus. And we do just that. We quickly gather everyone together and we follow the army jeep, rifles sticking through the open windows, down to the police station. The market is a scene of mass confusion, overloaded jeeps with luggage and sacks strapped to their roofs and sides, people riding on top of the sacks, the road out of town clogged with fleeing vehicles. As we enter the flow, I am thinking this must be a unique experience, fleeing Darjeeling in such a manner.

Little do I know that this is only the first of many times that I will find myself entering such an exodus to escape Darjeeling.

Vehicles fleeing Darjeeling

'We want Gorkhaland' stone sign in the Darjeeling Hills

8

THROUGH THE IMPERSONAL LENS

Two weeks after Gurudev's departure from Timi, I am outside the community hall in Namchi when Gurudev is due to arrive. Everything I had heard about him from others was so exaggerated that naturally I had thought none of it was true. I had been told so many times how lucky I was to be taken so close by him because his following was so immense. They told me that on his birthday 20,000 people come to his home village of Tukvar to bring him flowers. But they also told me he was a god, and not human. So where to draw the line?

Two hours before he is due to arrive, there are close to a thousand people waiting for Gurudev and the number is growing. They are streaming in from the surrounding hills, and they have come from as far away as Gangtok and Darjeeling. I am the only foreigner. The long driveway leading to the community centre is lined with people. Monks from monasteries in Namchi and beyond are drawing auspicious designs with coloured chalk on the pavement over which he will walk, blessing his way. They are burning incense to purify the air. Their cymbals and horns are ready for his arrival. Police officials and volunteers with special white kerchiefs and name tags are maintaining discipline, so if he suddenly arrives his way will not be blocked. Inside the community hall, which is a huge auditorium, volunteers are putting the finishing touches on the throne in the centre of the stage. It is overtopped by a silk parasol. Children are stringing great chains of flowers across the stage.

At the head of the driveway monks are creating an elaborate mandala of coloured chalk on the pavement, in the centre of which they place a coconut. A woman dressed in a white robe with wild, greying hair flying loose in the breeze stands before this mandala with a flower between her hands, which are pressed in an attitude of prayer. She starts rocking, and a chant arises from her throat in a voice that seems not her own. As the chant grows louder, her eyes roll up in their sockets, her breath becomes more laboured, and her rocking becomes more violent. I ask someone what she is intoning but nobody knows; she is a priestess of a sect with a language all its own, spoken only by its adherents, and only when they are in trance. Her incantation has a certain rhythm to it that quickly brings her

The coconut mandala

into a frenzied trance. Another woman, her attendant, also dressed in a white robe, stands behind her and grabs her by the shoulders when her frenzy reaches such a peak that she might do harm to herself or others. The monks blow into their long brass horns; drums struck with huge wooden clubs cause the very ground to vibrate.

Suddenly, the horns, the cymbals, and the chanting rise to a crescendo. They must have heard he's coming. Great heaps of pine-branch incense are lit by burgundy-robed monks, enveloping the gate and everyone around it in pungent, aromatic smoke.

Out of that smoke Gurudev's jeep appears.

There is a collective intake of breath, and everybody bows and starts mumbling prayers. The monks are blowing their long Tibetan horns, sounding their bells and cymbals. For his followers, just to see such a being is a tremendous blessing. His attendants jump out of the car and open the door for him. Dawa is not there. I don't recognize the others. Gurudev gets out and his face is different from how I remember it: he looks severe. There is no other way to describe it. His eyes are flashing like a captive lion's. It is as if the energy he expresses cannot be contained in a human body. I look again; is it really him? One of his attendants tries to straighten his robe, but he brushes him aside with a hard gesture.

Gurudev picks up the coconut that had been placed in the middle of the mandala and holds it above his head in both hands; then he brings it down with tremendous force and smashes it on the pavement, sending shards of coconut flying. His robe is splattered with the milk. He strides forward, barking out an order to one of his attendants with a harsh wave of his hand. The choreography is powerful. It is as if he were angry, but it is more than that. It is impersonal. He is expressing anger itself, or the wrathful aspect of some deity.

The crowd is torn between the impulse to surge towards him out of love, and to hold back out of awe and fear.

I watch the scene with probably more detachment than anyone else there, since I am not a devotee or even a believer, yet I feel an immense longing. I want him to take me as close as he did in Timi. But I am not sure how that will be possible at such a huge event. Now that I see something of the immensity of his following, and with what reverence he is treated by so many, I can better understand why people in Timi were always telling me how lucky I was. I realize they were right. His following is so big he won't even see me.

So I break from the crowd, run ahead, and position myself by the door to the community hall. By standing next to the door that he will have to pass through, we'll have to meet face-to-face. Most people get a glimpse of him and that is all. He had allowed me to get close to him before. I want to know whether he will again.

Gurudev is leading the huge crowd to the door. Behind him are his train of attendants, looking now more like bodyguards, keeping his way clear and making sure no one rushes him. It wouldn't be out of malice that someone breaks ranks. It would be like a moth, knowing better than to rush the flame, going full tilt into the light—an obliteration of self into source: it would be to fall unconscious into a halo of love by answering a maddened call.

Behind Gurudev and his attendants are the monks, their cymbals crashing in an endless crescendo, their horns a mad paroxysm of wildly concordant notes, clouds of incense billowing. And behind them, the huge crowd, a thousand strong, surging forward.

Gurudev climbs the stairs towards the door beside which I stand. His face looks rounder than I remember it. His skin is flushed and taut, as if bursting with energy or with blood.

There are beads of perspiration on his forehead as if he'd just walked out of a furnace. I can practically feel the radiation. He approaches the door to the auditorium and stops short directly in front of me. As if on cue the music suddenly ceases, the last crash of the cymbals slowly fading. It is as if the clouds of incense freeze as well in that moment of silence when Gurudev gazes deep into my eyes with a look both blank and intense.

'What is your name?' he asks. It is as if he isn't there, as if there is nothing personal left in him.

I tell him my name.

'Which country?'

'America.'

It is stunningly obvious he has no idea who I am.

His eyes, vacuous as deep space, which had fallen on me for a moment, shift to the door he is to enter and he continues inside, followed by the monks with their fanfare of horns and cymbals.

I stand by that door in a state of shock, jostled by the stream of people pressing to enter the auditorium. He doesn't even remember me! It hits me like a blow to my solar plexus. What was I thinking when I thought he had looked inside me and seen fertile ground for his teachings, worthy of close attention? The immensity of his following makes me feel tiny. So much for the ego! My first impulse is to flee. But I resist. I join the flow of people entering the auditorium and take a seat in the third row.

Gurudev sits cross-legged on his throne, the parasol rising above him in the shape of a cobra's head. Behind him are rainbow banners and *tankhas*, Tibetan Buddhist religious paintings. On the stage's backdrop is a huge image of the Hindu god Krishna, garlanded with flowers. To Gurudev's left, a line of robed Tibetan monks sit on burgundy cushions. They are performing a Buddhist ritual with small bowls of rice, occasionally flinging the dry grains to the various directions. Their chant is punctuated by the low bellowing of long alpine horns. To his right, a row of Hindu priests in white dhotis, foreheads smeared with gray ash, are reciting an ancient Sanskrit text. In a world in which religions usually mark differences, the admixture is stunning. It draws my attention away from myself and centres it on the single point where everyone's attention is focused: Gurudev.

Gurudev, sitting on his raised platform, is establishing his sovereignty. I haven't seen him like this before, fierce, barking orders, sending attendants scurrying to bring basins of water or find things for him, while others answer his questions and fan him with peacock-feather fans. It is almost as if he is playing with them, making a confusion out of which the mystery of his power will emerge.

People queuing across the stage to prostrate themselves before him are managed by the local organized force of devotees with their plastic name tags and identical scarves around their necks. The woman in the white robe is standing in front of his throne, the stem of the flower still pressed between her hands, reciting her incantation with fervour now, rocking from side to side, then shaking uncontrollably.

Gurudev sends his attendants away one by one to do this or that, even the one who has been fanning him. He sits alone now on his throne, gazing out over the priestess's head, above the line of people coming to touch his throne, and over the heads of an auditorium full of people. His gaze is fixed somewhere in space near the ceiling at the rear of the hall, his expression blank. Though his eyes are open, the impression is that he sees nothing. Like stone, he is simply being. Is this the ultimate expression of power, to not even see the people bowing down to you? Is he consciously deflecting the intense attention centred on him? Is this an expression of wisdom—an acknowledgement that the source is impersonal?

I realize that the more he looks out above everyone's heads at nothing and at no one—the more he releases his attention from the present—the more people's attention focuses on him. They are witnessing the mystery of a divine being commune with the Absolute. It is a masterful and paradoxical move—to release attention in order to focus attention. Children, and even babies strapped to their mothers' backs, are all silent now and, like everyone else, are staring at Gurudev with gaping eyes.

Gurudev holds this attention for but a moment. Then he begins to fidget. He is sitting on a pillow that does not suit him. It is uncomfortable. He leans over and plucks the offending pillow from under his buttocks. He looks at it like an impetuous toddler, flings it across the stage—and bursts out laughing.

And it *is* a moment of consummate absurdity, solemnity turned to mirth. The entire auditorium starts laughing too, uproariously, yet still in awe. They are seeing the mysterious, playful nature of their divinity. He creates a reality, then he takes that reality and with an infectious laugh and childlike innocence shows that it is nothing. Like making a figure from folded paper, then crumpling it in your hand and flinging it over your shoulder. He is only playing; yet how serious his game is, commanding the respect due a god-king. It is difficult to truly fathom what is happening. I am left only with my reactions, wondering about the reality.

People are streaming by him now for his blessing, leaving gifts on the altar before him—food, ceremonial scarves, money, potted plants. His attendants, who have reappeared, store these things away so there's room for more.

A beautiful young woman comes into the auditorium with a grace that makes heads turn. A silk scarf, knotted in the back, covers her mouth. In her hands she holds a large cup at the level of her forehead. She has come from across the road, from the dak bungalow, or government rest house. This is where Gurudev will spend the night. A special kitchen has been arranged there, where this woman with a scarf around her mouth—so she won't breath on Gurudev's food—prepares the pure food fit for a living god. She has come down the driveway of the dak bungalow, crossed the street, and walked up the auditorium's driveway. Now she enters the auditorium, climbs the stairs to the stage, and presents Gurudev with his tea.

Four little girls in frilly pink and blue party dresses enter the stage from the wings carrying huge bowls of flowers, which they place around Gurudev; then they bow and scurry away. Gurudev plucks a flower and shows it to one of his attendants, no doubt telling him the flower's medicinal properties. He laughs. His face is radiant.

Then he leans over to one of his attendants and whispers something into his ear. The attendant pushes his way through the crowd awaiting Gurudev's blessing and comes down into the auditorium. He makes his way over to me, causing people to scrunch their legs to the side, bends down, cups a hand over his mouth, and whispers into my ear, 'Gurudev is asking whether you're the one from Timi.' I nod my head. He returns to Gurudev's side.

Ten minutes later the woman with the scarf over her mouth walks across from the dak bungalow with a cup raised to her forehead. She enters the auditorium. She comes right up to my seat and ceremoniously presents it to me. 'It is from Gurudev,' she says.

It is a cup of hot milk with honey.

9

THE MAN BEHIND THE SHOW

They turn on the microphone and Gurudev starts addressing the crowd, his amplified voice ringing from the walls and broadcast through tinny loudspeakers to the overflow crowd outside, and throughout the neighbourhood. He speaks, sings, chants, speaks some more and generally holds people in rapt attention for about two hours, until night falls.

When he is through, a long line of people start flowing by for his darshan, or blessing, presenting him with flowers, ceremonial scarves, and other gifts. I notice that Tharbu, the monk from Timi, is among the monks sitting on the stage. He calls me over, so I sit with him and watch the line of people passing in front of Gurudev's throne. There are so many people backed up to see him that the rules have changed and prostration is not allowed. Each has but a moment to present an offering, put their head to the base of his throne, and be moved on by the volunteers with the white kerchiefs and plastic name tags. Some break ranks and prostrate themselves fully on the ground before him, which holds the line up and introduces moments of chaos in the otherwise strict proceedings. On either side of Gurudev stand the attendants who came with him in his jeep. They fan him with peacock-feather fans, clear the table before the throne of gifts so that there is room for more, and look for all the world like bodyguards. Gurudev sits in the middle of the mad swirl with a look of utter delight. He breaks bananas off huge bunches and hands them to people. He stuffs small wads of money into people's hands, and eats an apple that someone presented. I find myself watching him as closely as anyone, trying to decipher the meaning in everything he does, attempting to understand the man behind the show; and despite my best efforts, while trying to stand at a cool distance both to what I observe and to my reactions, I find myself falling under his spell.

Tharbu is introducing me to the other monks when Gurudev suddenly gets up to leave, obviously surprising everyone, especially his attendants, who start scrambling around. The driver runs out to pull the vehicle to the door. It seems part of his routine, to keep people guessing, never sure of what he'll do next. It maintains the mystery. As Gurudev passes by me, he motions that I should follow. At first I'm not sure that he means me. So I point my finger to my chest. He rocks his head Indian fashion and smiles.

I walk directly behind him. The auditorium is emptying, and everyone is pressing to see him leave. I can see them speculating about me. Outside, his jeep is waiting. Everyone is bowing down to him. An attendant opens the front door for Gurudev. Then one of the attendants opens the back door and tells me to please get in. My heart is pounding. I get in and I haven't a clue why—or where—we are going. Gurudev and the driver are in front, and I am at the back, and there are all these people bowing and jockeying for position just to get a glimpse, wondering who I am and what the foreigner's special connection to their guru is that he should be granted the extraordinary honour of travelling with him. Frankly, I'm wondering the same.

The driver starts the vehicle, revs the engine with a throaty roar, and—with a haughtiness usually reserved for the vehicles of Indian politicians or high military officials—muscles his way down the driveway, scattering devotees like chickens. Our journey is short. We cross the road and go up the driveway to the dak bungalow. The dak bungalow staff—from the manager, assistant manager and front desk staff to the cooks, cleaners, and gardeners—are all arrayed by the front door, their palms pressed together. Someone opens Gurudev's door. I get out, not quite knowing what to do, and am prodded to follow him up the steps to the rest house.

Gurudev is halfway up the stone steps when he sees a flowering weed growing between the cracks. He has the driver get his *kukri*, the ubiquitous Nepali machete and symbol of Nepali strength (which was hidden beneath the driver's seat), and carefully pries it free, roots and all. He instructs the driver to plant the weed in a flower bed. The driver pats the earth around the transplant and moistens it with a glass of water brought by one of the waiters. Only then do we continue inside. I hold back, thinking he will take his rest now after having been on stage for hours with the attention of so many centred on him. But one of his attendants pokes me in my back and tells me to follow.

So I follow Gurudev and the retinue down a hall and into the anteroom of the bungalow's master suite, which is adorned with oil paintings dating back to the British. The twenty-foot ceilings have filigree mouldings. I am conducted through this anteroom and into the master bedroom. Gurudev jumps on the bed and stretches out, as if to test its comfort. Then he sits up, delighted. A huge stuffed chair is opposite the bed and he tells me to sit on it. For a few moments there is a flurry of people in and out of the room. The woman with the scarf over her mouth brings us each a glass of water as others arrange flowers and scramble about.

And then I hear the heavy door click shut, followed by a sudden silence. I look around and I am alone with Gurudev.

The transition from the thronging, boisterous crowd of at least a thousand manoeuvring to catch a glimpse of God incarnate to being alone with him is stunning.

Gurudev sits cross-legged in the centre of the bed. Then he bounces on it like a child. It is a huge bed of beautifully carved wood. 'This bed, good bed,' he says. Then he tells me the Dalai Lama also slept there when he came to Sikkim. An energy of delight is emanating from him, like something a baby has. It is extraordinary in an adult.

The door opens and two men come in, closing the door behind them. One, wearing a suit and tie, is the mayor. The other is the manager of the dak bungalow. They enter with their backs bent, their palms pressed together in supplication. Gurudev calls the mayor over with a gesture of his hand. He whispers something in his ear and the mayor backs away from his bedside. Without turning his back on Gurudev, walking backwards, still bowed, turning every once in a while to see that he doesn't crash into something, he goes into the bathroom. There is the sound of running water. He returns a moment later with a plastic tub full of water, which he puts on the little end table next to the bed. The door opens to a crowd of people, who come into the room, each presenting Gurudev with a flower they plucked on the way and take a seat on the floor. He throws the flowers presented to him one by one into the tub.

Gurudev's attendants come in with his shoulder bag. They ask everyone to leave, even the mayor. I get up to leave too, but Gurudev motions that I am to stay. The door is shut. Again, we are alone. Then the door opens. There is a crowd of people all vying for position so that they can see what is happening within. A new group of people squeeze through and sit on the floor. Gurudev is whispering commands to this one and that, sending them on secret missions with the gravitas of a king sending his minister to negotiate with a foreign potentate. They pass through the crowd at the door, a look of urgent determination on their faces, only to return some minutes later, one of them with an empty clay flowerpot. Gurudev pairs the pot with a plant someone had given him, then gifts it to an old woman sitting in the back. Another's mission is to bring some old newspaper, which Gurudev uses to wrap the mangoes he is giving out. The atmosphere is a surreal mix of an imperial court and a children's playhouse.

One time, while whispering some order or secret advice into an old man's ear, his hand on the man's shoulder, he freezes for a moment and looks deeply into my eyes. His eyes are almost glistening with the significance he's trying to transmit. There is something confidential and intimate in his look, and I get the feeling he is trying to communicate something about the nature of the play that is unfolding. It is as if he is asking whether it isn't obvious. One can feel him above the show, looking on with a bemused smile. Like an actor on a stage, he seems to have distance from the role he is playing.

Is he suggesting I experience the unfolding play with the same gaze? I have the uncanny feeling that he is using the situation to show me something, that he is creating the conditions especially to instruct *me*. Yet why, really, do I think this, in a room full of people who are as enraptured as I am? It is only an impression; and like the vibration you feel near an electric transformer, there is nothing overt to point to. Yet even when he is putting his attention on the others, why do I feel his attention on me like a powerful laser? I feel on the verge of an understanding, as if there is a key just beyond my grasp, the acquisition of which would allow me to apprehend an elusive mystery hiding in plain sight, too simple to see.

There is a constant flow of people in and out of the room. Gurudev sits on his bed, charmed by his own creation in the middle of it all, speaking, telling jokes, hearing people's stories, and demonstrating his dexterity by throwing flowers into the basin of water. He is constantly having me take out my pocket notebook and write down the names of herbs. I can sense this is but an excuse and he wants me to take notes. Though I haven't mentioned it, somehow he's figured out that I write. Every time I put my pen to paper, he is happy. The woman with the scarf over her mouth enters with a tray of hot milk and cookies for Gurudev. Gurudev tells her to get another cup. He pours half his milk into the second cup and hands it to me.

10

FRONT-ROW SEAT

I am put up that night with a family of Gurudev's devotees. The next morning I wake early and rush through breakfast with my hosts, explaining that I want to go to the dak bungalow to see Gurudev. They tell me it is impossible, that I must wait for his public audience at the community hall. I feel they don't understand my close connection with him. That's what I think, at the same time wondering whether to think so is hubris. They detain me for some time; then I make some excuse for walking alone into the market and go straight to the dak bungalow, hoping that if I just show up there they'll let me see Gurudev. I want every opportunity to be with him. But when I arrive, they tell me he has just left in his jeep and won't be back until noon, when he has to be at the community centre.

I am walking through the middle of town on my way back to my host's house, disappointed that I have missed him, angry that I allowed myself to be detained, all the time feeling slightly silly for the disappointment I feel, when a vehicle pulls up short beside me and the door opens. It takes me a moment to figure out that the hand that grabs me and pulls me inside is a friendly one and that Gurudev is sitting in front with a huge smile. I squeeze in the back, suddenly back in Gurudev's movie. They turn the vehicle around, and I realize they had been on their way to the house to get me.

As we drive through town, people see who is in the front seat and they press their palms and bow their heads. We drive out of town and into the hills. Gurudev says, through an interpreter, 'I was speaking to the chief minister of Sikkim. I told him about you, that I have been spending time with an American; he was very pleased.'

Suddenly, Gurudev has the vehicle stopped. I always wonder why. This time a rock has rolled onto the road and three or four of us roll it off. 'Public works,' Gurudev says as we get back in and drive off. In fact, I never really know where we are going. Sometimes we are heading to a particular place; other times I have the feeling we are just driving. And even when heading to a specific destination, it is not unusual for Gurudev to suddenly have the driver switch directions. It is part of the mystery that surrounds him, that one never knows when he will arrive, or if he will arrive at all.

This time we end up in some devotees' house, and though they had no idea we were coming, they have a room in their tiny house—as do so many of his devotees—that is especially for him, ever ready for an unscheduled appearance. So Gurudev is conducted into his room and sits on the bed specially decked out for him. People flock for his darshan, to be in his presence, and to present him with a ceremonial scarf. Each holds the scarf forward with bowed head as they approach. Gurudev takes the scarf and consecrates it as he gives it back by putting it over the devotee's neck, which is a great honour. People bring him objects to bless, often *malas*, or Tibetan rosaries. By merely touching the object, he charges it with holiness. His blessings are obviously tremendously meaningful for the devotees. Does he truly think he possesses mystic powers and can confer them with the mere touch of his finger?

The play being performed is starring the god-man commonly known as Gurudev. 'Guru' means spiritual teacher.

'Dev' means divine or god. So his name translates literally as 'Teacher-God'. It sometimes seems I have a front-row seat at the Greatest Show on Earth. Yet to call it a show might make it too easy to then dismiss it: it is a show of enormous beauty, one that turns the minds of his devotees towards a sense of divinity. What is this divinity? By what power does he confer sanctity? How does a banana offered to him become sacred when coming from his hand? Is this an illusion he is offering? It seems he is creating something out of nothing. Is this the basis of his teaching? Is this what he wants me to see, and why he is always placing me by his side, on a level with him, to see from his perspective? Does he think me capable of such perception? What is it he is trying to show me? And what *is* his perspective? My mind swings from seeing it all as a great play of illusion, a chimera, a play of mirrors, to seeing that even if it is, it is one that generates love. Out of nothing, he creates an entire world. Maybe we all do, only with him it is conscious and therefore more obvious. Again, all I have are my reactions. There is something so vast and unknown about what I am experiencing. Fascinating and alluring. A rare gift he is giving me.

So we are in this house and it is getting on to midday. The lame are being brought in, and the sick. Gurudev is taking their pulse. He is breaking branches off flowering plants, wrapping them up, and explaining how they are to be administered. He cups his palm as if he is holding water, tilts it towards the patient and blows on it, conferring a blessing like a shaman of old. And as we are sitting in this room with an intimate group of fifteen or twenty people at a time, there are probably a thousand people back in Namchi waiting, buzzing with expectation.

When we return to Namchi the scene is as it was on the first day, when I had been waiting in the crowd for Gurudev, though this time I experience it from the other side. I experience what it is like to be in the vehicle, turn a corner, and ascend the driveway thronging with people who have been waiting in a state of advanced anticipation and excitement, all bowing deeply, the vehicle passing through clouds of incense, the drums and cymbals, the auspicious signs drawn on the driveway.

That day Gurudev spends the entire afternoon on the stage. First he performs a puja, reciting Tibetan texts with the ritual lightning bolt, called a *dorje*, in one hand and the bell in the other. The monks who flank him are chanting. Then he starts talking and telling stories and singing and it goes on for three hours. The crowd is entirely absorbed and delighted. He must be a wonderful speaker, for he holds the crowd enthralled. At one point, I find someone who can translate. Gurudev is saying that it doesn't matter what religion you are, that all religions are one. The ultimate god is the God of Love, and all religions are religions of that one god. To be religious is to be loving, and one should be loving and compassionate to all living beings.

After Gurudev finishes his talk, a long line of people forms to receive his darshan. While this goes on, they set up a microphone on the side of the stage and people—a Hindu priest, a schoolteacher, a local official—start giving talks. The Sikkimese community TV station is there filming it all. A local doctor approaches me and offers to interpret if I would speak, and I agree. I say what is on my mind. I tell the assembled people that since I am a foreigner, many people ask me what religion I am, expecting me to say I am Christian, but that I always respond by asking them, 'What religion is God?' I explain how my response usually elicits an uncertain smile. Then I say I believe all religions are only pointing at something beyond, say at the sun. So there is Jesus, pointing at the sun. There is the Buddha pointing at the same sun. There is a Hindu finger pointing. But what often happens is that the followers lose the message of the master and worship the master and not that to which he is pointing. In other words, they make the dog's mistake of looking at the tip of their master's finger instead of at that to which the master points.

Jesus was on the side of the prostitutes, the poor, the lepers, those dressed in rags. Yet if one of them would come to a Christian church today where everybody is scrubbed clean and in their Sunday best, they'd be looked down upon, if not outright barred. In a Buddhist monastery in Sikkim there is a golden Buddha. What has that to do with the teachings of the Buddha? 'I want no religion,' I conclude. 'I go for what is beyond.'

When the event is over for the day and I am whisked back into the vehicle with Gurudev, he gives me the thumbs up. 'Very sweet talk,' he says.

That night Gurudev sleeps in the house where I stayed the previous night. We don't get there until 10 p.m. A bed is made for him with a Tibetan rug, and the multitudes start streaming in. I think again about what he is doing, in light of my talk that afternoon. I had said we shouldn't get caught by any finger pointing at the Beyond, but we should each become an arrow to the very heart. Watching the crowds flock to him brings up in me a reaction that is visceral. Once again, I wonder how he can bask in the attention given a god-man and still be a man of truth. In his presence, everything is centred on *him*. And though I try not to be, I too am inexorably drawn to him. Despite myself, I feel like a bee drawn to a flower.

The woman of the house is radiant: Gurudev is staying at her house, which is now the centre of the cyclone that forever revolves around this one man. Her kitchen is now the master's kitchen. People with scarves over their mouths are cooking his food. 'So many people want to see him,' she exclaims. 'The stairs [this was on the fourth floor] are totally full!' I go to the stairwell and see that the stairs are packed. I also see how much Gurudev is giving her simply by being in her house.

Through one facet, I see that the world I've entered is far greater than my native world. Here, there is a place for the divine human being. Gurudev plays that part, and provides thousands with something to love, teaching universal love, the religion of love. He makes them laugh. And he makes the mother of this family overflow with love and awe. It is beautiful to see.

I am forever confronted with questions of reality, factual reality vs reality that has no basis in fact. I have noticed while wandering through Sikkim that every town has many different ways of being spelled. Ravangla, for instance, was spelled 'Ravangla' on one road sign and 'Ravongla' on the next. The school says the name of the place is 'Rabang' while the police station announces it as 'Rabong'. While one might both imagine and wish that there would be a single spelling for a single place, it is clear that this is not the case, and equally clear that it bothers nobody. One realizes that facts aren't so important here. Here is a god-man walking. Here are the devotees full of love.

The next day, the third and final day of the ritual, is the big day; it is called the *wang*, or blessing. Many people are too busy to come on the other days, or they don't want to sit through the teachings. But everybody comes for the *wang*. Everybody wants the blessing. And in Namchi, 4,000 people come. Two huge fires are set up for a *yagna*, or fire ritual, in the courtyard in front of the community hall. One fire is overseen by the Tibetan Buddhist monks chanting Tibetan texts; the other, right next to it, is presided over by the Hindu pundits, chanting from ancient Sanskrit scriptures. How rare to see rituals of different religions happening side by side. This proximity brings looks of surprise, and delight, on many people's faces. It is an almost revolutionary statement of Gurudev's teaching of the unity of religions.

Only a fraction of the people can fit inside the auditorium; the rest have to listen to what is happening through loud-speakers mounted on bamboo poles.

At mid-morning, Gurudev suddenly gets up and the car is brought around. I am whisked up and brought to the car and we just leave. Four thousand people came from all over Darjeeling and Sikkim, and we leave! I ask where we are going. To Jorethang, I am told, a town about an hour away. I ask why. Gurudev laughs. 'Shopping,' he says.

They drop Gurudev and me off in the middle of town, and the others go shopping. I follow Gurudev through an alleyway and up a grungy staircase, into a flat where there is a bed set up for him. He has me sit next to him. Tea is brought for

Yagna, or fire ritual, Namchi

us, and later, a meal. People start arriving for his blessing. A lame man is brought up the stairs on the back of his blind wife. Many come seeking medical advice. Pema appears with a razor blade and leads Gurudev outside. With a growing crowd of devotees watching, some of them bowing flat on the ground before Gurudev, Pema shaves his head. Meanwhile, his driver is in the market filling the vehicle with vegetables, fruit, bars of soap, pens, shirts, underwear—things Gurudev will give out later. Like the alchemist of old, his work is the transformation of common material into a blessed substance.

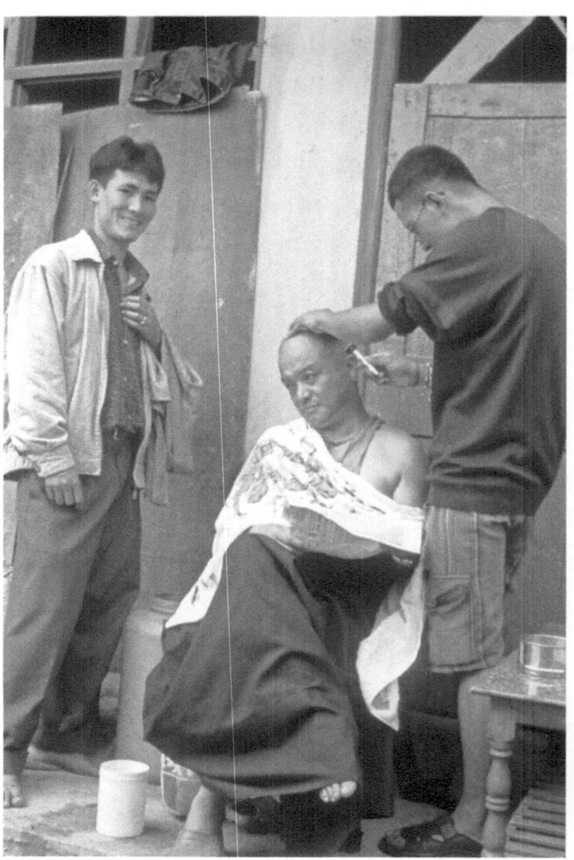

Pema shaving Gurudev's head

We drive back to Namchi and there is another ritual, followed by the *wang*, when everybody queues and passes before Gurudev's throne. He has a long stick known as a long-life arrow with coloured cloth wrapped around it, and he touches it to each person's head, one at a time. All those thousands. This is how these long pujas end, with this individual contact with the teacher. The people come with presents for him, some with a flower, some with money wrapped in a scarf, and then they move down the line of monks. The first pours a few drops of holy water into each person's right palm. The next monk gives out a little sweet ball called a long-life pill. Then some sweet powder; then something that looks like salt. Finally, they are each given a protection cord, which is a string with a special knot in it that you tie around your neck. The line of people filing by him goes on for four hours. I go behind the stage and on the side, in the wings, directly behind the line of monks, there is a big stuffed chair. And there I sit for all those hours, just watching Gurudev and the incredible unfolding scene. He sees me sitting there, and has tea brought to me. He calls me forward and gives me a plate of pistachio nuts. Occasionally, he stops the line and gives something special to one of the passing people, a flower, a branch of some bush. And I know these people will cherish these things, press the flower between the pages of a book, keep these things forever because they had been singled out by the god-man. Never have I seen such devotion and love by such a multitude. And each comes with his own devotion, his own way of looking upon the most high.

At one point, Gurudev reaches out and rests his open palm on a baby's head. Then he looks at me, his hand still on the head; he is gazing at me with an open, quizzical look, asking me again whether I understand. I catch a glimpse. Even if no greater mystic power comes through him, even if it is just the greatest show on earth and is all smoke and mirrors, I can't help but feel the love it generates. He provides something—himself—for these people to hold as the absolute highest. There is such love on these people's faces: the little children in awe of so great an event they can't even begin to understand; old Tibetan women, bent with age, tears streaming down their cheeks, prostrating themselves before him; teenage guys, styled, cool, in black dungarees, still humbled by the power they bow before. It brings tears to my eyes. What a miracle it all is. All question of believing in it all or not dissolves in the love that is undeniable.

A little later, a man approaches Gurudev pushing before him his reluctant seven-year-old son, who is clearly afraid of drawing close. The boy looks up at Gurudev and presses his palms. As he starts to bow, Gurudev's hand flies out and grabs something that the boy had tucked in his pants under his shirt. Then Gurudev holds in his hand a stick that the boy had fashioned into a pistol. The boy is frightened at first, having been found out by the Most High. The father is naturally embarrassed and words of apology start sputtering from his mouth. Gurudev takes the gun, tucks it under one of the pillows he is sitting on, and laughs. Across the boy's face flashes the realization that he'll never get his beloved toy gun back. Gurudev's laughter is infectious. Soon there is an entire hall of people laughing at this boy having been caught with a gun by Gurudev. Then Gurudev hands the boy a fifty-rupee note. This sum, equivalent to about one US dollar, is a labourer's daily wage, a veritable fortune for the boy, who walks offstage clutching the money, delighted by what his worthless piece of wood has turned into.

A little further back in line is an ancient Tibetan woman, gnarled with age, her face as creased as the mountains she fled over after the Chinese invasion, huge chunks of turquoise elongating her earlobes, her thin ponytail of grey hair braided with colourful strips of cloth.

Two young men, probably her grandsons, are practically carrying her to Gurudev's throne. Though the long wait has obviously been trying for her, the burden seems to lift as she draws close. Her face is radiant, her eyes full of love and devotion. She puts the single flower she has been clutching with her arthritic hands on the pile of flowers before the throne and, with the help of her grandsons, prostrates herself. They help her to her feet, and after tottering a moment she regains her equilibrium.

Gurudev reaches under the pillow and with a huge smile gives the old woman the wooden gun. The woman looks at the gun incredulously. Then she looks up at Gurudev, who is just breaking into laughter.

The next morning, Gurudev is leaving for Tukvar in Darjeeling. He is ushered into the jeep. There is a crowd to see him off. He calls me to his window and has me take out my pocket notebook. He has me write down the Nepali word for car, road, and tree. 'It is funny,' I say, 'to come to the feet of a master to learn Nepali.' He laughs. 'What to do?' he says. I tell him I am beginning to write about my experiences with him, and he laughs again. He hands me an orange and gives me a thumbs up. Then he invites me to come with them to his home village. I would want nothing more than to prolong my time with him; yet having escaped Darjeeling twice, I decline. Gurudev seems to understand.

The driver starts the engine. Everybody presses their palms, bows their heads, and amid a loud call of 'Jai Gurudev!' they drive off.

The moment he is gone, it is as if the lid has been taken off a pressure cooker. Everything is so concentrated in his presence that it is actually an incredible relief to see him drive off, and to know one can experience normal life again. Tharbu is there, the monk I knew from Timi, the one who said, 'Life is a flower, and death is death.'

He turns to me.

'Life is a show,' he says.

He gets it.

11

CRAZY WISDOM

Tharbu walks me into town so that I can book a seat on a shared jeep to Gangtok.

'Gurudev,' he says as we jostle through the crowd in the market, 'he's the real lama. For me, being a lama is sometimes like a job.'

And I suppose it is true. Performing rituals is Tharbu's profession; it's how he makes money. There is a conflict in Tharbu, which I appreciate very much. Later, I visit Tharbu in his home village in west Sikkim and find out he has a wife and kids.

We are approaching the jeep stand when a jeep comes screeching to a halt beside us. It is a man I recognize from the community centre. 'Thomas! Jump in,' he says, throwing the door open, 'Gurudev has sent me to find you. I've been searching for you for over half an hour. You must hurry, Gurudev is waiting!'

I can hardly believe it. 'I thought the show was over,' I say to Tharbu. And it had been a relief.

'For the true show master,' Tharbu says, 'the show is *never* over.'

I jump into the jeep and pull Tharbu in after me.

We speed to the edge of town and the man leads us running up a footpath to a large house in the middle of terraced fields. An elderly couple I've never seen before are standing outside the house, calling out as we draw close, 'Thomas! Hurry, hurry! He is waiting!'

I am ushered to the end of a long hall and into a room. I hear the door close behind me and I find myself alone with Gurudev. He is sitting cross-legged in the centre of a bed upon which has been laid a Tibetan rug.

A few minutes pass in what for me is a perplexing silence. Then others slip in. It is Gurudev's inner circle—his attendants, a few monks, the couple from the house. We all stand in a semicircle around the bed.

Gurudev picks up a *damaru*, a small hourglass-shaped drum with beads at the ends of leather chords that act as strikers. With a flick of his wrist he starts sounding it. Then he begins chanting in Tibetan; the monks join in with their low, sonorous voices. Gurudev is capable of projecting a presence that is so deep and elemental that one is sure one is partaking in something infused with the ancient powers that set the first dawn in motion. One realizes the power of the oral transmission of the ancient sages of the East. To be in that room, present at that moment, feels like the greatest privilege I have ever had. Everybody is gazing at Gurudev with looks of both awe and tremendous love. The energy he is expressing is the love that he speaks of, the universal binding force. You can feel it, and practically hear the hum.

Gurudev lifts a bowl of rice with two hands above his forehead and blesses it. He puts some into each of our open palms. Then he hands us each a flower. A ritual commences in which we throw rice to the four directions, to the Above and to the Below for the good of all sentient beings. By means of this ritual, all the energy that the thousands who attended the three-day puja centred on this one man is discharged; it is given back. All that was accumulated is given to all beings in the six directions for their benefit. That is blessing. It is a moment to swell your heart. The love we feel is not for him; rather, it is the gratitude for the presence and expression of love itself.

Gurudev ends with a sonorous Sanskrit chant that returns us to the very same moment first evoked by the ancient sages that composed the chant in the dim beginnings of time. And when he finishes, a deep silence descends on us, which is then broken by Gurudev, who waves his arm towards the corner of the room and says, 'Bring that.'

He is referring to a *chamor*, a stick with the long hairs of a yak's tail attached to its end, which is used in rituals. They wave them before things of the highest sacred order, like gods and sacred statues, to show great respect, like the fanfare before a king.

Dawa hands it to him and he takes it and flops it on his bald head as if it were an unruly wig. He puts his hand on his puffed out chest, bursts out laughing, and says in an exaggerated, boastful way, 'Me Sai Baba,' drawing an obvious parallel to the big hair of one of the most famous Indian gurus of the twentieth century.

The room breaks into laughter at the shattering of the sacred moment, this act of consummate absurdity.

It is Gurudev's ultimate statement: to create an atmosphere so packed with a single significance, to create a reality both rarefied and precious, and then to turn it all on its head. It is as if a crack formed in each of our heads that let in a beam of light, a beam that tickled us into a thigh-slapping laughter.

I have somebody translate 'Crazy Wisdom' for him. Crazy wisdom is the wisdom that is so high it seems crazy to the conventional mind.

Gurudev runs his hand over his head and gathers some of the yak hairs that have stuck to his shaved stubble. He rolls the hairs into a ball and gives it to me to keep as a holy relic.

'Yes,' he says, his eyes twinkling, 'Crazy Wisdom.'

❖ ❖

Tharbu walks me back to the bazaar in Namchi, where I get a seat on a shared jeep to Gangtok. While I am squeezing in and settling amid the impossibly numerous passengers, Tharbu disappears. He is rather like that, a bit enigmatic, a monk, yet not a monk, somehow struggling through his role as monk and family man, a bit cracked by his own admission, and very dear to my heart. He returns just as the driver is starting the engine, and as we begin to move, he presents me with a little gift, a small packet wrapped in newspaper, which he had just bought at a shop. 'This will help you think about it all,' he says with a twinkle in his eye. 'Open it later.'

Tharbu stands, his palms pressed at his forehead, until the jeep rounds the first corner. During the four hours it takes to reach Gangtok—passing through steep forests, bamboo groves, and villages, by cascading waterfalls and mountain streams we have to ford—I feel buoyant, like someone in love. Gurudev asks nothing for his love.

In Gangtok, I get out of the jeep at the jeep stand, which is on the edge of the town, backed up by a slope falling away in pine trees to a distant river flowing through the valley like liquid silver. Sitting on a stone overlooking the deep to relax a moment before moving into the city, I remember the little package Tharbu gave me. I tear off the newspaper, and it is a packet of cigarettes.

As crazy as it was for Gurudev to put the yak hair on his head and declare himself Sai Baba, so it was for Tharbu to present me with a packet of cigarettes. Not only because I don't smoke, but because of the taboo he broke in buying it, dressed as he was in the burgundy robes of a monk. It would be rather like a Catholic priest in the West going into a pharmacy and buying a package of condoms. While Tibetan lamas, especially in Sikkim, can drink, smoking is considered impure.

My mind wanders over the last days with Gurudev and his way of creating a reality and then placing a crack in the reality he has just created. It is as if we condense energy to create what we think of as a reality. In the breaking of the form a tremendous amount of energy is released, as when the

Tharbu, taking his leave from Gurudev.
The sunglasses were borrowed and put on for the photograph.

atom gets split. There is a mystery in this that can perhaps only be understood by experiencing it, and then experiencing it again. Sometimes I get a glimpse of what Gurudev is doing. I often have the feeling he is manipulating the situation in order to afford me this glimpse. Perhaps my not being a part of the culture around him gives me an added chance, since alien cultural forms are easier to see through than one's own.

Gurudev is a superlative actor. He manipulates everyone around him to take part in a movie to which he alone seems to have the script. I sometimes try to attribute motive to his actions—secretly playing the psychologist, wondering why he must always create a swirl of activity, like a cyclone with him in the centre, even speculating what might have happened to him as a child to create an adult with a pathological need to control—but I can never keep this up very long. Whenever I place myself in an adversarial role he outsmarts me, like a superior player at the game of chess; and his strategy is always the same: he wins the game with love. That is the incredible beauty. What he reveals through his self is universal love.

Universal love cannot manifest in just any situation. The ground must be laid. A situation must be created that can hold, if for only a flash, a quicksilver such as that. Gurudev's powers are such that if his motives were anything less than the highest, if he mixed the impurities of ego into the magician's game of making present that universal binding force, it would be an egregious manipulation, playing with people's longing for his own ends. That is what charismatic dictators and cult leaders do, with often tragic outcomes. With this in mind, I find myself scrutinizing him, unable to quite believe that what I stumbled upon by wandering without aim, like the Zen archer who hits the bull's-eye blindfolded, is the real thing, a spiritual master—especially because I wasn't even consciously pulling back the bow or aiming for the target. I test him continually, and he knows it. I even think he appreciates that I am testing the purity of his gold. I am the first Westerner he's come to know, and I think he is interested in how my mind works.

I find myself honoured that he allows me the position from which to observe him so closely and to find myself, despite myself, manipulated into a place of awe. The very fact of his affording me the opportunity is deeply mysterious and leaves me wondering at my luck. It also makes me incredibly grateful, especially as I sense the material coming together for this book. It has always been my experience that one cannot go out searching for a story to write. It is when the story comes knocking at your door that you know you are suited for it and that it is a story that only you can tell.

Sitting on a rock at the edge of the Gangtok jeep stand overlooking the wooded mountains, what I feel now is deep separation, and even longing. The river running through the deep valley reflects the distant sun. While I harbour the heightened energy that hums around Gurudev within me, I can feel it already dissipate. As if his presence were a drug, I feel his absence like a glow losing intensity. I am in a world now without a centre. People's motivations seem quite common, to sell me a ticket on a jeep to wherever, to sell me a packet of crackers. It is like coming back to earth after experiencing flight for the first time.

When I fled Darjeeling the second time, I had told my family that if they ever heard me say I wanted to go back to Darjeeling, someone should take me out behind the barn and shoot me.

I inquire about jeeps to Darjeeling and book a seat for the following morning.

PART II

THE RETURN

12

THE DIAMOND MIND

The first thing I do when I arrive in the town of Darjeeling is to walk down Nehru Road. This main tourist road is now bustling as if nothing's ever happened in Darjeeling—or as if darkness has been forever conquered and half the population of Kolkata as well as people from Mumbai, Delhi, and who knows where have come to celebrate along with representatives from most countries in Europe, not to mention North America and Australia. It is April, the height of the tourist season. Entire extended Indian families—grandmas in saris, granddaughters in tight-fitting jeans, children munching popcorn and licking ice cream—are snapping photos of each other, no doubt to be framed and hung on a wall back home. Knocking into each other in the frenzy that is found wherever too many people are gathered having too much fun, they are wrapped in newly bought scarves with knitted hats propped on their heads. Though preposterous in the heat, these knitted goods will be brought back home as proof of their journey to the high mountains.

I am braving the jostling crowd because I want to buy Gurudev a present. One cannot present oneself to the master without bringing something. Since I am going to his home village, I am expecting it to be an extended stay. Therefore the present must be something special. Choosing a present for Gurudev is different from getting one for anyone else. The thought process is entirely different. For you know from the outset that though you are giving it to him, he will give it away, probably before your very eyes. He will be but the conduit, the agent for the present's rightful recipient. There is something hugely liberating in this, something so contrary to the normal, his actions imbedding a teaching in both selflessness and unwarranted acts of kindness, that it is a constant wonder and constitutes much of his allure. This is especially skilful on his part because by acting as the conduit, he in effect turns others' actions into acts of kindness. This is part of the high people get in his presence. By participating in Gurudev's selfless acts, those who come bearing presents are themselves acting selflessly, and this is why they do it. Few of us would buy something, turn around, and give it to a stranger.

I take refuge from the crowded road in an equally crowded shop selling all manner of inexpensive 'authentic' Himalayan souvenirs, sweaters, and gems to an eager clientele comprised mostly of haggling Bengalis. I look first at the shelves of Buddhas and Hindu gods, then linger over the case of gems and decide upon a present. It isn't a diamond, but it looks like one. It is a cut zircon. The highest teachings of the Tibetan Buddhists are called the Vajrayana or Diamond Vehicle. A diamond reflects the many facets of the world, yet itself is clear and retains no image, just like the enlightened mind. That is the theory, and that is my present.

Halfway down Nehru Road I nip into Glenary's, a fancy bakery and coffee shop with windows overlooking the mountains. I order a pot of coffee, which is actually Nescafé. Even so, it is a rare treat in a land of sugary milk tea. Just when my ersatz coffee is brought, an acquaintance of mine walks in. We'll call him John. A student of Tibetan Buddhism, John is from England and he has been living in Darjeeling for about five years, studying both Buddhism and the Tibetan language.

I invite John to sit down, get the waiter to bring another cup, and begin telling him about this lama I met in Sikkim. My enthusiasm is obviously infectious; his face lights up as I recount my tales. Then he expresses wonder that he's lived all this time in Darjeeling and never heard of this lama. He asks me the lama's name.

'Gurudev!' he exclaims when I tell him his name, his expression suddenly one of both shock and contempt. 'Of course I've heard of Gurudev. That's Subash Ghising's guru!'

It feels like a kick to my solar plexus.

'You're new around here, aren't you?' John says, eyeing me closely. 'If there is an opening of a government project or the commemoration of some special day,' he goes on, 'there's Ghising paying homage to Gurudev—and Gurudev, as far as I can see, sucking up to Ghising. This is an old story in India, the unholy alliance between politician and so-called holy man. Yet how can an authentic holy man play ball with politicians, especially one like Ghising? You know who Ghising is, don't you? It does seem you haven't been here long.'

I stammer something, largely incomprehensible, about how of course I know who Ghising is.

'You better be careful,' John warns. 'You might not know what you're getting into. Remember when Ghising was ambushed?'

How could I forget?

'Ghising came out publicly and said it was only by the grace of Gurudev that he survived. It was reported in the newspaper that as Ghising lay crouched on the floor of his Ambassador car, the bullets whizzing by, he called upon his guru for protection. Apparently, there was some talk about Gurudev driving along the same stretch of road where Ghising would, a few days later, be ambushed. Gurudev had stepped out of his vehicle and stood for about five minutes at the very spot where the ambush would take place, blessing it. Then he had got into his vehicle again and continued on his way. At the time no one knew why. That's the story, and it's widely considered a miracle. Apparently though, the driver thought they'd just stopped, as they sometimes do, to urinate in the bushes.

'It is well known that Gurudev gives Ghising advice on how to stay in power, telling him the propitious days to go out in public, and days when danger lurks. That's what they say, anyway. All this begs the question, of course, as to why he didn't warn Ghising when he knew what was going to happen on that lonely stretch of road. Nancy Reagan had her astrologer; Ghising has Gurudev. It's a very strange alliance.'

John calls the waiter over and asks for another pot of coffee.

'Ghising rules these hills as if they were his fiefdom,' he continues, 'and he does so with the constant threat of violence. Not that he himself wields the *kukri*. He's got his boys for that. And especially feared is his councillor from Tukvar and Singamari, Bimal Gurung. He's the one people fear most, even more than Ghising. He's got the boys. And where do you think Bimal lives? In Tukvar, not far from Gurudev. And did you know that Gurudev is Nepali? Though he's a Tibetan Buddhist lama, he's a Gurung, born in a village of tea pluckers. He's also known around here as the Gurung Rinpoche. The Gurungs are one of the Nepali ethnic groups. Obviously, Bimal Gurung is also a Gurung. Who knows what the connections are. Just remember, your lama is the party's spiritual leader.'

I stagger out of Glenary's, reeling at John's claims, and run into a friend of mine, a local Nepali who, when I tell him I am going to Tukvar the next day, puts a hand on my shoulder and gives me a warning: 'I don't know if I'd go down there. During the agitation in the late 1980s, they were the most militant. They still are—and the biggest supporters of Ghising. That's Ghising's stronghold. It's a rough area. We call the people who live there the Mexicans, like bandits. You be careful.'

❖ ❖

The next morning I walk to North Point, at the northernmost point of the ridge upon which Darjeeling is built and take the ropeway, a gondola, which plunges with the precipitous Himalayan mountainside, skirting over the tops of bamboo groves and soaring above steep slopes of tea bushes, where lines of women pluck tea and throw it in baskets strapped to their backs. In my gondola are three young guys from Bangladesh who are visiting Darjeeling on vacation. Having never seen or heard of a gondola before, let alone been in one, they are terrified. I counsel them to close their eyes and think of home. It doesn't work. They take photos and holler with fright the entire way.

The ropeway over tea bushes

At the bottom of the ropeway is a collection of tightly packed wood-plank tea stalls set up for tourists, selling milky sugar tea and cheap trinkets. Asking for Gurudev's village, I'm directed to the road, which descends the steep slope of tea bushes in a series of tight switchbacks. Between the tea bushes and along the margins of the road wildflowers are in bloom. Huge butterflies ride the gentle breeze collecting nectar. Puffy white clouds scud across the deep blue mountain sky. After some time I ask a boy for

Gurudev's house. He becomes my guide. We take a shortcut down packed dirt paths through the tea bushes, enter a village, cross the paved road again, and go down a narrow alley between houses. We come upon a little house on the right; its sheet-metal roof is covered with dozens of cooing pigeons. Outside, a man sits on a wooden chair in the sun. A small white dog is sitting under the chair with his head sticking out between the man's legs. A goat is nibbling at some vegetable scraps the man is holding out. He looks up, sees me, and calls out, 'Hello Thomas!'

I have never seen him before.

'Come this way, Gurudev's been telling us all about you. He will be very happy.'

The Saint Francis of Tukvar

He leads me into the small house and there sits Gurudev on a bed, the window open beside him, the mountains beyond. It looks like he's just woken up from a nap. Dawa comes in through another door with a cup of tea held to his forehead. It's like walking back into the same movie. They both flash me broad smiles when they see me.

The room is small and I sit on the floor. Dawa sits next to me.

'It is difficult to be apart, isn't it,' Gurudev says gently, expressing my sentiments exactly. My heart had been pounding with more than just the altitude when I stepped inside.

I take out the zircon crystal and present it to him. He opens the white tissue it is wrapped in, picks it up between his thumb and forefinger, and holds it to the open window. The snow peaks splinter in its many facets. 'Clear, just like mind,' he says. 'Empty *and* full.'

He tells Dawa to find a mirror. Dawa runs out with his usual enthusiasm and returns a moment later with a round pocket mirror. Gurudev places the crystal on the mirror, which he holds in his palm. He slowly starts tipping the mirror but the crystal doesn't slide. Dawa and I are holding our breath as the mirror becomes vertical. Then Gurudev keeps going and turns the mirror right upside down—and the crystal sticks to it. Dawa's eyes widen. Gurudev looks at Dawa and then turns to look at me, wanting to see the effect his feat has had on us. Then he turns the mirror back over, takes the crystal off, wraps it in the tissue it came in, and motions for Dawa to put it in his shirt pocket.

Gurudev jumps up; Dawa helps him with his slippers, and Gurudev goes to the outhouse.

I am alone with Dawa.

'So what did you think of Gurudev's trick with the crystal?' I ask him, emphasizing the word *trick*. He obviously thought it a miracle. Sensing my scepticism, he smiles without answering. 'Let me see the crystal,' I say. He hands it to me. 'Now where's the mirror? I bet I can repeat his trick.' From the beginning in Timi, Dawa and I have had a friendly banter going about Gurudev's miracles. Needless to say, he is always seeing them, and I am always debunking them. He gets the mirror and I unwrap the crystal. He has a big smile on his face. While gullible, he has a keen intelligence and is open-minded enough to relish an experiment.

Wetting my forefinger without him seeing, I moisten the largest facet and then press it onto the mirror. To fully contrast Gurudev's show, I turn the mirror upside down without ceremony and the crystal sticks. For a moment Dawa looks at me as if now I've acquired supernatural powers, then catches himself. Just then, Gurudev returns. I put the crystal back into the tissue and Dawa slips it back in his pocket.

A little later an old man comes in, and Gurudev invites him to sit. It is an intimate moment. Gurudev is in a good mood. He puts some pillows behind his head and lies on the bed. We are sitting on cushions on the floor, leaning against the wall. Gurudev and the old man speak, and I enjoy watching them.

Then Gurudev asks Dawa for the crystal. Dawa takes it from his pocket and gives it to Gurudev, who presents the crystal to the old man, indicating that he should make it into a ring. The man is elated to receive such a gift from Gurudev.

Dawa leans over, and with a twinkle in his eye whispers in my ear, 'Did you see the miracle Gurudev just performed? He took a piece of zircon and he made it into something infinitely more precious than diamond. Now that man will treasure it for the rest of his life.'

The old man takes his leave. Dawa, Gurudev, and I sit quietly for some time. Gurudev dozes off. Dawa and I watch him sleep for some moments.

Dawa leans over and starts to whisper, taking up our conversation where we'd left it before. 'I know you don't believe in Gurudev's miracles. I think this is because you do not understand yet who Gurudev is. He is not one of us. Gurudev knows everything, every single thought that goes through our minds.'

'You're right,' I say, 'I don't believe it.'

'We were recently in Mirik, a town towards the Nepali border,' Dawa whispers, a huge, open grin on his face. 'Just outside Mirik, on the road to Darjeeling, two brothers live in houses next to each other. One brother, Karma, had a potted plant of a type that no one there had ever seen before. It seemed to grow larger by the minute and it was always filled with the most remarkable velvety red flowers whose smell could fill an entire house with sweetness.

Dawa

'The other brother, Pema, admired the plant every time he stepped into the house. In fact, he liked the plant so much that he even asked Karma if—since they were brothers—he could have the plant. Karma said, blood tie or not, he would not give up the plant. This went on for months, but Pema's repeated requests met with the same refusal.

'So we were coming back from Mirik and Karma happened to be in front of his house when we were passing. He noticed us and pressed his palms together in greeting. Gurudev told the driver to stop. Gurudev gave Karma a bundle of carrots as everyone from the adjacent houses, including his brother Pema, came to get Gurudev's blessing. Karma invited Gurudev into his house for tea, and Gurudev accepted. Mind you, the brothers had been to Gurudev's pujas, but neither of them had ever spoken personally to him. There is no way Gurudev had heard about the flowering plant.

'Everyone followed Gurudev into the house. Gurudev has a keen eye for all things natural; he knows his plants—flowering, medicinal, and otherwise. He had never seen a plant like the one in Karma's house. He exclaimed at its beauty.

'Karma, seeing Gurudev take such a liking to his plant, picked it up, held it out to Gurudev, and in one of those spontaneous acts of unselfish kindness that occur daily around Gurudev he said, "This plant is my prized possession and I would like to offer it to you." Gurudev took the plant, admired it a second, turned around and handed it to Pema. Everybody in the room burst out laughing, awed by the scope of Gurudev's limitless knowing. Now everybody in Mirik knows this story, and Gurudev's fame there has spread.'

Dawa and I both laugh at this remarkable story, inadvertently waking Gurudev up. He opens his eyes and looks at me. His eyes are glistening with tenderness.

He speaks. Dawa interprets: 'Gurudev is saying that with you he feels as if a close member of his family, who happened to have been born half a world away, has come.'

Gurudev smiles and closes his eyes. Dawa and I watch him fall gently asleep, his breath becoming deep and rhythmic. He offers his entire life, even his afternoon nap, to the scrutiny of others.

There is something about Tukvar that is very sweet. Though Gurudev was born and grew up in another tea garden across the valley, it is Tukvar, at his family's house, that is his home—if anywhere is. Gurudev has neither possessions nor home. Like a wanted man with a bounty on his head, he never spends more than a few nights in one place.

Gurudev gently awakens. He opens his eyes and turns his head to look at us. He asks me whether I like his village. 'This very simple place,' he says in his broken English. 'Here no song, no music. No dance. Only fooding and lodging—everything. But this home heaven like. Many-many people coming, eating fruit, vegetable, rice, ginger, tea for everybody. All with no money. All without paying. How possible? No miracle—but god bless. Your god good, my god good, you good, me good, other person also good. All good. All God, love. No crying. Why? Why? Love. Love is God. God is loving. Same-same. But outside looking—no god, no god outside, temple, church. God inside. But what I know? I no education man.'

'Gurudev,' I ask, 'why do you travel so much? Why don't you stay here, in your village, so your devotees can all come to you?'

Dawa puts my question to Gurudev and then explains his answer: 'If Gurudev did that,' Dawa says, 'only his rich devotees could see him. So many of his devotees are very poor, and few could afford to travel or take time from their fields. So *he* must go to them.'

Gurudev closes his eyes and goes back to sleep.

Dawa whispers in my ear that for years Gurudev travelled on foot, walking all over the hills, staying in his devotees' houses. Then someone gave him a vehicle. He only had it a short time when he met a taxi driver who had just lost his vehicle in an accident, didn't have the money to buy another, and was having trouble feeding his family. Gurudev asked his own driver for the keys, handed them over to the taxi driver, and simply gave the vehicle away. Gurudev started walking again.

Dawa then tells me something that opens a topic I feel reluctant to bring up on my own. He tells me that Gurudev's present vehicle was a gift from Subash Ghising. 'Ghising gave it to Gurudev,' Dawa says, 'on the condition that he promised not to give it away.'

'Though I've never met him,' I say in a whisper, both of us with our eyes on the sleeping Gurudev, 'most people say Ghising—how can I say this diplomatically? Well, I can't. Everybody says Ghising uses violence to maintain his power. He's not the type one would normally associate with a spiritual master. Holy men usually stay away from these men of power. What do you make of it?'

Dawa laughs nervously. Gurudev moves in his sleep. Dawa waits some moments, his eyes on Gurudev, making sure he goes back to sleep. Then he says in a whisper, 'None of us knows why Gurudev does anything. And you'd better be careful. I think you are now starting a long association with this area. I think you'll be coming back here for years. You don't understand all that goes on here. There are certain areas you shouldn't make inquiries into. You must be very careful.

'Ghising is building Gurudev a monastery outside Darjeeling worth millions of dollars,' Dawa continues. 'People have tried to settle him down before. They've built monasteries for him, one even in Nepal, but he never stays in them. Never. I don't think he'll stay at this one either!'

Dawa laughs again. Gurudev wakes up and asks him what is so funny. Dawa is obviously reluctant to tell. But Gurudev waits and Dawa is under the imperative to always speak the truth to his master. Besides, he believes Gurudev knows everything that goes on in his head, so there'd be no use lying. Dawa recounts our conversation. Gurudev, on hearing Dawa's opinion that he won't stay at the monastery Ghising is constructing for him, claps his hands like a child and laughs. It is impossible for me to tell whether Gurudev finds it funny that Dawa would think that or whether he is laughing at the idea himself, perhaps because that is his plan.

The subject of Gurudev's relation to Subash Ghising had obviously been on my mind ever since John mentioned their connection. Now I have confirmation of the connection John had alleged. I don't want this shining light to be tainted by the same darkness I'd experienced everywhere else in the Darjeeling Hills. This is obviously my moment. I understand the inherently explosive nature of even asking about Gurudev's connection to Ghising. Yet the situation is perfect: only Gurudev, Dawa, and I are in the room. I trust Dawa, and he is an excellent and intelligent interpreter. I am just formulating my difficult question in as tactful a way as I can when a commotion stirs outside. It grows louder and soon the door flies open and a group of devotees comes flooding in. My moment has passed, something I will later learn to regret.

The village in which I find myself lies in the Tukvar Tea Estate, about halfway down the 5,000-foot slope from the town of Darjeeling towards the Rangeet River at the border with Sikkim. It is a collection of perhaps one hundred homes. There are some sheds for goats and the occasional cow, a few shrines, and on clear days an unobstructed view of the snow peaks of Mount Kanchenjunga. In every direction the village ends in steep slopes of well-tended tea bushes. For this is a company town, so to speak: while the individual families own their houses, the land the houses stand on are owned by the tea estate and the people living in them are all workers. Tukvar is the oldest tea estate in Darjeeling; it was first planted in 1852. And while the Tukvar Tea Estate is owned by the Birlas, one of the richest families in India, the workers living there are quite poor. The women pluck tea and the men do the heavier labour on the plantation and work in the factory where the tea is processed. They have done so, in most cases, for generations. Along the road are a few tea stalls and small shops. Despite the warning I'd been given in Darjeeling, Tukvar is a very friendly place.

The house where Gurudev lives is like any other in the village—wood-slat walls, plank floors, and a corrugated tin roof. Though there are internal walls and thin wooden doors, one can hear what goes on in every room. Gurudev's room is partitioned in two by a low wall, open at the top. His bed is in the back; I never know which member of the family sleeps in the bed in the front, for they put me in that bed every time I come. It becomes my room for the duration of all my stays there. The window next to my bed looks out on a clump of bamboo and the stone steps leading down to the outhouse.

My first morning in Tukvar I awake at dawn. The door next to my bed, which opens to the mud track in front of the house, is ajar. An old woman with bare feet comes stealthily in, holding a yellow flower. She is followed by her grandchildren, a girl of six leading a toddler, both clutching wildflowers in their little fists. The woman folds back the curtain that serves as a door to Gurudev's room and peers through it. The girl is trying to keep her little brother quiet. I sit up in bed, but they don't really notice me—or that they're passing through my bedroom. Gurudev lets out a loud bellow. 'Hooooe!' The old woman smiles with delight, and the three of them disappear into his room. I hear the woman prostrate on his floor; he comments on the flowers. There is another door to Gurudev's room and I hear Dawa come through it. Soon others pass by my bed, people taking a short detour on their way to work in the tea garden or just as part of their morning routine, each holding a flower to present to Gurudev and receive his blessing in return. I go into his room and sit on the floor and watch the morning procession. After everyone lays their floral offering before him, Gurudev dips the tip of his right ring finger into a small dish of sandalwood paste and marks their foreheads—protection for the day. Everybody kicks off their sandals before entering and there is an ever-changing mound of sandals outside the door.

Here in the village there is an intimacy between the people and Gurudev, the elders having grown up with him, the youngsters having always known him to be a part of their village, spiritual uncle to them all. As the morning progresses, the children come in their school uniforms, backpacks full of books. Laughing, scrubbed clean for the day, they come bearing flowers to present to the living god, so happy that he is from *their* village. How better to start the day than by seeing a six-year-old girl walk into Gurudev's room with a flower in her hand and come out beaming, her flower transformed into a banana or an ear of corn?

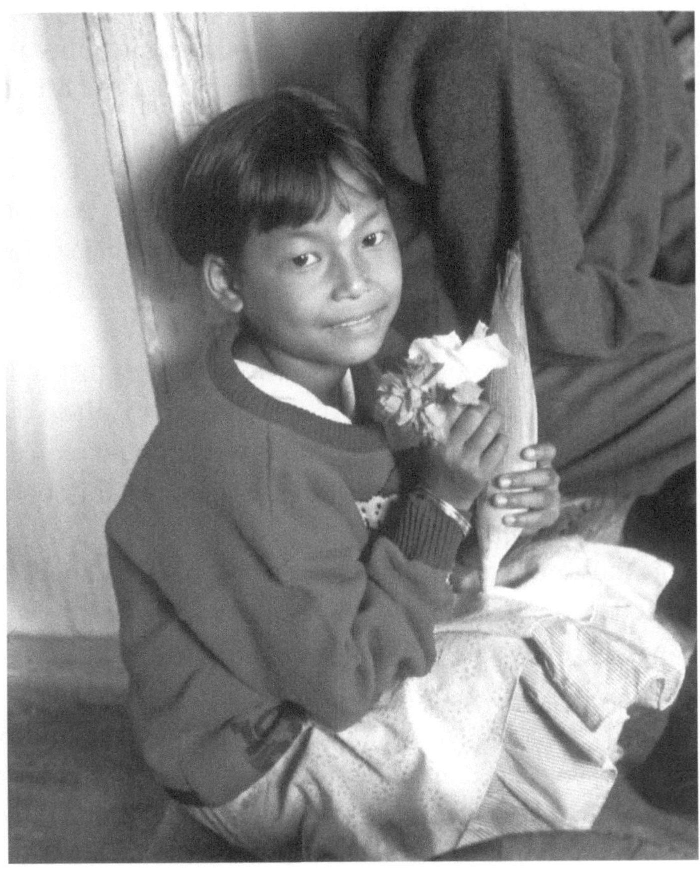

Gurudev must have seen the delight in my eyes. 'Many children here,' he says, 'mommy daddy no having money. No good food no vitamin many health problem. Here every child fruit—every day!' He hands a little girl a melon that almost dwarfs her. 'No charge! No problem. Apple vitamin, banana vitamin. No problem!'

Later, Gurudev is sitting on his bed. I am on a chair opposite, and we are eating breakfast when the village idiot comes in. I use the term 'idiot' advisedly and in a non-derogatory sense. While people with severe mental and physical handicaps are shunned and institutionalized in the West, they are looked after by the family and indeed entire villages in the Hills. While children, especially boys, sometimes play pranks on them, they have a place in the society and I've often seen them shown great kindness.

The idiot of Gurudev's village is a man with a permanent smile plastered on his face, protruding useless ears, and a throat that produces only animal grunts. It is clear that not only is he deaf and mute, but his brain is also wired in a pretty simple way.

His entrance is accompanied by the most delightful, happy sounds we all might produce if we ceased to filter our joy through the medium of language and found a truer expression, more directly expressive of delight. It is impossible not to be infected by his simple joy.

He is holding in his hand a dusty, half-crushed flower he plucked from the side of the road, which he presents to Gurudev. Gurudev takes the flower and throws it across the room into a bowl of water that has been placed at the base of the family shrine. To the idiot, this minor feat of dexterity is a miracle. You can see it in his widened, wonder-filled eyes. He claps ecstatically, squealing with delight. Gurudev motions him closer and hands him a ten-rupee note. The idiot takes it between his thumb and forefinger and examines it as if he were a mime examining a dirty rag. The tragic look on his face, the way he points at the offending note, makes clear what he is saying: 'That's all? Only ten rupees? I might be a fool, but even *I* know this is next to nothing.'

Then, to show that he is deserving of more because of recent misfortune, he puts the money in his back pocket and demonstrates how he has recently lost money from that very pocket. He turns all his pockets inside out to demonstrate his destitution.

The idiot turns everyone into a mime. Gurudev lifts an imaginary bottle to show that if he gives him more money he would buy drink with it. But no, the idiot shows, I've had a great misfortune: I had money in my back pocket, and it fell out. He throws the money on the ground and pretends to walk away.

Gurudev turns to me and speaks. Dawa interprets: 'He is saying that you cannot change a man's fate. If you give a drunkard money, it only increases his misfortune.'

Finally, in exchange for a promise that it won't be used for drink, Gurudev gives him another ten rupees. The idiot is ecstatic. Gurudev takes a *khata*, a ceremonial scarf, and ties it around the idiot's head. He takes a peacock feather and tucks it under the scarf. The idiot is crowned for the day. He leaves, making little noises of delight.

13

THE MEANING IN RANDOM EVENTS

Gurudev has a genius for finding meaning in the random events of everyday life. Somebody presents him with a large fruit wrapped in newspaper. He unwraps the fruit and puts it aside, hardly noticing whether it is a papaya or a pomegranate. It is the newspaper that interests him. Examining the headlines, he tears out a few words. Rarely is it an entire headline. A word or two—or a phrase—usually suffices. These scraps he ensconces in the folds of his robe or hides under his pillow. Under the pillows of Gurudev's thrones are troves of treasure—a veritable arsenal of spiritual wisdom. He reaches into the deep, concealing folds of his burgundy robes or pulls up the corner of his pillow or blanket to reveal his little hidden treasures. He picks out a scrap, often without even looking, and hands it to some unsuspecting devotee placing a flower on the low table before him—a special message from Gurudev gleaned from a random scrap of newspaper, something especially for that person to take home and ponder. Gurudev has the uncanny ability of coaxing significance and meaning from the seemingly random. He is often right on the mark, answering with a scrap the question that hasn't yet been put to him.

One time, Gurudev held up a newspaper photograph of the Mona Lisa and asked me if she were a movie star. Another time, he was sitting enthroned before a crowd of thousands, the monks on either side of his throne blowing their huge alpine horns. When those who had pushed to the front of the crowd started rushing the throne and touching their heads to the ground before him, an almost exaggerated look of boredom crossed his face. I have noticed this look before, especially when the fervour of worship hits a crescendo. So he picks up a newspaper and starts leafing through it, scratching the corner of his mouth and yawning. To say he looked bored would not be accurate: ironic would come closer to the truth, the corners of his lips suggesting an enigmatic smile, as if he, like the Mona Lisa, were continuously verging on a laughter that never came. He steals a glance at me. 'What to do?' he says. He is saying that he is a being like any other, under a law, having to fulfil his role in this life. His, it sometimes seems, is to live up to others' expectations of what a master should do.

As the crowd continues in an endless wave to press their foreheads to his throne, he folds the newspaper back to expose a half-page-sized photo, holds it up, and slowly shows it to the crowd, first to the people on his left and arcing towards the right, where I sit. I am the last one to see it—a photo of Marilyn Monroe, her neck exposed and her breasts bulging. He turns to me. 'This one goddess?' he asks. Then he turns the paper over and holds it up again. The huge headline reads, 'Another Time, Another Place.'

Since imitation is the greatest form of flattery, I decide early on that I too can play this game. Why should he have all the fun? So one afternoon in Tukvar, Gurudev is sitting on his bed surrounded by devotees and I am sitting on my bed on the other side of the partition. A scrap of newspaper on the floor catches my attention, too good to let lie. The headline reads, 'You Cannot Escape the Third Eye'. I rip it out and hand it to a little girl on her way through to see Gurudev, and gesture that she is to give it to him, just as Gurudev would do, in a commanding but friendly way. So she brings him the scrap, explaining that she was instructed to do so by the foreigner. I can hear Gurudev asking someone for a translation of the headline. Gurudev bursts out laughing. 'Third eye!' he calls over the partition wall. 'Good one,' as if we are now comrades, able to find consequence in the inconsequential, meaning in the meaningless, a point where there is no point, significance where there are no signs, sense in the senseless, and messages in the random scraps of everyday life.

'Another time, another place'

Gurudev has a book that could easily have been the subject of a short story by Jorge Luis Borges, the great Argentinean writer of metaphysical tales. For this is an endless book, a book bursting its own binding, two times its natural thickness, stuffed with headlines and scraps of paper. He produces it at odd moments from under a corner of his bed and uses it as a book of divination. He always handles this book gingerly not only because it is holy, but because its binding is torn and many pages are loose. He leafs through it as if to gain inspiration, sometimes as if looking for something that he might have lost there as long ago as in a previous lifetime.

The book originated as an English–Nepali dictionary. Maybe sometimes he is simply looking up a word. But often he flips through it. Then he glances in a significant way at someone sitting on the floor. He flips some more pages, picks out a scrap of paper, puts on his reading glasses to read it, replaces it, turns a page, and peers over the rims of his glasses at that person again while everyone in the room waits for the pronouncement of the magical dictionary. It might just change the course of that person's life. Sometimes Gurudev holds the book in his hands and has someone open the book at random. Without looking, Gurudev puts his index finger on a word in the dictionary and from that word tells something about that person's condition or fate.

The book of divination

One time a friend from Spain came with me to see Gurudev. She spoke neither English nor Nepali, and I was forever having to translate from her Spanish to English for someone to translate to Nepali so that Gurudev could understand her words. She opened Gurudev's book at random in the middle of the English Ps. Gurudev put his finger on a word. It was the word 'polyglot', third definition, which reads, 'a mixture or confusion of languages'.

14

THE ROAD CREW

I frankly do not know how long I spent in Tukvar that first visit. The days followed a certain rhythm, which at the time I would have been happy to have continue forever. The day invariably started with the villagers and their children lined up outside the hut, each with a flower for Gurudev. This would be followed by breakfast, which I'd usually be allowed to take with Gurudev, followed by any number of groups coming to receive his blessing or seek his advice. Though a constant curiosity, I was accepted as an honoured friend by all. The family took me in as one of their own. Gurudev transformed that village of tea pluckers, and at times the atmosphere was imbued with the magic of fairy tale. Once, when it was raining, I walked out of his room and stood gaping at the puddles in front of the wood-slat house, incredulous that such a being could be found along a muddy track—and not one paved in gold.

Many evenings a bald-headed old man, whose small frame was made even smaller by the curvature that more than ninety years had put into his spine, hobbled over from his house nearby with a cane in one hand, holding in the other the neck of a one-stringed instrument. The roundness of his head bespoke a roundness of spirit; he exuded wholeness, a calm that only those possess whose lives bear the fruit of a lifetime of spiritual practice. He would come into Gurudev's room, which was invariably full of people, bow before him, touching his head to the ground, then sit on the floor cradling his instrument on his lap.

At a certain point Gurudev would prop himself up with pillows, lean back, and motion for the old man to begin. The old man would start by twanging his instrument's single string with his finger, filling the room with a rhythmic drone, at once monotonous, hypnotic, and evocative of mystery. He'd close his eyes and sing in a voice that opened the heart, not forcibly, but with the penetrating force of gentleness alone. His voice had both the frailty of an old man and the collective strength of a centuries-old tradition.

Many of the songs the old man sang were mystical in nature, and though I couldn't understand the words, they never failed to move me deeply. Other songs were obviously devotional, dedicated to the guru and singing his praises. And yet others were full of puns and extemporaneous turns of phrase, which must have been both brilliant and hilarious, especially coming from such a withered, old fruit on the human tree. It was then it hurt me not to understand more than an extremely rudimentary Nepali, for though Gurudev sometimes had someone translate what the old man sang, it was pure poetry, and as Robert Frost once said, poetry is that which gets lost in translation.

Then one day, it was perhaps after a week or so, I could sense a change. Much as a dog reads the subtle signs that tell him his master will be leaving, I knew Gurudev would be going on the road. I felt that nervous excitement of balancing between hope that I'd be allowed to come along and despair that I'd be left behind. And it wasn't until the last minute, when the family were lined up on the sides of the dirt lane along with half the village with their palms pressed, the vehicle waiting on the side of the motorable road, that

Dawa came running. 'Where's your pack?' he said, his eyes gleaming. 'We're leaving!' I grabbed my pack—I had readied it just in case—and thus began my sojourn on the road with Gurudev and his road crew that must have lasted six weeks. We went from event to event set up for him across the width and breadth of the Darjeeling Hills.

While there were always both Tibetan Buddhist monks and Hindu priests at Gurudev's events, those he travelled with, his travelling retinue—excepting Dawa—resembled a band of young toughs rather than those whose role in life was to see to the needs of a living god. Gurudev's devotees sometimes complained, asking why he surrounded himself with such rough characters, guys who in another context one would cross the street to avoid. It *was* curious—another of the strange contradictions about Gurudev—why it was never quite possible to feel comfortable around him. Not only did he not shy away from contradictions, he seemed to relish them,

The road crew

using them as tools of befuddlement, which were ultimately used as tools for giving teachings.

Or were they?

The confusion I felt around Gurudev at the beginning never abated; it only deepened. I think this is good. It always seemed that once one set of confusions was cleared, he'd throw up another, as if one's time with him was an endless course of hurdles. In my more cynical moments, I wondered whether he resembled less an incarnate god than a figure very much like the Wizard of Oz.

Gurudev's main attendant, the person undoubtedly closest to him and without whom he rarely if ever went anywhere, was his nephew Pema. I call Pema his nephew, though I'm not sure whether Pema was strictly speaking his nephew. In a land where cousins, and even friends, are called 'brother' it is often hard to tell. Regardless, Pema was a close relative, and since it was through him that Gurudev's events were all scheduled, he was the only one who knew the intricacies of our schedule, which often included two events a day and involved many hours on the road. Pema was in his mid-twenties. He tended to wear dark glasses, military cargo pants, black army boots, and a black T-shirt with a design on it of intertwining long-fanged serpents. He would stand beside Gurudev at the big events, his darting eyes hidden behind dark lenses, his hands clasped, exposing his muscular body in all its force to anyone who would consider doing Gurudev harm.

I don't doubt for a moment that Pema would have put himself between Gurudev and an oncoming knife. His stance at Gurudev's side seemed studied; and if it was, he got it from Hollywood, taking his cue from the depiction of the Secret Service security detail around the American president, or maybe from the protection detail of a Mafia don. Pema moved at ease in all circles, and though he was young, he was shown great respect by everyone, from jeep drivers and tea pluckers to political leaders and high incarnate lamas. Once you got to know him, his rough and even menacing exterior seemed to be just that—an exterior; for he could also be quite sweet

Pema

and gentle. Still, he seemed most at home with some of the darkest characters we encountered, and I often had the feeling he was continually tempered by Gurudev's presence, as if without Gurudev's influence he would be capable of dark deeds. I was always very careful with Pema, and to the end there was something about him that frightened me. Pema was always with Gurudev. He slept in Gurudev's room, often on the floor next to his bed, almost every night, be it in Tukvar or while we were on the road.

Our driver's name was Sangam. He had rather long hair and a round face. An unlikely character to be driving an incarnate god, he would have blended in well in any Nepali roadside watering hole. As with Pema, he was in his early twenties and was surprised to find out he was close to forty. When you saw him in his blue jeans, crawling out from under the jeep with a greasy wrench in his hand, you'd never guess the fervour with which he would prostrate himself before Gurudev every morning. He was an excellent mechanic, fixing the vehicle with ease when it broke down, which was rare since he anticipated impending troubles with a pre-emptive turn of a wrench or tweak of the engine. He washed the vehicle often and attended carefully to the two flags that

Sangam, the driver

flew on little metal masts at the front of the vehicle, the one on the left the multicoloured flag of the Buddhists, and the one on the right the red triangle of the Hindus. It was largely by these flags that people walking on the sides of the roads, working in their fields, or looking out of their windows would know it was Gurudev, and come flocking for his darshan, to get his blessing.

I always had the feeling Gurudev had saved Sangam from some kind of trouble, that Gurudev was forcing to the straight and narrow someone who had been in danger of going off the deep end. Each of us had our own story to work out with Gurudev, and Gurudev was working on each of us in his own way.

Then there was Rabdin, not at all the ruffian in a denim jacket; he tended to wear beige knitted sweaters and his shoes were always polished. With an inborn and genuine gentleness, it was as if he were there to offer contrast to the rough-boy look of the others. Whether he had started out a ruffian, I do not know. His dedication to Gurudev was complete. Whenever we left the vehicle, he would carry Gurudev's orange shoulder bag, which contained his personal items, with total devotion. He would stand beside Gurudev at the big events, the image of the perfect attendant, arranging Gurudev's robes when he sat cross-legged on his throne so that the folds of the material were just so, as if he were dressing a mannequin. His duties on stage included fanning Gurudev with whatever was at hand—be it a peacock-feather fan, newspaper, or a piece of cardboard—collecting the offerings, and clearing away the flowers that were continually piling up before the master to make room for more. He was always solicitous of the woman of the house wherever we stayed and seemed to gain true satisfaction in serving tea.

And then of course there was Dawa. Dawa was from Gangtok, the capital of Sikkim, and had first heard of Gurudev from a book written about him. The book itself was controversial, not because it contained every fanciful miracle story ever told about him and would make any non-believer cringe with its credulity, but because the book won a major Darjeeling literary prize. The prevailing opinion among those who were not Gurudev's disciples was that the book won the prize only because Subash Ghising had ordered the judges to choose it, the book being about his guru. I had occasion while travelling with Gurudev to meet the author of the book a few times, and once got into a pointed discussion with him about certain photographs in the book that supposedly showed a spiritual glow emanating from the master. My reasoned proof that the glow was the result of the camera's flash and would of necessity occur no matter whose visage was caught at that particular angle, both caught him off guard and produced abject denials, proving the immunity of faith to reason.

Some two years before I met him, Dawa had read the book and was amazed to hear there was such a Celestial Being as Gurudev living in Darjeeling. A short time later he chanced to hear that Gurudev was coming to Gangtok. When Dawa walked into the hall and saw Gurudev sitting on a raised platform in the centre of the stage, he was immediately drawn in. He went to the front and sat on the floor so that he could watch him closely. Buddhist monks sat on the floor to one side of Gurudev's throne, Hindu priests on the other. The hall was full. A long line snaked to Gurudev's throne and everyone held something to give to the master, for you don't present yourself before the lama without an offering. And when they reached his throne, attendants moved them along so that each had but a moment, enough time to lay the offering before him, press their palms, and maybe touch their heads to the throne before

Gurudev's image for sale in the Darjeeling market

they felt an attendant's hand on their shoulder. Some broke free of the attendants' grip and prostrated themselves fully before this being they perceived as infinite light.

With the Hindu priests on one side of the throne and the Tibetan Buddhist monks on the other, Dawa knew—even before Gurudev opened his mouth to speak a single word—that Gurudev's message was revolutionary. He had read in the book that while many of Gurudev's Buddhist followers believe him an incarnation of Padmasambhava, the wizard credited with bringing Buddhism to Tibet, his Hindu followers believe him an avatar of Vishnu and an incarnation of Krishna, who incarnates when times are tough and a guiding hand is needed again amongst the suffering peoples of the earth.

Dawa saw that Gurudev defied traditional categories defining what a religious man is or is not. By bridging the gap between different religions, bringing Hindu priests together with Buddhist lamas, Dawa grasped Gurudev's message of universal love and of a god beyond distinction. And even though Gurudev was not speaking when Dawa sat down, the scene was choreographed to give the message, his teachings most powerfully put by his example, rather than by any verbal admonition.

Dawa was wearing a gold ring, which I think he had inherited. He fingered the ring, twirling it on his finger, and then he got up. He waited in line for Gurudev's darshan, and when he got to Gurudev he slipped the ring off his finger and held it in his palm; in a subtle way, so no one could see—he didn't want to draw any attention to himself—he gave the ring to Gurudev. Gurudev took it, saw what it was, and after putting it under the pillow he was sitting on, gave Dawa a banana and a flower. Dawa then took his place on the floor in the front again and continued to watch this being, whom he was now certain was his teacher. A few minutes later, Dawa saw Gurudev put his hand under the pillow, take the ring, and reach down and tap one of the Hindu priests on the shoulder. He held out his hand and dropped Dawa's golden ring into the priest's hand. The priest tried it on and the ring fitted perfectly. A stream of tears rolled from the man's eyes, which he could not stem. Dawa found out later why the man cried at the sight of the ring: the priest had had a silver ring, which he had worn for over ten years. It was a lucky ring, one that meant a lot to him, having been a gift from a great sadhu, or holy man, who had since died. The day before, the priest had been washing at the river when the ring slipped from his finger, fell into the swiftly moving water, and was lost. And though he was greatly saddened by the ring's loss, he had mentioned it to no one. And now Gurudev had replaced his ring, this time in gold! That was to be the first of many miracles Dawa would experience in the presence of the one who would become his spiritual master.

So this was the travelling crew: Sangam driving and Gurudev in the passenger seat in front; Pema, Rabdin, Dawa, and I in the back. And since the back was only meant for three, it was a tight squeeze. Being the last one to join the crew and feeling privileged by chance for being there, I took it upon myself to always be the one to lean forward with my buttocks only partially on the seat, hanging onto the back of Gurudev's seat when we rounded tight turns, and otherwise facing the discomfort I didn't think it fair to impose on the others since my presence in the vehicle, though it stretched from days to weeks, was both temporary and the cause of the discomfort. Sometimes people would join us for a single journey and would squeeze in the way back with the luggage and vegetables.

We travelled together to many obscure corners of the Darjeeling Hills, to one ritual gathering after another, one tea garden after another, and wherever we went crowds flocked to see him. I got so used to having people on the sides of the roads bowing as we passed that it felt strange when one day I drove in another vehicle and no one paid us any mind.

Once we were at a three-day event at a tea garden which over 4,000 people attended. On the second night someone was stabbed and killed in a nearby bazaar town. We heard about it in the morning. We immediately piled into the jeep and drove down to the town. Gurudev and I walked down the main road of the market with Dawa. Gurudev had Dawa buy bundles of vegetables and load them into the jeep. Gurudev and I continued until we reached a grain dealer. We went in and Gurudev bought some things, which he then immediately gave to a man walking by. The man came in and sat down, as did more and more people as word spread that Gurudev was there. Soon the shop was packed with people and more clogged the road in front of the shop, all trying to see him and hear what he was saying. He was beaming with joy and making everyone in this small bazaar, where someone had been murdered only hours before, laugh. And this went on for two hours.

Gurudev at the grain dealer's shop

15

THE CHILDHOOD OF GOD

One day we went to Siliguri, the large town on the plains just out of the mountains, where Gurudev had been invited to a wedding. It was a good three-hour drive on a road that switched back and forth down the slopes of mountains to the Teesta River. Then we followed the course of the river until the mountains suddenly stopped and the vast north Indian plains stretched out before us. As mentioned earlier, the contrast between mountain and plain is not only geologic. Culturally also, it is a vastly different world down there, where the people are Bengali and not of Himalayan descent. When the river hit the plain it widened to nearly half a mile—or rather the riverbed widened, for it was the dry season and it was mainly stone and dried gravel. We passed through a huge tropical forest in which large, thick leaves were falling one by one through the heat-baked air onto the parched ground. Deep in that forest lived rhinoceros and elephants.

Siliguri was a dreadful city: large, ugly, and polluted. We entered the city and went down narrow lanes, which opened into an area of new development—a mixture of shanty town and concrete buildings with the pretension of something greater. Then we turned in at a gated place with a uniformed guard. And though I thought this was where the wedding would take place, as usual I had no idea of the programme.

This was the house of Gurudev's father's younger brother and his family. The place was huge. Six storeys high. The uncle's son, who also lived there, owned a large distillery of what they call 'country liquor'.

That morning I had had a dream that I was riding an elevator with Gurudev, which upon awakening I found funny since there was probably not one elevator in all of the Darjeeling Hills and Sikkim. When we walked into the front hall of the house, there was a button on the wall. Dawa pushed the button and I suddenly found myself riding an elevator with Gurudev.

Set amid such squalor, they had a little palace. I immediately noticed the fine original paintings on the walls and commented on them to the uncle's son. He was a collector of the works of some of India's finest painters and he showed me through room after richly furnished room on multiple floors, all hung with colourful canvases. He appreciated very much that I noticed his passion and enjoyed the paintings so much. This branch of Gurudev's family was quite wealthy and secular. They treated Gurudev with respect, but not devotion. I got the impression they were bemused by the show, rather than taken in by it.

One hears stories about Gurudev, many of them fantastic. His greatness is bound up in the layers of ambiguity that surround him. And the closer you draw to him, the thicker the fog becomes. He is like a magician pulling himself continually out of a hat, creating himself anew, showing himself, but always as if in a mirror, his true self—what he really is—standing apart from what he is showing. Yet that which stands apart seems to be of no more substance than the reflection, demonstrating that we are all actors and that the world is our stage. One time, some people were taking pictures. They had me sit next to Gurudev so that I'd be in the shot. He put his arm over my shoulder and we smiled for the camera. As the shutter clicked, he shook his head Indian fashion and said, 'Acting.' Then he put his fingertips to his chest and said, 'Acting director.'

The acting director

I decided to ask Gurudev's uncle what Gurudev was like as a child. He would know, and I had the feeling he would not embellish mercilessly as so many of his followers did.

The uncle told me that when Gurudev was born, he was in the army stationed in Dehradun. 'I heard that my older brother had had a child and that he was extraordinary,' he said. 'One hears stories, you know, but I didn't really believe them. Yet I was curious to meet the boy. The first time I met him something happened that impressed me greatly and made me realize there was something to the stories.

'I was on leave from the army and I came to visit my family, whom I hadn't seen in a long time. Gurudev was only four or five years old. I walked into the room and there he was with a woman I had never seen before. She was an overly fussy woman, very proper. You could tell by the way she dressed and the care she put into her appearance that she was fastidious and very concerned with form.

'When I walked into the room she was lighting a stick of incense. She put it in a wooden incense holder and handed it to the boy. The boy said a little prayer and put it on the floor.

'"No, no," the woman said with a condescending tone. Of course I can't remember her exact words after all these years, but this is the gist of it. "You mustn't put it on the floor," she said. "That's very naughty. You must put it on the table." There was a little table there, you see, like a side table.

'To this the boy said, "What does it matter if the incense is on the table or on the floor? It is our prayers that are important. The gods are as close to the floor as they are to the table. Surely, the smoke can reach them with our prayers as easily from there."

'Remember, the boy was only four or five years old. His level of understanding impressed me greatly, those words coming from a boy who had only recently learned to walk!

Gurudev with his mother

'Not long after that, people started coming to him, and he started preaching, giving talks. Even when he was eight or ten years old. One time—I think he was only eleven—he addressed a crowd of thousands in Darjeeling. He has had a following his entire life. He would suddenly start chanting Sanskrit mantras and texts even though he had never learnt them. It was most extraordinary. It was the same with Tibetan, as if he knew it all from before.

'Even though I am Indian,' the uncle concluded, 'I am thoroughly modern in outlook. I am not a religious man. Yet these things impressed me greatly. I have no explanation for them. It merely lets me know there is more than can be encompassed by my understanding.'

I hesitate to write about Gurudev's past. Most tellers of tales when it comes to Gurudev are not as level-headed as his uncle, and it is difficult to draw the line between fact and fantasy. Most of the stories seem to begin on one side of the line and then cross over.

A case in point: When Gurudev was a child he lived in a village in the Phoobsering Tea Estate, where he was born. One day he untied all the cows, goats, sheep, and pigs in the entire village. They say he was motivated by compassion for the animals. Regardless of his motive, the animals' motive for what they did next is clear: hunger. They went into the fields of ripening corn and grains, filled their bellies, and ruined the village's crop. The police were called in, Gurudev was caught, and to appease his angry neighbours and to avoid a hefty fine—which the family could not afford—the boy was sent to jail. This part seems to be fact. But like every other story about Gurudev's past, the story doesn't stop there.

While he was in jail, the story goes, he told the guard, 'I am now in your jail and you can control my body, but you cannot control everything that happens in your jail: you cannot control my mind. My power is still greater than yours.' The guard took this as a challenge. 'I'm in control here, and if you're not careful, I'll prove it to you.'

Gurudev reached his hand through the bars in his cell's window and tore a bud off a plant that grew there. He held it in his open palm and said, 'This flower bud is in your jail. If you control everything in your jail, command it to open. Tell it to become a flower!'

The guard thought this boy, who had caused the destruction of his entire village's crop, weak-minded. 'Nobody can do that!' the guard exclaimed.

'Then just watch,' Gurudev said. 'I will make it open.' He held the bud in his palm and commanded it to open, and right there in front of the jailer the bud transformed into a flower. The guard, greatly shaken, left the cell. Later, he came back to bring the boy some food. He peeked into the cell and there was Gurudev in the full-lotus meditation posture. He was levitating a few feet off the ground, glowing with an unearthly light. The jailer opened the door, prostrated himself before the boy, and apologized. 'Please forgive me,' he said, 'I didn't know who you were. You are free to leave.' And thus ended Gurudev's time in jail.

The more fantastic the stories, the more I would hold stubbornly to facts, insisting on the rational even though I knew there was a universe beyond the rational. Perhaps it is the imagination that truly sets humanity apart from the other beasts in the jungle—but not fantasy. I often wondered why the people surrounding Gurudev needed such stories to believe in him. It always seemed symptomatic of a lack of faith, rather than its opposite.

Another tale I heard many times was that when he was a child, Gurudev used to ride backwards on his donkey all the way from his village up to Darjeeling. And when he got to the city he would take out a flute and play while he rode backwards, laughing so much the whole time that people thought him mad.

So I asked him one time, through Dawa, 'Gurudev, did you used to travel backwards on your donkey through the streets of Darjeeling playing your flute?'

'Yes,' he said, 'I did.'

'Gurudev, why did you ride your donkey backwards?'

'If we were going up to Darjeeling, my donkey knew the way. So why should I also look where we were going? If you have two flashlights, why should you point them both in the same direction?

'I saw no difference between that donkey and myself. Actually, I see no difference between anybody and myself. We are all one being. But that donkey and I were especially close. It used to follow me everywhere, like a dog.'

Gurudev went on to tell me another story: 'One day I was riding the donkey up a steep path in the thick fog. I came upon a Hindu priest, who of course was a Brahmin, the highest caste. Donkeys are considered lowly and impure in our culture. I was a boy. He was an old man. The path was steep. I asked him if he wanted to ride the donkey but he refused, saying if he merely touched the donkey he would become impure and no one would have him come to their house to perform the rituals. This was his source of livelihood. But I convinced him. "Surely you know purity comes from the heart," I said. "Aren't your powers greater than a donkey's? How could he defile you? Besides, you'll be the same man before and after riding the donkey, only you'll be more tired if you walk. Why don't you ride? The fog is thick. No one will see you."

'So he got on the donkey. We were approaching the village when the fog suddenly lifted and everybody saw the Brahmin priest riding the donkey.' Gurudev burst out laughing.

I had heard many times that his present incarnation was his third. His first incarnation was as a Tibetan lama born in Tibet. His second was as a Hindu priest born in Nepal. This explains how he started speaking both Tibetan, the language of the lamas, and Sanskrit, the language of Hindu priests, when he was a young child without apparently ever learning these languages. He simply started speaking them.

People told me that when he was eleven years old, Gurudev wrote a paper for a class in his tea garden primary school in a script that his teacher couldn't read. So the teacher brought the paper to the village monastery to ask the lamas. The lamas said it looked like Tibetan, but they too couldn't read it. So the lamas brought it to a bigger monastery where the abbot, who was a great scholar, recognized it as an old form of Tibetan writing. The abbot was greatly impressed and asked who wrote it. When he was told it was an eleven-year-old boy living in a village on a tea estate outside Darjeeling, he was astounded. He and some other lamas went to see the boy.

The story goes that around this time Gurudev started saying he had been a lama in Tibet in a previous lifetime. When the lamas came, they wrote down the details he was able to furnish. They sent those details up to Tibet, and they all checked out—names, place names, dates. Some high lamas from Tibet came to test the boy, to see whether he was the reincarnation of this lama. Then in 1956 when Gurudev was eleven years old, the Dalai Lama came from Tibet to India for the 2,500th anniversary of the birth of the Buddha. He crossed the pass into Sikkim and then continued down to Kalimpong, the second largest town in the Darjeeling Hills. The lamas brought Gurudev to the Dalai Lama, who tested the boy himself and then declared him a reincarnation. He also gave instructions that Gurudev be specially trained and maintain a pure vegetarian diet.

Gurudev meeting the Dalai Lama in Darjeeling, 2005

I wanted to know what he had to say about this. So one day when it was just Gurudev, Dawa, and me alone in the room, I asked him. 'Gurudev,' I said, 'they call you a *tulku*. That means you are a reincarnated lama. They say the Dalai Lama himself tested you and proclaimed you an incarnation. Is this true?'

'This was when I was a boy,' he said. He asked Dawa to massage his legs, and it was clear he wanted to speak no more about it. Dawa started massaging his legs and said to me, 'He cannot speak about himself like that. It would be a mark of pride. To find out about him, you must ask others.'

But I pressed him. 'Did you meet with the Dalai Lama in Kalimpong when you were eleven years old?'

'Yes, I did.'

'Did he declare you an incarnation?'

'He said I should be given no meat or eggs. That I should be specially trained. Yes.'

After eating a midday meal with the uncle's family and taking a nap, we got back into the jeep and drove further into Siliguri, down increasingly narrow alleys through which the jeep barely squeezed until we reached the little hall where the wedding feast was taking place. There was a tremendous commotion when we arrived. The crowd parted for Gurudev. He got up on the little stage and with the newly wedded couple before him, gave a little speech. I asked the man standing next to me what he was saying. 'Gurudev is saying we should all be peaceful and loving,' the man replied. 'He is speaking about the brotherhood of man.'

Then Gurudev called for me to come to the front, which I did, mainly because I couldn't refuse. So the crowd parted and I got up on the stage. Gurudev handed me two ceremonial scarves. 'Blessing,' he said. So I put one around the bride's neck and one around the groom's, muttering platitudes about how happy I was for them and wishing them a wonderful life together, a moment that was recorded for all time in this couple's wedding video.

Then we rushed out of there, got back in the jeep, and headed back to the mountains. Along the way Gurudev grilled me on the wildlife in the area where I lived, and I whistled all sorts of bird calls and kept everyone laughing. I even sang a Spanish love song of my own creation, made up on the spot and making no sense. Gurudev was very good at making puns, even in English. Mainly we laughed our way through the mountains, stopping to give out vegetables, money, and bars of soap.

We were headed to Tinchulay, where another branch of Gurudev's family lived in the mountains about an hour from Darjeeling. Just before we got to his relatives' house, we stopped at a house where there was a huge crowd. As usual, I had no idea what was going on. I knew this couldn't be a puja set up for him since even his relatives didn't know we were coming. As we got out of the car, Pema told me it was the funeral of an eighty-seven-year-old woman, a woman who was blind from birth, whom Gurudev knew since he was a child. We were greeted by the woman's eldest son, who was wearing white and had a white scarf tied over his head, which he had shaved upon his mother's death.

I went with Gurudev up the embankment to where everyone was sitting on chairs outside, eating the funeral meal. Many came to press their palms and greet Gurudev. I followed Gurudev and the son up a path between fields to where his mother had just been cremated. Flowers covered the still-warm ashes. Gurudev was walking in front. He reached down, picked up some of the flowers, and crushed them between his fingers as if wringing his hands. He turned away, and when he turned back I could see he was weeping. Huge tears flowed down his cheeks. It came over him in an instant and in an instant it was over. He recited an incantation and we went back to where the others were. We were led into the house, sat, and were brought tea. Then we left.

When we arrived at his family's house, they ushered Gurudev into a special chair in the huge living room, almost like a throne, between two huge couches. No one else ever sat in this chair, even though Gurudev might be absent from this house for months at a stretch. They sat me next to him and brought us tea. Gurudev was tired, so they left us alone in the room where we sat looking at old magazines and watching TV.

Gurudev spoke of himself, as he rarely did. He said, 'I never sad. I never cry.'

'But just this afternoon—'

He cut me short. 'I no feel sorrow,' he said. 'I weep, but just like that,' and he snapped his fingers. 'My tears, for the son. Very meaning for him.'

He was silent a moment.

'Before long time,' he said, 'when I young, I get angry; but that like putting gold into fire.'

After some time they opened the door and people from the village started coming in with flowers for Gurudev and to bow down before him, touch his feet, and sit a while talking in the most gentle way.

The next morning we set out again. We travelled from puja to puja, every day a ritual at another tea garden, sometimes two in a day, spending hours careening around tight mountain roads, the jeep never going straight for more than a few feet before taking the next hairpin turn. And everywhere the crowds, flowers, pressed palms, ritual, incense.

16

CUTTING A BANANA WITH A SPOON

One evening we were staying at a devotee's house. In the room were Gurudev, Tharbu, Boron (one of Gurudev's relatives, who speaks English reasonably), and I. I asked Boron if he would interpret for me a question I had for Gurudev. In so many words, I asked Gurudev this: 'According to Buddhist teachings, there is no difference between nirvana and samsara, between the enlightened state of the sage and the level of the ordinary man. The ordinary man believes there is a state called enlightenment, which it is possible to strive towards by following a spiritual path; he imagines there is something to be achieved by attaining enlightenment. But these teachings proclaim that there is nothing to achieve; in fact the moment one ceases to believe the myth that something is lacking in the present moment, the moment one ceases to desire more than exactly what is—it is at that very moment that the bubble of illusion pops and one realizes enlightenment is already our basic nature, and that by achieving that understanding, we have in actuality achieved nothing at all.'

Needless to say, it was no small feat for me to put my question clearly enough for Boron to understand and to be able to interpret to Gurudev.

In the exchange between Boron and Gurudev and my trying to make sure Boron understood my question, I didn't notice that Gurudev had picked up a banana. He held the banana in the palm of his hand, looked me deep in the eye, and slowly pulled back the peel, exposing the fruit. Still staring me in the eye, he picked up a spoon and proceeded to slice the banana. Then he said in slow, deliberate English, 'You can also cut a banana with a spoon.'

My first reaction was, so what? But the way he was staring at me, I suddenly understood: this was his answer to my question!

To my question about the ultimate nature of enlightenment and illusion his answer was, 'You can also cut a banana with a spoon!'

Like a Zen master, he was answering the most profound with the highest absurdity.

'That's it!' I exclaimed. 'The perfect answer.'

Tharbu and Boron, who hadn't understood that this was his answer, suddenly got it too and started laughing, their foreheads almost shining with the glow of such a clear and absurd answer.

Then Gurudev said something to Boron. 'He is asking,' Boron interpreted, 'what you understood by his answer.'

For a moment I hesitated. What to say? I tried to think of a response, and somehow I was just left with the absurdity. I answered something about how, if everything was the same, the highest wisdom was also contained in the most mundane, even in the fact that you could cut a banana with a spoon. At the same time I was saying this, I knew I was failing the test, because the only correct answer would have been a spontaneous statement of even higher absurdity.

Then Gurudev started speaking; Boron interpreted: 'There was a kingdom ruled over by a king who had a daughter who was the wisest person in the entire kingdom. Even the high priests and the oldest and wisest sages in the kingdom had to admit that the princess was wiser than them. She had the unique ability to both ask a question and answer any question the wisest ones could put to her without uttering a single word.

'When the time came for the princess to marry, the king announced that the princess would marry the one who proved to be the wisest suitor. The king had a chief advisor who had a son of suitable age. This advisor thought it natural that his son should marry the princess. So with much fanfare he brought his son to see the princess. But the advisor's son was a crude young man without any glow to him whatsoever. It didn't take but a moment or two for the princess to determine that there were many in the kingdom wiser than the advisor's dull son.

'The king then commanded his chief advisor to find a suitor for the princess. This was a bitter pill for the advisor to swallow since he still thought it only just that his own son marry the princess. But a command is a command and the advisor set out in search of a suitor for the princess.

'He was walking through the forest when he came upon the most ragged woodcutter he'd ever seen, a man dressed in dirty rags with matted hair, perched high in a tree. He was sawing the very limb he was sitting on, and just as the limb was cracking with his own weight, the advisor stopped him. "This fool will prove my son the worthy suitor," the advisor thought; so he brought the man, again with much fanfare, to the princess.

'When the rough fellow was brought before the princess he didn't even know to bow or to sit in a chair. So he stood before the princess. The princess got up and stood right in front of the man and raised one finger in the air, forcefully shaking it there as if to make some point. The woodcutter flinched before the princess's sudden movement. "Good," the advisor thought, "whatever wisdom she is expressing, he's only afraid the princess wants to poke out his eye!" When the man raised a finger menacingly in her direction, the advisor saw that he was threatening her now. And when he pointed two fingers menacingly in her direction, threatening to poke out both of her eyes if she made an attempt at one of his, the advisor already started planning what glorious robes he would wear when his son married the princess. The man then lowered one of his fingers and again shook a solitary finger at the princess, at which the princess fell to her knees with tears rolling down her cheeks. To the utter dismay and disbelief of the advisor, she kissed the ragged man's filthy feet and, speaking for the first time in the interview, announced that she had finally met someone of sufficient wisdom to marry.

'The advisor was beside himself and demanded an explanation. She said that when she raised a single finger she was indicating that everything, the entire universe and everything in it, was one. When he then raised a single finger, she said, he was agreeing with her. Then when he raised two fingers with such force of emotion, he was saying that out of the One comes the Many. That, she explained, was a statement, while not of great wisdom, at least of tremendous understanding. But at the end when he put up a single finger again, she explained, casting a look of loving devotion at this man whom the advisor had deemed so foolish as to cut the very branch he was sitting upon and thought not much more than a beast, she knew that he was the wisest man in the whole kingdom, worthy of her hand in marriage. For he was saying not only that from the Many the One can be found, but that God, the One, can be found in the Many—that there is no separation and they are one and the same.'

Gurudev finished his story. Tharbu and Boron laughed, delighted at his story. But something about it bothered me. It took me a moment to realize what. He was saying that the wisest one, the princess, misinterpreted the fool's fear of getting his eyes poked out for high wisdom. Why would he be telling me this story at this particular moment except as a way to say that his banal statement that one could cut a banana with a spoon was just that, a banal statement, no further implications or teachings intended. Any high wisdom I saw in his statement was a reflection of my own quixotic nature.

Hadn't I seen this in others, how they interpreted everything Gurudev did as a miracle? How many times had I been sitting next to him when the look of wonder on the others' faces revealed their perception that a miracle had just occurred? On these occasions, Gurudev had taken to leaning towards me and whispering, 'No miracle,' with a confidential look. I was happy for his taking me into his confidence and admitting his very human status against the tide of opinion of those around him that he wasn't a human being but a living god. In fact, I had come to believe that what was extraordinary about Gurudev was that he was actually nothing at all, a true blank mirror, a mirror into which everyone was free to project their own image of the highest and get it reflected back unsullied by any trace of ego. In that way he could be a miracle-working god for the village folks, and for me, an embodiment of wisdom and a philosopher.

Gurudev had started speaking with Boron about something else, but I interrupted. 'I have another question,' I said. 'Ask Gurudev if I am in the position of the princess in his story, imagining wisdom where none was even intended.'

Boron interpreted my question. Then Gurudev spoke. Both Boron and Tharbu slapped their thighs and laughed at what he was saying. It was obviously brilliant. 'Gurudev is saying,' Boron said, 'that he hadn't yet told the end of the story. The true end of the story was that the rough woodcutter, whom the advisor had found like a fool cutting the branch he was sitting on, *was* in fact the wisest man in the kingdom. But he was poor. He knew he hadn't a chance to even appear before the princess. So he had dirtied himself and dressed in rags and waited for the advisor to come along to begin sawing the branch. He knew the advisor would choose the candidate least likely to outdo his own son, and thus he was chosen. And when he raised his fingers—first one, then two, then one again—he was only pretending that he was afraid of the princess poking out his eyes, but was actually espousing the wisdom that the princess thought he was. And it was all this the princess saw. She could see it in his eyes. And that is why she chose him.'

This said, Gurudev laughed so hard at pulling the rug out from beneath my feet for the third time that I couldn't help but see that he was in fact the wisest one in these hills.

17

NIGHT OF SHIVA

We were driving one morning out near Mirik, not far from the Nepal border, when Dawa told me we were headed to Raniban, a forested place below Tukvar, a place of caves and huge boulders washed by a river plunging through a ravine. The name Raniban means 'Queen's Forest'. It was just below the village Gurudev grew up in, not far from Tukvar. Gurudev had lived there in a cave for some time when he was perhaps in his late teens (be it for days, months, or years, I never could get straight, though I heard each version). Back then, he declared the place sacred to the god Shiva. Now he usually only goes there once a year, for Shivaratri, the night of Shiva, the big festival to Lord Shiva, creator and destroyer of worlds, often depicted with the damaru—a mini drum—in one hand, fire in another. The drum beats the birth of time and creation; the fire consumes the creation at the end. I don't think it was Shivaratri, but it must have been another festival for Shiva for we were going there and I was told many people would be there throughout the night.

On the way we stopped at an ancient stone Shiva temple situated by a stream in another wooded ravine. It was a tiny place in the silence of a distant forest inhabited by a single priest who lived in the rough. Dressed in nothing but a torn loincloth and the sacred thread of a Brahmin, his eyes were wild and bulging. When he saw us descending through the forest he ran to greet us. Gurudev led the tiny procession down the steep trail to the temple where we could hear other sadhus beating drums and singing devotional songs. The priest followed one step behind, bounding like a monkey, squatting to take a pinch of dirt from each footprint left behind by Gurudev's plastic sandals. He put each pinch of sacred dirt into an old scrap of newspaper to preserve as a holy relic. He hadn't the facilities to offer us tea, but he did add fuel to the sacred fire so we could stay warm in the cool mountain air, which was gusting with the passage of clouds through the forest. The temple was built over a small cave inside of which was a natural Shiva lingam, or rock in the phallic form, flower petals sticking to the ghee with which it had been anointed.

When we were leaving, the priest turned to me, jutted his finger towards the heavens, and said:

'Who has seen the wind?
Neither you nor I.
Yet when the leaves are moving,
The wind is passing by.
God same-same.'

We arrived in Tukvar at sunset. They locked up the family house, and everyone piled into a few vehicles. We drove about twenty minutes down the switchback road from Tukvar towards the Rangeet River until we were in hot country and there were groves of orange trees. We stopped where the footpath led to Raniban. Someone took out a *kukri* and cut a piece of bamboo for Gurudev to use as a walking stick.

By the flickering light of crude kerosene-and-rag torches, Gurudev led the way down the footpath through strips of forests and across fields, past isolated houses and animal sheds, to where the mountain folded together on itself into a steep forested ravine with a river raging through it. The water roared through the narrows in the darkness as it plunged into pools and came up frothing. The mountains ascended straight to the sky. Only a strip of stars was visible high overhead. Huge boulders, some of them the size of houses, were thrown about, a few so large that trees grew on them. Crossing a crude wood-and-bamboo bridge, we were greeted by over 200 people who were awaiting our arrival. The place was decked out with colourful ribbons and long garlands of flowers. A huge tarpaulin awning covered an area large enough for perhaps a hundred to sit. Under the awning was a stone throne, which had been constructed for Gurudev.

Shiva, painted on a market wall, Darjeeling

Having declared Raniban sacred to Shiva when he was young, the place was now full of stone altars to the various Hindu gods. There was even a committee that looked after the place. Gurudev sat on the stone throne and had me sit next to him. A circle of musicians playing tabla and harmonium started singing bhajans, religious devotional songs, while the torrent raged in the background.

After some time, Gurudev had some of the boys give me a torch-lit tour of the various shrines set up at special rocks. It was like a theme park dedicated to the Hindu pantheon. A rock with the shape of a curved trunk, for instance, was now a shrine for Ganesha, the elephant-headed god. There was a cave that my guide told me reached all the way up to, and connected with, the cave on Observatory Hill in Darjeeling. They told me the only one who ever went all the way through the cave was Gurudev. Pema later told me the cave ended just around the first bend.

When I came back from my tour, Gurudev was gone. Someone told me he had gone to sleep. A few minutes later, one of Gurudev's relatives passed by, saying he was going to Gurudev and that I could come with him. So we climbed the slope towards a torch burning in the darkness through the jungle. The flickering light was illuminating a huge cave, really an overarching rock face over 100 feet high, jutting out over the ravine. And at the base of this sheer rock face, at the deepest point of the cave, was a rock shelf, like a naturally carved bed or throne etched into the stone.

Sitting cross-legged on this throne on a pile of blankets was Gurudev, another blanket wrapped around himself against the evening chill, torches casting huge dancing shadows on the rock behind him. On the flat stone before this throne sat about a dozen people. Among them was Pema. Gurudev had me sit next to him so he could interpret. Pema put his arm around my shoulder, and we looked up at Gurudev.

This was a throne worthy of Gurudev's natural powers; all the others—those in people's houses throughout the hills, fashioned by placing a rug on a bed or a plush pillow on a chair, thrones made of wood or even concrete and stone—were but cheap imitations, man-made approximations of this one. Created by the collision of continents, the rock face was ringed by thick flowering vines. It was set in dense jungle with a waterfall and pool in front of it.

With a gesture of his arms to encompass the entire scene, Gurudev said, 'This place natural place. Everything grows here: fruits, nuts, wild green vegetables, all growing naturally. Food, lodging—everything! Everything is here but salt and gold.

'This place just like Tora-Bora. Tora-Bora—Bin Laden. Just like Tora-Bora,' and he burst out laughing.

'But this place no fighting-fighting. This place peace place.'

Then he said, 'One time I lived here seven days, and every day a cobra snake came and I gave it a bowl of milk. Every day it came back for the milk.

'That was long ago, and I thought, this is beautiful, natural place. So I told all the people: "This place sacred place, sacred to Shiva." I told them that so they wouldn't cut the jungle. Other jungles, all cut-cut. Nobody even takes one branch from this place.

'Many places I go, natural place. I say, this place sacred to this god, that place sacred to other god. Now all natural parks. All preserved.'

There was a spring just below the cave, a fissure in the rock where a trickle of water issued. I had heard the miracle stories about it, how when Gurudev was a teenager there was a plant growing out of a crack and he pulled the plant and a spring of medicinal water gushed forth that had been flowing ever since. Just another story, I supposed. As Gurudev was sitting there, he said, 'Many people come here to get water from this spring. Holy water. They come for healing. Those that are healed, stay. Those that don't get healed, they go away.' He raised both hands in a gesture as if to make light of the entire world.

'What to do?'

The light of the moon was filtering through the high branches. 'Moonlight can help us see at night,' Gurudev said. 'But it can also help the thief. Yet the same moonlight is the enemy of the thief. It is by the light of the moon that the thief can be detected. The poison of the cobra is used as the medicine, isn't it?

'Once there was a dog that had puppies. The mother died, and those puppies were suckled by a wild pig. Is it true that Tarzan was left alone in the jungle as a child and was suckled by a lion?'

I had to confess my ignorance, but I told him the story of Romulus, the founder of Rome who, along with his twin brother Remus, was suckled by a wild wolf.

He motioned to the long vines that spilled over the stone high overhead and reached almost to the ground. 'The longest vines have the biggest fruit. Why is this? No knowledge without college.' And he laughed.

'When the air is humid, it is possible to extract the water from the air. You can even put it in a glass—and you can drink it. But you cannot drink the air…' Pointing to the heavens and twisting his wrist as if he were spinning a ball—or the earth itself—he burst out laughing.

'If you come to me with a flower, I will give you a plate of fruit. And even if you do not give me a flower, still I must give you a plate of fruit.'

He raised his hands with a shrug.

'What to do?' he said, and laughed, having expressed the imperative under which he lived.

He let a period of silence pass between his proclamations. Properly enthroned, he was now speaking from his full power. Like the stories of Sufi masters, there were levels of meaning behind levels of meaning. As often with Gurudev, the sublime was followed by the absurd, nipping at its heels, as if to show that just as the rich man invites a thief, so wisdom and folly are never far apart. But one never could be too sure, for in his expressions of the absurd his highest wisdom was hiding.

Sometimes mere words, the communication of thought by verbal means, can set fire to one's understanding like a flash of lightning. One sentence can reveal what volumes cannot. It is genius that can express with words that which is beyond words. It is a master who can express the highest. For what was Gurudev expressing both in his life and in his statement about his obligation to give equally to all, regardless of whether one gave to him or not, but an expression of the overflowing nature of the creative force of the universe itself?

The parable he was living was about receiving flowers or not, and about giving a plate of food. Other masters have spoken of the nature of the sun—that it shines equally on the rich man and the poor, upon the generous and miserly, the wise man and the fool. Doesn't it say in the Bible that whether you are a sinner or a saint, the grace of God is on you?

Gurudev expressed this power, this energy, this overflowing bounty like a spring gushing from the depths, and he did so continuously, from the moment he woke up in the morning until he went to sleep at night. That was what was so remarkable. The ceaselessness of it, and his unflagging cheerfulness.

Gurudev was holding something in his hand. He reached down and indicated I should take it. It was a little branch with three leaves connected to one stem. He pointed to each leaf in turn.

'This one Brahma, this one Vishnu, this one Shiva. Three gods, one stem. All one. All gods one god. All is God. Me God, you God, tree God, rock God, tiger God, elephant God, everybody God. All same-same.

'Atom, atom, atom, atom—all atom God.

'God father, God mother, and also children.

'Lord Krishna say every person, every animal, and every atom equal. In each and every atom is the same spirit of God as within us.'

The torches played with his shadow, casting it huge and flickering onto the rough stone wall behind.

Soon he sent everyone but Pema and me back down the hill. He threw me a blanket and I lay on the stone below his nature-hewn bed. Down by the river, the devotees were staying up all night singing devotional songs to Shiva and to Krishna, whom they considered Gurudev an incarnation of. There were scattered fires in the jungle. Through the thick canopy of leaves the stars shone.

At dawn, people started arriving with incense and flowers and they all touched their foreheads to the stone at the base of Gurudev's natural throne.

'One time, long ago,' he said to me, 'there was a queen. She no sleeping at night. Why? Because there was one—what do you call—seed, one mustard seed, under her bed. Last night I have dream. I dream one monk sleeping next to me couldn't sleep. Why? Because there was a thorn in his bed. He has no sleeping until he remove that thorn.'

The night before, while walking up to his cave, I had stepped on a thorn that had pierced my flip-flop and gone deep into my foot. Though I had taken the thorn out, as I was trying to sleep my foot ached and I lay awake a while, worrying about infection.

18

CANCELLED LUCK

One day we were on our way to a village where Gurudev was to perform a puja—don't ask me where, but it was up the side of a mountain and down a curving road and through a large jungle of towering trees, wild orchids, and thick vines. The jungle, they told me, was full of wild boar and leopards. We were passing in and out of the clouds and it was cold and damp, the kind of damp that goes right to the bone. We came out of the forest and entered a large village perched on the crest of a little ridge, which was engulfed in cloud. A vegetable market was in full swing. Pema jumped out and disappeared into the fog. People started coming to Gurudev's window for his blessing. He had collected a few stones and twigs along the way, which he now gave out. Pema returned with a huge armful of bunched carrots, which he put in the back. Then he disappeared into the fog again, to emerge this time with a sack of tomatoes and another of apples. He disappeared a third time but he returned quickly, empty-handed, with something of obvious importance to discuss with Gurudev. Pema jumped into the jeep and we turned around and returned the way we had come, through the jungle. Adding to the mystery of what went on around me was always the barrier of language. In other words, I never knew what the hell was going on—let alone what was about to happen. Dawa sensed my confusion and told me that Pema had run into the man who was organizing the event to which we were headed. The man was on his way to Gangtok, where his sister had taken ill. So the event had been cancelled. Since we suddenly had some time, we were headed now to a government-run tourist bungalow for a rest. These tourist bungalows were run by Ghising's Darjeeling Gorkha Hill Council and each had a room set aside for Gurudev.

So we wound back into the jungle and turned left onto a road that took us up the side of a cloud-enshrouded mountain of thickset pine trees. We passed through a huge iron gate and pulled up to the door of the bungalow. The driver blew the horn to announce our unexpected arrival.

The staff arrayed themselves at the door, bowing deeply. Gurudev and I were ushered into a room with Gurudev's portrait prominently displayed on the wall. They sat Gurudev on one bed and me on the other. They gave us blankets to wrap around ourselves to keep out the raw dampness of the room. They brought us tea. Then hot water bottles. Wood was brought and soon there was a fire roaring in the fireplace. The staff came in and prostrated themselves before Gurudev.

Three women with babies strapped to their backs burst into the room. They bowed, and then started crying, telling Gurudev some tale. They showed him a letter. It was in English and he couldn't read it. Dawa translated for him and then handed the letter to me. It was from the Darjeeling Gorkha Hill Council saying the little food stall these women ran just outside the gates of the tourist bungalow had no permit and therefore must be torn down within three days. The letter was dated three days before. So the stall had to be torn down that very day. They were weeping. This was their only livelihood—how they put food in their children's mouths—and they didn't know how they'd survive.

Gurudev heard their story. Then he summoned one of the young men who worked at the bungalow and instructed him to go to Darjeeling and tell Ghising personally that Gurudev wanted him to issue a permit so these women could keep their business. He called Dawa over. Dawa produced a wad of money; Gurudev peeled off a few bills, which he gave to the young man to pay his jeep fare. Bowing deeply to Gurudev, the young man set out for Darjeeling. And like that, it was done. Dawa was proclaiming another miracle. The women left the room with tears of joy. One event cancelled, a sudden decision to take a break at a rest house, and these three women's source of livelihood was saved.

I thought of my friend John, the foreign Buddhist living in Darjeeling, and his condemnation of Gurudev for his connection with Ghising. His claim that Gurudev was closely associated with Ghising and his party I now knew was true. What I didn't know was how to deal with it. Here I was in a DGHC rest house with a huge portrait of Gurudev on the wall with his hand in the open-palm expression of 'do not fear'. Frankly, the nature of this alliance baffled me and proved to be the largest and most enduring source of befuddlement during my time with him. It placed Gurudev in the wider context of the struggle in the Hills, and for the life of me I did not know which side he was on. While in this instance Gurudev was clearly using his influence to do good, it wasn't always so clear.

We often went to events that were sponsored by members of Ghising's Gorkha Hill Council. Some were large public events attended by thousands and for which the politician/sponsor was the honoured guest; other events connected with the politicians were private, when we would stay at the sponsor's house and the event would be attended only by the sponsor's family, friends, and associates.

Regardless of the nature of the event, it was the custom for an event's sponsor to escort Gurudev and the entourage (either in our vehicle or more commonly in his own, which would then drive immediately behind us) to it. In response to the attack on Ghising, each member of the Gorkha Hill Council now had a military escort dressed in camouflage, armed with a rifle. This meant we sometimes travelled under armed guard.

On one occasion we were travelling with a councillor to his home in Kalimpong, a journey of a few hours, in a motorcade of three vehicles. Gurudev's vehicle always travelled in front. In what seemed like every village, Gurudev had the driver stop in front of a little shop. Gurudev would go into the shop, followed by the councillor. The military guard would keep watch outside. I'd squeeze in as well just to see what would happen. And what happened in every shop was just about the same. Gurudev would buy whatever was on offer: sacks of rice or beans, cartons of biscuits, soap, and produce. Because the councillor was the sponsor, he had to pull out his wallet at every stop and peel from his thick wad of (probably ill-gotten) 500-rupee notes enough to cover Gurudev's purchase. Some of the items would be packed into the back of our vehicle to be given out later. But other things were given out on the spot. Gurudev would see someone passing in front of the shop and call him or her over and give away what he'd just bought with the councillor's money. This form of wealth distribution seemed all right for the councillor the first couple of times. He even seemed bemused by Gurudev's ways, as if this was all to be expected and was an expression of his wisdom. But as his stash of 500-rupee notes began to thin, you could sense behind his false smile an increasing sense of dread whenever he'd follow Gurudev into another store.

Once, we stayed at a councillor's house at the edge of a village. It was a beautiful, newly constructed house, the largest in the village, with ample room for Gurudev and the entire crew. I even got my own room. The councillor and his wife spoke English perfectly and were gracious hosts. His children, who were on holiday from private schools in Dehradun, were interesting, intelligent, and well educated. The food was hygienic, the water filtered.

When I told a friend in Darjeeling afterwards where I had been, he told me that it was a well-known fact that this councillor (who shall here remain unnamed) murdered the man who held his seat on the Council before him. How very strange, to travel with a saint to the house of a murderer.

On another occasion we went to an event in Singamari at the northern edge of Darjeeling town, where the local councillor for that area, Bimal Gurung, was sponsoring a public event. A cavernous tent had been erected, at one end of which was a raised platform with the customary array of Buddhist monks and Hindu priests. In the centre of the stage was a raised platform piled high with cushions on top of which sat Gurudev. The tent was overflowing and the crowd filled the surrounding football ground. All morning there had been a line of wooden chairs in the centre of the front row that stood empty, waiting for the councillor and his retinue.

I stood on the edge of the stage, watching Gurudev and the crowd, my stomach tied in a knot. Even at that time I knew of Bimal Gurung's reputation as Ghising's right-hand man, the one to whom the duty of dealing with political opposition was often delegated. Gurung and his band of young men—most often referred to as his goons or gundas—were, in a place where politics was ruled by fear, the most feared of all.

How could Gurudev allow himself to be glorified by these people? He had just accepted the hospitality of a murderer, and with him so had I. Now he was sitting on the throne at an event sponsored by the most feared man in the Hills. Though I tried not to judge, and to observe with an open mind—figuring a mind free from agitation would be in a better position to understand—the contradictions were just too great.

Was he using his connection with the party to raise his own star and gain fame? Was he that ambitious? People had told me that Gurudev's fame had indeed grown quickly with his connection to Ghising and the party. Was the party, in return, using him to gain support under the cover of a saint? Gurus and politicians have had nefarious links in India for ages.

Or was he using his association with these unsavoury characters to positively influence them? After all, who would benefit more from the society of a saint? Since I had never seen Gurudev act from any motive but the highest, it was difficult to imagine him acting out of greed. His central teaching was, after all, one of love and of selfless giving, which he demonstrated continuously. Yet he was more than happy to stand centre stage in the role of living god, all-knowing, never contradicting devotees' erroneous delusions concerning him, spouting words of humility while people prostrated before him.

Gurudev and Subash Ghising at the inauguration of the Shrubbery Nightingale Park, Darjeeling; Pema stands guard behind Gurudev.

I happened to be outside the tent in Singamari when Bimal Gurung's motorcade arrived. It consisted of two police jeeps with lights flashing, packed with armed men in uniform, followed by Bimal's expensive black vehicle. The motorcade muscled its way arrogantly through the crowd and stopped in front of the tent. A crew from a local TV channel suddenly appeared to film the arrival of the leader, no doubt at his request so that he could make the most of his sponsorship of the event. I had wanted to observe this man I'd heard so much about and try to glean something from his interactions with Gurudev, but I knew, as the only foreigner in the huge gathering, that if I showed my face it would subsequently be broadcast on TV. Gurudev was sure to call me up on stage when Gurung was there. So I slipped behind the tent to where huge vats of food hung over wood fires. I waited in line and received, along with the others, a free meal.

Gurudev posing at one of the many sites he inaugurated for Ghising's party

Tea garden ritual site (above) and procession (below)

19

BLADDER AND OTHER MIRACLES

Schoolchildren lining the road at our arrival

Travelling with Gurudev was like being in a pressure cooker. Questions raged through my mind I could not ask. I was alternately ready to flee and feeling blessed that I was even allowed to be there.

It was shortly after the event in Singamari with Bimal Gurung that we went to the biggest event of our entire tour. The local schools had been closed for the day and the driveway to the field, where huge tents were pitched for the event, was lined with schoolchildren as we arrived. Gurudev sat on his throne before 4,000 people and again he had them all laughing—for eight hours! An amazing feat—as was the fact that in those eight hours he didn't once get up. This posed for me a tremendous mystery. They were continually bringing him tea, and for eight hours he spoke and sang and chanted and cracked jokes and never got up to relieve himself. How miraculous, I thought. Though I was always questioning his superhuman reputation, his bladder did seem rather remarkable.

It was later that I saw his ruse. Gurudev always sat on his raised platform cross-legged. In front of him was a long, low wooden table, which was closed in front towards the audience but had a shelf accessible from the back. I was standing to his side as he was singing when I noticed him fiddling with his robes, opening them towards the shelf. There was a jar on the shelf, which he put under the folds of his burgundy robes, very subtly so that no one would notice. The low table shielded him nicely. He manipulated the jar into position. Then he placed his hands on his knees and finished the song. He looked out over the crowd with a faraway, blissful look, his lips parted in an enigmatic smile. To the assembled multitude, he was entering a trance-like state.

Gurudev enthroned

Appearance and reality were often at odds in Gurudev. A man who can urinate in front of

4,000 people without them knowing clearly has the powers of a conjurer. And in fact, there were times when I saw his entire show as one continual play of illusion, especially if I took the testimony of his devotees. I sometimes looked at them all as positively delusional and felt myself surrounded by fools.

A case in point: That evening I was alone in the room with Dawa and Gurudev. Dawa got a plastic basin and Gurudev sat at the edge of his bed as Dawa washed his feet. It was like a scene out of a Bible picture book. We talked a while and then Gurudev stood up, took a few steps, slipped into his sandals, and walked out of the room. Dawa leaned over towards me, wonder filling his eyes. 'Did you see,' he said in a hushed, reverent tone, 'he left no footprints! His feet were wet and he left no footprints!' Dawa's losing track of the time it took for Gurudev's feet to drip-dry had been transformed into a miracle.

Then, as if to compound his folly, Dawa leaned over again and said to me, in an earnest, confidential tone, 'You would be surprised, but Gurudev actually knows English.'

'Come *on*, Dawa.'

I was so tired of hearing fantastic and clearly farcical stories about Gurudev.

'I can tell you exactly how much English he speaks,' I said, 'Gurudev knows some words; he can put together simple sentences. You know this too: why else would you always be interpreting for us?'

Dawa neither refuted my argument nor saw my point.

Instead, he told me that Gurudev spoke German too and that he had been to Germany. He started telling me a story that had echoes of the life of Jesus. There were twelve years, Dawa explained, when Gurudev was a young man and no one knew where he was. Gurudev had told Dawa that for some of that time he had been in Germany. He had devotees there, people who became his followers, but it was before he was a master. He told Dawa that he wanted to return one day to show them what he had become.

Gurudev came back in and I decided to test what Dawa said. How did I know where Gurudev had or hadn't been? The story sounded ridiculous—I doubted it greatly—but it was worth a test. So I picked a moment when all was quiet. I watched him closely and said, '*Wie geht es Ihnen*,' which means 'How are you' in German. If he knew German, something would register. It didn't.

While travelling with Gurudev I had only a small daypack with me, the same pack I had when I met him in Timi on the second day of my pilgrimage in search of the present moment. It contained not much more than a change of clothes and a toothbrush. The very nature of my pilgrimage was definitely not to find, but to dispense with, any intermediaries I might encounter. Nothing could have been further from my intention than to find a guru, especially one so shrouded in mystification, one whose followers were so delusional. There is a saying in Buddhism: 'If you find the Buddha, kill the Buddha.' Meaning: find out for yourself. Experience yourself. I wouldn't have to kill the Buddha; I could simply lift up my light pack and start walking, wherever I was. All roads are equal when you have no goal but present living. I couldn't imagine Dawa was lying to me when he told me what Gurudev had told him about Germany. Yet it was incomprehensible: Why would Gurudev make up such a story? Was he playing with Dawa's credulity? Was he telling him these stories, knowing Dawa would mention them to me? I already knew that Dawa reported to Gurudev on our private conversations. Were we all actors in Gurudev's movie? I bristled at the notion. What was I doing there?

It was with my hand on my pack that I confronted Gurudev. It was my turn to test him. One wrong move and I'd be out of there, happily wandering down the road without a backward glance.

'If you are a man of truth,' I asked him, 'why is it the closer I come to you the more I seem to be surrounded by illusion?' Dawa was in the uncomfortable position of interpreting what I said next: 'Take Dawa, for instance, your close disciple. He is full of illusions about you. All you have to do is take three steps and he'll see a miracle. He literally believes you speak all languages. He says you speak English. Do you speak English?'

'No,' Gurudev responded. He seemed both detached and slightly amused at my fiery, defiant expression.

'Dawa told me you speak German. Is this true?'

'No.'

'He also told me you've been to Germany. Is this true?

'I have only been to India, Nepal, and Bhutan.'

'Everywhere I go with you, people are telling me you are not really a human being. They say you are a god. What are you? Are you a god?'

'No,' he said, 'this is only what my disciples say. I am not a god. I am a human being. I am a teacher, a guru. I am a master. That is all.'

'I understand the goal of Buddhism is to dispel illusions,' I said. 'Yet the people around you are full of illusions. I've never seen people so deluded. How can this be? How can it be that the closer you get to a man of truth, the more deluded the people are? Does this mean you are not a good teacher? Why don't you correct them? Even Dawa says you are a god.'

My defiant tone fell like a stone in a still pond, plunging without causing a ripple. Gurudev was unflappable. I had the distinct impression he liked my recalcitrance, as if he were playing with the reality around him out of a sense of compassion, for the purpose of creating conditions for others to wake up. If this were true, no matter what my reaction, it would be an opportunity for my awaking.

'A disciple is like a plant,' Gurudev said. 'All you can do is give it the right conditions. You can put it in the sun. You can give it food. You can water it and you can give it love. But you cannot make it come to bud. You cannot make it flower. You cannot make it come to fruit. These things, given the right conditions, come on their own, in their own time, by nature.'

For a brief moment my mind unhinged from its habitual ruts and I had a flash of understanding. Gurudev was just busy being what he was. He neither asked disciples to gather round him nor did he invite or invent stories about himself. Nor was it his function to correct others. He took others exactly where they were. His nature was like a spring, overflowing with love. In a way, he was absolutely nothing. His answer made me see how much of my reaction to him was just that, a reaction, originating in myself—reflecting me and not him. And what better function for a teacher than to provide the opportunity to know yourself. He then said something very beautiful, a metaphor for compassion. Because the roads are so steep in the Himalayas, there is a rule of the road that is observed there, which he then cited: 'The car going up the hill has the right of way.'

20

THE PRESSURE COOKER

The next morning we set off for another puja in a tea garden. Our journey took us through the town of Darjeeling, where we stopped in the vegetable market. My new-found understanding of Gurudev was put immediately to the test when Gurudev started barking out orders at Dawa. He sent Dawa across the street to buy some vegetables and then he called him back gruffly. I didn't know what had been going on between them to elicit such behaviour, but still it bothered me. The more imperious Gurudev acted, the more Dawa grovelled. And, I might add, the more I felt like inciting Dawa to rise against tyranny. These revolutionary feelings arose spontaneously within me. Here Gurudev was again, acting like a god, demanding the respect due a god. It was by acting in this way that his disciples treated him like a god, which he then said he wasn't. He demanded it. Then he denied it. Grand creator of illusion. His words of the day before now seemed hollow. He once said, 'The tree laden with fruit naturally bends low,' meaning the man of wisdom is naturally humble. I watched him from the back seat, my little daypack on my lap. I was very clear with myself from the beginning that I would fall into no one's trap. I could resume my pilgrimage in search of the present moment at any time and at any place. It was important for me to remember how I'd entered Gurudev's movie, and that I could exit by the same door. I had one hand on my pack and the other on the door handle. It would be that simple. I felt claustrophobic, like the pressure cooker was malfunctioning and we'd have to rely on the emergency release valve to prevent an explosion. If Gurudev were to treat me in the way he treated the others, I would have been gone in a flash. I had my dignity. It made me doubt the others, both for allowing themselves to be treated in such a way and for worshipping Gurudev in return.

Dawa brought a huge quantity of green leafy vegetables and filled the back of the jeep with them. Then Gurudev sent him back for bundles of carrots. A constant line of people came by for darshan. I couldn't help myself from thinking what a pompous ass he was, a fraud, saying he was not a god yet revelling in the attention due one. It would be easy being a mere observer, but I was not; I was still trying to discern whether the man sitting in the front seat was a true spiritual master and whether my understanding was just not great enough to realize it.

We drove out of Darjeeling and went past the Dali Monastery. Just as we were entering Ghoom, we stopped across the street from where a man was selling three-foot-long squashes. Dawa jumped out, went to Gurudev's window for instructions, and then ran across the street. I had the feeling if Gurudev told him to jump in front of a speeding truck he would do so, thoughtlessly. Dawa came back. There was a problem. He had no small bills. Gurudev got angry. Dawa got in the jeep and we continued but a short way before stopping again, this time in front of a house.

Our sudden arrival obviously surprised the house's occupants, who quickly made ready and led Gurudev into a room they kept just for him, as was the case in so many of his devotees' houses. They were pulling the sheets up and covering with a thick blanket the bed that was 'only for him', upon which it would be a sacrilege for anyone else to sleep, even if Gurudev didn't show up for a year. Gurudev saw the state of the room, turned around, and went to the bathroom.

Dawa led me through a door into a dim room and bid me to sit on the floor. In the back of the room was a shrine glowing from the light of oil lamps. Some people sat cross-legged on the floor in the room's centre. I sat with them; and it was only then I noticed a woman dressed in a white robe sitting cross-legged on a wide bed, exuding the unmistakable radiance of tranquillity. She was mildly observing with half-closed guru eyes all that was occurring in the room. And now she was looking at me, but in a way that neither demanded her attention nor called for my response. It was with a certain holy indifference that her eyes went to whatever occurred in that room.

The people on the floor were all facing her and there was the most beautiful silence. I was happy just to sit there and observe this woman. Darshan: to be in the presence of. I had no idea who she was, but there was a special atmosphere in her presence. She said something in Nepali to one of the men sitting next to me and they started conversing in hushed tones with extended silences between responses. An old woman came into the room and presented the woman with a ceremonial scarf. Then Dawa opened the door and motioned for me to come.

As we walked down the hall towards Gurudev's room, I asked Dawa who this remarkable woman was. 'She is known as Mataji,' he said. 'She says she channels Sai Baba. But Sai Baba has said he will never allow the spirit of Sai Baba to be channelled through any other vehicle than himself. So her claim is false. We don't like her.' We entered Gurudev's room. And there he sat, just like Mataji, on his little throne, people sitting on the floor reverently beholding a human incarnation of God. How very absurd, I couldn't help thinking: two of them in one house, and rivals.

I sat on the floor. 'This room my room,' Gurudev said. 'This bed only for me.'

But I was there when we first got to the house and saw the bed being quickly made up and smoothed out. So did he. So why did he bother? Whom was he trying to impress? Since it was so unlike him to boast, it crossed my mind that he was saying this to push my buttons, to elicit exactly the response I was now experiencing in order to light a fire under me.

The daughter of the house (whose room 'his' room appeared to be) came in. Gurudev motioned for her to take the women's underwear and shirts off the curtain rods, where they had been put to dry.

At that moment I felt incapable of being in his show any longer. What did he want with me? Why did he allow me to get so close to him? Never had I been around someone I could see from so many angles and think so many contradictory things without being able to draw any stable or lasting conclusions. Sometimes I thought he was just the most ambitious person I'd ever known—aspiring to be a living god and succeeding, at least in the eyes of his community. As a Westerner, I probably added a little shine to his presentation.

Dawa, having finished arranging Gurudev's robes, sat down next to me on the floor. I leaned over and whispered, 'Is there a shop nearby where I could buy a razor?' When travelling with Gurudev it was often difficult to figure out how one was supposed to wash oneself. The stubble on my face was becoming unseemly. I had caught a glimpse of the bathroom, and there was a proper sink with a mirror above it. This was my opportunity. Dawa told me where to find a shop, so I excused myself and bought a razor. When I came back in, Dawa told me to follow him into another room where we were to have tea. 'But I want to shave,' I told him. I was tired of listening to people's orders. Gurudev's word was always a command, and now Dawa was insisting I come for tea. I protested that I wanted to shave, but to resist would only cause a scene. I sheepishly followed him and accepted the proffered cup, which I downed quickly, scorching my mouth. Then I excused myself and went to the bathroom.

I was halfway through my shave when there was a hurried knock at the door. 'Thomas, hurry.' It was Dawa. 'We are leaving! Hurry!'

'Tell God to wait,' I said.

'What?'

'Nothing. I'm coming.' I scraped as best I could the rest of the hairs growing out of my face and darted down the stairs to the waiting vehicle, and we were off. In Ghoom, we stopped and Dawa went dashing around doing his master's bidding. It took him some time because he still only had large bills and had to find someone who could change them. This is a common problem in India. Dawa had been in such a hurry that he had left the door open. I looked down and saw a scrap of newspaper on the pavement. As always in Gurudev's presence—no matter how much I wanted to deny it—everyday coincidences yielded meaning. It was time once again to play Gurudev's little game. While Gurudev was busy giving blessings—and vegetables—to a long queue of people that had formed outside his window, I reached down and picked up the piece of newspaper. I cut out the picture with the caption and when Dawa came back into the car and we started moving, I handed it to him and motioned for him to give it to Gurudev. It was a picture of a lion trainer dressed in a fur loincloth, holding open the mouth of a lion. Underneath, it said, 'Circus Master'. Dawa interpreted, and Gurudev turned to look at me and smiled uncertainly. We drove off into the hills.

Dawa leaned over and whispered in my ear, 'If Gurudev is the circus master, we are his trained animals.'

'Not me,' I shot back. I felt my half-shaven cheeks. I could have stayed in that bathroom and finished the job but hadn't. Gurudev was a good trainer and I resented it.

Gurudev started speaking and Dawa leaned forward to catch every word coming from the master's mouth. Then he interpreted in the reverent tone he always used when telling me the latest wisdom coming from the sacred spring. 'Gurudev is saying one must always have small bills when one goes shopping.' For Dawa, this was obviously a tremendous revelation. To me it was an absurd truism, something every child knew.

We stopped at the edge of a small village where some women were selling huge bundles of carrots and radishes. I got out with Dawa, both to help him and to alleviate the pressure I felt by being in that vehicle. Another car stopped. It was a Bengali tourist couple, and they bought some carrots. Gurudev opened his window and called them over. They didn't know why, so they hesitated. Gurudev was holding out a bundle of carrots. He tried to hand it to them but since they already had carrots and since they couldn't figure out why this lama was trying to hand them more, they tried to refuse. Then Dawa said in a reverential tone, 'He is a mahatma, a great soul. It is prasad, a blessed gift.' How absurd, I thought. Always shoring up the image. If he was such a great soul, weren't people supposed to be able to feel it themselves? Did he need Dawa to advertise? It all smacked of religion to me, the organized form of religion that I so vociferously rejected. If you meet the Buddha, kill the Buddha. And as I said in my speech in Namchi, to which Gurudev so readily agreed, don't get stuck on the one who points to the mystery that lies beyond. Move beyond, yourself.

The man stepped forward and cautiously took the proffered gift.

We drove on.

Something happened. I honestly cannot remember exactly what it was, but it was a little coincidence, what they would call a miracle, that was immediately attributed to Gurudev. I must say that coincidences did tend to abound in Gurudev's presence. Like that scrap of newspaper with the picture of the circus master appearing at exactly the right moment. I do not dispute the miraculous nature of the event—or, for that matter, of the entire universe. What bothered me was saying these things happened by the power of the guru. When I was on my pilgrimage in search of the present moment I was both open and present enough that things started flashing, and these little miracles were almost constant; yet I did not say they occurred because of my powers or anyone else's. It was the miraculous nature of the universe itself that was manifesting. It can do that. To attribute it to anybody was to miss the point. And dangerous. If the goal is to directly experience unity, nothing and nobody should get in your way. If you see the Buddha, kill the Buddha. They were worshipping the Buddha, attributing the miracle of the entire universe to one man.

Since I didn't see him correcting them, I took it upon myself.

I leaned forward on the back seat and actually poked Gurudev's arm. 'This is a human being,' I said. 'He is flesh and blood, just like the rest of us. Spiritual power, God, whatever you want to call it, is in him. Of course it is. But it is in me as well. It is in all of you. It is in the rock. If in the end all is One, then it is equally everywhere. If the little miracles of daily life happen, why attribute them to him? It is the nature of the universe! Why worship him as if he is the one who causes it all? Maybe the little miracles happen because I am here—or because of any of you. It is nature of the fabric itself. It's what we are all made of!'

Firstly, the boys were not used to someone questioning the master. It just wasn't done. Secondly, they had no idea what I was talking about—and it wasn't only because of language. We were from different worlds, thrown together in the pressure cooker of that vehicle hour after hour, day after day, and now week after week, plying the twisting roads of Darjeeling at the command of the Master Director himself. He said stop, we stopped. He said go, we went. It was easy to see where the boys' contention—that everything was caused by Gurudev—came from.

It was Sangam, the driver, who first manifested the anger they must all have been feeling because of my words: he started turning the wheel erratically, jerking the vehicle around curves and driving faster than he should have. After speeding up on a blind curve, he had to swerve away from an oncoming car. We almost hit, and the impact would have been right at the back door where I was sitting. Then there was a rattling noise, and the multicoloured Buddhist flag at the front of the vehicle fell off. Sangam stopped, opened the door, and started walking back to retrieve it.

Dawa whispered in my ear. 'You aren't going to believe this; it is another of the miracles: whenever there is tension in the jeep one of the flags falls off. This has happened so many times, always when there is trouble.'

My hand was on the door handle, my pack within easy reach. I was a free man. Nothing held me. At that very moment and on that stretch of empty road I could simply open the door and start walking. Thousands flocked to be in his presence and I had practically unprecedented access. People were continually telling me, often with a hint of jealousy, how lucky I was. I felt as if he were offering me his kingdom and I was on the point of refusing it on the grounds that it somehow wasn't good enough. One wrong move on his part and I would have been out of there. It was one of those razor-edged moments. Everyone pointed to him and said he was the cause of all miracles. All he would have had to do was agree with them, to say, 'I have acquired certain powers,' and I would have been gone in a flash. The devotees always felt like a veil, covering and obscuring the truth of what he really was. And still I wondered: who was he really, behind the tremendous show?

So I asked him, 'How is it that these little miracles happen?'

Gurudev turned around to look at me. I was afraid he'd be angry for my defiant stance. I could feel it in the others. But he wasn't. As always, he was happy and calm. He asked if I remembered the greens we had eaten at breakfast. We had eaten rice and greens that morning at a devotee's house and he had explained to me that the greens were gathered wild in the forest. 'It is like those greens,' he said. 'These things happen by nature. It is *prakritik*.' He motioned for me to write the word down in my little notebook. I released my hand from the door handle. Like a trained animal, I pulled the notebook out of my pocket. Dawa helped me with the spelling and he interpreted for me: *prakritik* means 'natural'.

He understood. It was by nature itself, and had nothing to do with any individual. He claimed nothing for himself, despite what his followers believed. Yet why he didn't correct their erroneous notions?

As if he picked up on my thought, he said something which Dawa at first didn't want to interpret. Gurudev made him. 'Gurudev is saying that it is always the ministers that bring down the king.'

Sangam returned with the flag. He put it back in its little holder, got in, and we drove off.

We wound through a pine forest to a place where there were monkeys on the sides of the road and a little stone Hindu temple, probably to Hanuman, the monkey god. Gurudev had Sangam stop and he did what he did with all his devotees. He fed them. He threw bunches of bananas out of the window and a scuffle ensued as dozens of monkeys descended on the fruit.

Shortly after that, we took a left turn down a small, steep dirt road that switchbacked through the tea garden where the next event would occur. We came upon some women with tea pluckers' conical wicker baskets on their backs. We stopped, and they came to Gurudev's window, palms pressed, huge toothy smiles on their open, dark faces. He gave them bundles of carrots. Then we came upon a man walking alone. We stopped. He obviously didn't know who we were. Gurudev held a bundle of carrots out of the window for him, and like the Bengali couple, he hesitated. Dawa leaned out of his open window. 'He is a mahatma, a great soul. He will be doing a puja tomorrow at the temple.' Trying to drum up business.

A half-hour later we arrived at the village, where preparations were under way for the next day's gathering. Outside the village temple, men were busy constructing a bamboo scaffolding on which a colourful tarpaulin would be put to shade the overflow crowd. Others were hanging colourful banners. Someone was lashing a loudspeaker to the top of the scaffolding and they were already testing the sound system, which was cracking and popping and screeching with feedback.

As usual, there was much fanfare at our arrival. But somehow I was deeply unimpressed. What was all this show worth, if it was all to greet a man who was not a god, playing the part of one? It's fine for them, if they need it, I thought, but I have no need.

We were led to the house where we were to stay, and I tagged on behind, carrying Gurudev's shoulder bag. It should have been an honour, but I felt like calling his bluff; the urge arose within me to hand him the bag. Why couldn't he carry his own bag? The tree that bears fruit naturally bends low. Hah! I would be veering seriously from my course in life to sit under the shade of this tree. So I left him with his bag and went back outside. The loudspeakers were now blaring out in tinny squawks some canned Tibetan religious music. It grated on my ears and nerves; I just couldn't stand it. What if there were people in the village who weren't followers of Gurudev, who didn't want to hear this music? It was all so overbearing. It felt like a Christian revival meeting. Over the music, someone announced the arrival of Gurudev and invited everyone to the puja, which would begin the next day. I walked by the jeep, and Sangam was on his back under the vehicle, trying to fix the holder for the flag that had fallen off because of my intransigence. He scowled at me as I passed.

'Where are you going?' he asked.

'For a walk.'

'By yourself?'

'Yes.'

The need to be alone: that's something Indians seem unable to comprehend. He looked at me as if I had truly gone crazy, which maybe I had. There was a dirt track leading up a slope of tea bushes. I started walking, the harsh amplified sounds like whips lashing my back, driving me on.

It took me twenty minutes to get beyond the loudspeaker's reach. Free at last! No more miracles but for the simple miracle of nature and green growth. I climbed up a huge flat stone and laid on it, surrounded by green, bird song filling my ears, the sun beating down. Not a soul in sight. I lay there all afternoon, getting up only once to go to a little spring that flowed from the base of the rock to wet the razor, which was still in my pocket, and finish my shave, which had been so rudely interrupted. I didn't return to the village until it was dark.

❖ ❖

The next morning as the sky blushed red in anticipation of the rising sun, I went outside and plucked a flower from a bush. I brought it to Gurudev, who was just awakening and sitting up in bed. I presented it to him and told him I was leaving.

'But you will come back?' He looked shocked, almost hurt, if that human emotion was possible for him.

'No,' I told him. 'I will go to Darjeeling where I have some things to do. I will come to Tukvar for your birthday in three or four days.' Gurudev's birthday was the biggest event in his yearly calendar. Shortly after that, I had to leave for Delhi and my flight back to the United States. The woman of the house came in with two cups of tea. Gurudev took the lid off his cup and took a sip.

'Whatever you want, you will get,' he said. 'The guru is like that. If you come to the shopkeeper and ask for one rupee of sugar, you will get one rupee of sugar. If you ask for one hundred rupees of sugar, you will get that also.'

He took another sip of tea. 'In Tibetan there is a saying: Sometimes it takes seven years for the master to test the disciple; it can also take seven years for the disciple to test the master.' He smiled. 'The wood of the sandalwood tree has a very beautiful smell,' he said. 'If another tree grows near sandalwood, after seven years the wood of that tree also smells like sandalwood.'

He picked up the lid to his cup.

'We also say in Tibetan, when a man finds his teacher it is as if the teacher puts a lid on his cup,' and he put the lid back on his cup. 'Meaning: disciple protected. Nothing can happen to him.'

Tears welled up in my eyes.

Here I was, practically rejecting him, and still he was showering me with love and protection. We sat in silence, drinking our tea. Then I stood to leave. He put a ceremonial scarf around my neck and I took my leave. I felt as if he'd blessed me for reclaiming my freedom.

I started walking in the early dawn. The sun was just rising, bathing the world in a rosy hue. I was on the road again and free. It was a tremendous release. The lid was off the pressure cooker. The morning fog clung to the slope of the mountain like undulating curtains. Women were already plucking tea, their conical baskets strapped to their backs. I was filled with joy. The birds were singing and I was happy.

It took me over two hours to climb the small dirt track through the tea garden to reach the main road. I turned right and headed towards Ghoom and Darjeeling. I was a bit apprehensive about walking past the Hanuman temple with its many monkeys for fear they would gang up and challenge me, thinking there was food in my pack. I found a length of bamboo to use both as a walking stick and to brandish if the monkeys become aggressive. Peace through strength, I thought, as I passed through thick forests and groves of bamboo growing between huge moss-covered boulders.

A jeep came up from behind, honking as it passed. A familiar face poked out of the window. It was Dawa. It stopped a short way in front of me.

'Jump in.' Dawa called.

'No way! I find God on the open road with the birds and the trees!'

'But Gurudev is here!'

I walked up to the waiting jeep. I think Sangam had taken Gurudev's vehicle back to Tukvar to help get ready for Gurudev's birthday. Someone must have lent them this jeep and they were headed to the market or to some devotee's house before the ritual began down in the tea garden. I knew the routine. Gurudev was sitting in front. They had draped a huge towel emblazoned with Disney characters on his seat, a simple attempt at a throne.

'Jump in, Thomas,' Dawa said again, his eyes beseeching me to be reasonable. 'Gurudev is saying we'll give you a ride.'

Gurudev motioned to the back, where there was room.

'No way!' I exclaimed.

'*Please*, Thomas, just get in.'

None of them could comprehend: when the master says to do something, you do it. If Gurudev had told any of them to jump off a cliff, they would have. As attendants, it was their responsibility to smooth everything to the Master's will. It was an awkward situation to say the least, one at which I couldn't help but start laughing, illuminated by the immanence of the One in the All, and the total absurdity of the mindset of a devotee, worshipping the illuminated person and not the illumination itself. But Gurudev got it. He started laughing with me. They stared at him as uncomprehendingly as they had been staring at me. His eyes were shining. He told the driver to continue. I ran beside the car for a short while, laughing, waving them on.

Around the next corner the temple came into view. As I had feared, there were dozens of monkeys lining the road. But Gurudev had smoothed my way. The monkeys were all happily peeling back the skins of bananas Gurudev had thrown them. They let me pass unmolested.

21

THE BIRTHDAY

Before leaving Darjeeling to go down to Tukvar for Gurudev's birthday, I went to the Oxford Bookstore on the Chowrasta and bought a copy of *The Emperor's New Clothes*. The book tells of an emperor who has some tailors make him a new set of clothes that they claim can only be seen by those who are wise. When the emperor goes to see the clothes being made he cannot see them, for they are cutting and sewing air, the tailors being swindlers. The emperor says nothing out of fear that he will be thought unwise. When they are finished he parades through the streets in his new clothes, but actually he is stark naked, a fact that some are deluded enough not to see and others dare not admit, even to themselves. Everyone admires his new clothes until a child calls out, 'But the emperor's got no clothes!' Being a tale of a collective delusion surrounding a commanding figure, my thought was to present the book to Gurudev.

I took the ropeway from North Point down to Tukvar and from the terminus I walked down the steep switchback road through the tea bushes to Gurudev's village. Along the way, people I'd never seen before greeted me by name.

Tukvar was buzzing. Banners strung over the road and in the alley leading to the family house wished Gurudev a happy fifty-seventh birthday and greeted the thousands who would come to celebrate. Gurudev was not yet there: he was still at the tea garden where I had left him. They were in the middle of constructing a new house across the alley from the old one where I had always stayed. It was a huge concrete structure of many storeys that had just popped up and was still growing. The whole place was a frenzy of excitement and action. They were covering the flat roof of the new house with a multicoloured tarpaulin suspended from a bamboo scaffolding, under which was Gurudev's throne where he would give darshan. Ribbons were strung everywhere. Big pots of food were boiling. More and more people came and happy activity abounded.

Late the next afternoon someone came to get me. Gurudev was arriving. I hurried to the road, where he was just getting out of the jeep. I had been feeling intense ambivalence towards him, like a bee towards a flower, cautious lest the flower be one of those exotic ones that trap the insects they attract. I was brought to the front of the waiting crowd. When Gurudev saw me he smiled. 'You have come,' he called out to me, and he beamed. He was genuinely happy I was there.

My ambivalence was not strong enough to withstand the look of love in his eyes. I pressed my palms in greeting.

The air was electric in his presence. My sense of touch was almost sensitive enough to actually feel the vibration. He was obviously no ordinary human being. He led the crowd back down the alley to the house, stopping along the way to break a branch off a flowering bush and give it to a woman with the instructions to put it in a pot and grow a new plant.

A constant stream of people converged on the house, many of whom I knew from events across the Darjeeling Hills and in Sikkim, and the many devotees' houses we had visited. The next day would be his birthday. The festivities had begun.

The entourage followed Gurudev to his new bedroom upstairs in the new building. Gurudev sat cross-legged on his bed. The room filled. Pema sat next to me, and Gurudev said he wanted Pema to interpret. Gurudev looked at me a moment in silence. He rubbed his open palm over his shaved head. Then he spoke.

'He is saying,' Pema said, 'that there is a fountain of water; the water comes from the pool and splashes back down. But there is another water, water that comes straight from Heaven. It is the lucky fish that can swim up and catch the drops that fall from Heaven. Those drops, when you drink them, make pearls inside you. There are rocks, and there are pearls. Like it says in the Bible: don't throw your pearls before swine.'

A delegation of monks arrived from the Dali Monastery. They were headed by a high reincarnated lama, a man of about thirty who wore dark sunglasses and had a big gold tooth. Cushions were set for them near Gurudev's throne for the next day. The reincarnated lama from Dali also had a throne, slightly lower than Gurudev's. They had come to perform various chants and rituals during the celebration of Gurudev's birthday.

I was called down into the new kitchen on the first floor for dinner. When I returned, Gurudev's bedroom was packed. More were pushing to get in. I didn't even try. I was squeezing by his door so that I could go up to the roof where they were setting up for tomorrow when I noticed a scrap of newspaper being trampled beneath all those feet. I picked it up and ripped out the headline. Squeezing through the crowd, I got far enough into the room to reach out above the people sitting on the floor and handed it to Gurudev. He had someone translate: 'Good chemistry for tomorrow.'

That night I slept on a mat on the floor in Gurudev's room.

❖ ❖

In the morning, I was the first to wish Gurudev a happy birthday. We could hear the sounds of a crowd gathering outside the closed door. The Hindu priests were singing devotional songs. When one of the women in Gurudev's family brought us tea, she had to fight her way through the crowd and slip in through the door, shutting it carefully so as not to close it on anyone's head.

When we were through with our tea, Gurudev motioned for the door to be opened and the crowd surged in, everyone holding bouquets of flowers. One man presented Gurudev with a bottle of milk and told him the outcome of a conversation they had had a few months earlier. The man's cow had been pregnant and he had asked Gurudev when the cow would give birth. Gurudev had said it would give birth on his birthday and that it would be a male, a bull. The man was there to tell Gurudev it happened exactly as he predicted, the bull having been born just before sunrise. He presented Gurudev with a bottle of the cow's fresh milk.

And thus began a stream of people to get his darshan and give birthday greetings, a stream of people that would last well into the night. At times the line of those waiting, often a dozen people wide, extended from the roof of his family's house, down the stairs and the dirt alley, and stretched a full mile down the road. People waited for hours, slowly inching towards Gurudev, love in their eyes, flowers in their hands, excitement mounting as they neared him. And once they presented him with the flowers and the other gifts—ceremonial scarves, money, and fruit—they went down another set of stairs behind the house and were each given a full plate of food. Somehow, a meal was provided for 15,000 people.

It was one tremendous love fest. A pile of flowers grew on either side of Gurudev's throne. By afternoon, the piles were higher than he was. Gurudev was in great form, radiating

Line of people on Tukvar road

tenfold the love directed to him, a vortex into which everyone poured their offerings and out of which those same offerings flowed, increased by having passed through his hands, imbued with love, holiness, happiness, and joy. And the magic was there to see. There was a small army of people cutting fruit and making packets of prasad, which everyone received after having his darshan. And the people themselves brought the food. Someone might present Gurudev with a bunch of bananas, which would then be thrown by Dawa or one of the other attendants across to the people preparing the prasad. By the time that person reached the stairs in the back and was handed a packet of prasad, it might very well contain pieces of the same bananas he had just brought. But now they were consecrated, partaking in the holy blessing. When people presented Gurudev with ceremonial scarves with money wrapped in them, he handed the money out again. His energy, his gifts, and you could even say his divinity, were all conferred upon him by the devotees. It was as if 15,000 people shone their

Making prasad

lights in one direction and then marvelled at the sparkling splendour.

Late in the afternoon, as the piles of flowers surrounding Gurudev grew to little mountains, I was watching him from a short distance off. He was radiant. Someone handed him a pomegranate, which he handed out to the next person in line, who immediately pressed it to his forehead.

Gurudev called out to me over the heads of those assembled, his hands raised in a gesture that made light of the entire world.

'Loading ... Unloading ... What to do?'

We both laughed. And he was right. I knew exactly what he meant. The night before he had said the birthday wasn't for him. It was the devotees' birthday. He didn't call for such a birthday bash. He was doing it because so many were attracted to him and wanted to show their love by bringing him a flower on his birthday. These flowers were now piled higher than his throne. They poured all their energy into him; *he* had nothing to do with it. It happened by itself; it happened, as he would say, by nature. It was also the nature of a person in such a state to give all those gifts right back to others. So both loading and unloading were just happening. Though he was the central point of it, he had nothing to do with it. Nature was overflowing through him, that was all. And what can you do about the course of nature?

In our lives, we cannot help loading and unloading. Earning and spending, eating and defecating, loving and losing, being born and dying—all expressions of loading and unloading. But being aware of the 'loading and unloading' nature of the universe was not enough. Gurudev's brilliance shone in the last part of his formula: 'What to do?' The man at the centre—focal point of it all, surrounded by mountains of flowers showered on him—was keenly aware that *he* wasn't the cause of any of it. Fifteen thousand people converging for the sake of love itself: love was the prime mover.

Gurudev was in an ecstatic state. It was late afternoon and still the line of people wanting his darshan snaked through the village and into the tea garden. I was standing not far from him. Again, he called out to me. He patted his shoulder, his chest, and his leg. 'This one,' he said, meaning his body, 'rest house.'

'This one,' he said, pointing to his eye, 'window.' Then he pointed to his ears, nose, and mouth. 'These ones—all windows.'

I was standing near Gurudev when he leaned forward towards a young teenage girl flanked on either side by two women who, as I found out later, were the girl's mother and aunt. Gurudev was repeating the word namaste, hello, with clear enunciation, *na-mas-te*. The girl mouthed the word and tried to make the sound, but it was obvious the girl was probably deaf and definitely mute. Her first attempts to repeat the word after Gurudev produced not much more than an animal grunt. Slowly what issued from her throat became vocalized sound and eventually she repeated the word, trembling with excitement. And by the expressions of mother and aunt and

People queued for hours

Everybody offered a flower

everyone else present, it was clear I was witnessing something extraordinary. I could not help the tears welling up in my eyes. Gurudev started on another word, enunciating it clearly. The girl watched his lips closely; after a few tries, she was able to repeat the word. She was so excited she hugged her mother. Gurudev held up the line a few minutes longer mouthing words with such love and tenderness, getting her to speak. It was like a scene out of the Bible. He gave the girl a beautiful peacock-feather fan and showered her mother with flowers, fruit, and a big wad of money. I followed them down the stairs and outside and got their story.

They came from a very remote area in eastern Nepal. The girl was twelve. When she was five, she had had a high fever that lasted a month, during which she became deaf. She spoke her last word fifteen days after the fever ended. Someone told them about Gurudev and his powers so they came, walking four days to reach Tukvar on his birthday. The words I heard her utter were her first in seven years. They were all still giddy with excitement.

People had told me over and again that I didn't understand how lucky I was being so close to Gurudev. I was beginning to understand. There are vast mysteries and possibilities beyond our reckoning. He taught always that there is but one religion: the religion of love, and that God is love. He embodies that love. This might sound crazy. I am truly the Doubting Thomas. I have no room for belief. I have to see or experience, and then I know. That afternoon I experienced something vast and moving.

A little later, a group of people came through. They were from the Dooars, a region south of Bhutan in hot country. Gurudev had visited their place some time back. When he was there they said to him, 'If you are really the incarnation of Lord Krishna, play a flute and call the cows in.' Krishna, of

The deaf girl

course, is often depicted as a flute-playing cowherd. Gurudev said he wouldn't do that, but he would call the elephants. So they handed him a flute. He played, and eight elephants came out of the jungle. He went inside the house and the elephants stayed. The villagers were frightened. Wild elephants cause a lot of destruction. They told him the elephants wouldn't leave until they had his darshan. So he went outside and showed himself to them, and they went back to the jungle. Nice story. True? Who knows? But these people had journeyed all that way to be with him on his birthday. They came with fresh coconut, sugar cane, papaya, and other tropical fruits from their land. They were talking about the elephants and I was told the story.

Some time later, I was sitting on a chair, minding my own business and watching Gurudev, the centre of the vast vortex of energy. I was nostalgic already about leaving, wondering how I would ever capture the scene in words for this book, when an old man I'd never seen came, tapped me on the shoulder, and handed me a little scrap of yellow-lined writing paper. The way it was torn, and by the partial handwritten letters above and below, it was clearly ripped out of a bigger piece of paper, like a child's school paper. It was torn such that only some words remained. It said, '... who can tell the story?'

I grabbed onto the man's arm. 'Who gave you this paper?' I asked.

'A monk,' he said.

'Which one?'

'He just left,' he replied. 'Perhaps Gurudev gave it to him. I do not know.' He disappeared into the crowd, leaving me alone to contemplate the message on the scrap of paper that was delivered into my hands just as I was thinking of how I would write about the scene, '... who can tell the story?' I turned the paper over. On the back, by chance, torn from their context, happened to be the words, '... you the pen?'

In the evening, when the line of people waiting for darshan came to an end, Gurudev jumped off his throne and went back to his room. I went with him. Food was brought. Gurudev was not tired, but charged from the long day.

Just when we finished our meal, we could hear the Hindu priests coming up the stairs, boisterously singing devotional songs. The door flew open and the priests, who had been performing their rituals and chanting from the Sanskrit texts before the sacred fire, came in with the fire's red-hot coals

This mind, very big magnet

on a brass plate. It was billowing with smoke from incense that had been sprinkled on the coals. They had drums and clacking metal instruments and they smudged Gurudev with the smoke, then stood before him singing devotional songs. After some time, Gurudev invited them to sit, and they sat with me on the floor and the mood was jovial. They sang more devotional songs; then Gurudev took the drum and sang a funny song with a pun in it about a woman wearing woollen socks walking to Tibet. One of the priests I got to know had the habit of pointing to his ash-smeared forehead, rocking his head in the Indian fashion, and saying, 'This mind—very big magnet. I speak all language.' It did seem he knew a smattering of many languages, even French, German, Italian, and Spanish. During the birthday celebration we took some long walks together and he told me he was retired from government service. He had been a priest for the Indian Air Force. I asked him what that entailed. 'When plane go up,' he said, pointing to the heavens, 'I do ritual. I pray: no-come-down, no-come-down, no-come-down.'

Tea was brought for all, and Gurudev told funny stories that had everyone laughing. He told them that at the big event in Namchi, during the blessing on the last day when he was giving darshan, I sat in a stuffed chair at the edge of the stage the entire time. He said that chair was actually put there for the chief minister of Sikkim! This made everybody laugh. Then he said in English, 'Today's student, tomorrow's leader.'

The old man from the neighbouring hut came in with his primitive one-stringed violin. He propped the instrument on his feet and plucked out a beautiful folk tune, singing with a raspy voice. The front of the instrument was stretched with animal skin. The sound was raw and soulful; the old man's singing was full of feeling. He was from a Nepali caste of itinerant singers and storytellers, the ones that have travelled from village to village since ancient times singing the news from other regions. His father, grandfather, and great-grandfather all the way back were musicians. Some of his songs caused tears to roll down people's cheeks; others caused the people to roll on the floor with laughter.

Then Gurudev poured water through his conch shell and handed it to one of the priests to blow. The conch shell is an important part of Hindu ritual. The tip of the spiral, the very tight point, is cut off and one blows through it as if it were a trumpet, with one's hand cupped in the shell's spiral opening. The priest blew into the shell and made a resounding sound that shook eardrum and wall alike. Then Gurudev motioned for the next priest to try it. He had trouble making it sound. It takes a great force of lung. So Gurudev had him pass it to the next priest sitting on the floor. He was able to blow with enough force to make the deep reverberating sound break into a higher overtone. Then Gurudev took the conch. He poured water into the cut end until it ran out of the shell's spiral opening. He shook the shell and then put it to his lips. And he blew. It looked as if it cost him no effort, yet the sound that issued from that shell reverberated and made my head ring like a bell. It was a pure sound, of such a volume as to set every molecule dancing. Then he broke into a higher overtone and one above that, each pure and distinct, each piercing right through the last to a higher level. And somehow by breathing in through his nose while still blowing, he was able to make the shell sound without end. Then he picked up another conch shell, a rare one whose spiral turned clockwise, and he blew both at once in an ecstatic frenzy. When he was through, there was an awed silence in the room. Even the old Hindu priests had looks of wonder. Gurudev turned to me and said, 'A bowl can only hold its capacity, and it does not diminish the ocean.'

The Hindu priests sitting on the floor opened their scriptures and chanted from some of the oldest writings in the world. Gurudev watched them in a bemused way. He caught my eye. 'Indian culture,' he said. 'What to do?' Then he started whistling like a bird, in rhythm to the chant and to the chant's two notes. Then he said, 'This is very ancient—like bird song.'

The roof where he had spent the day giving darshan was crowded now with people awaiting him, so he moved out to his throne. There was a small group of musicians on harmonium and tabla. They played music late into the night as one person after another got up before the assembled crowd and danced traditional Nepali dances to the whoops and delight of all.

The next day hundreds of people were still there and the festivities continued. In the late afternoon, the monks from the Dali Monastery did one final puja for the inner circle of Gurudev's family, at the end of which the family would pay the monks for their services. Just when they were about to begin, the sun, which had been hidden behind dark clouds all day, broke through, casting long shafts of golden light across the scene. I squatted next to the throne where the reincarnated Dali monk sat, and photographed the family, first with their palms pressed together and later holding rice in their open palms to throw to the four directions, to the Above and the Below. It was a beautiful, warm, and intimate moment. At one point Shanti, Gurudev's aunt and the matriarch of the family, came forward and with tears running down her cheeks put a ceremonial scarf around my neck and

Above & Opposite:
Women of Gurudev's family

said, 'My son.' The moment the ritual was over, the clouds closed up again and the sun set.

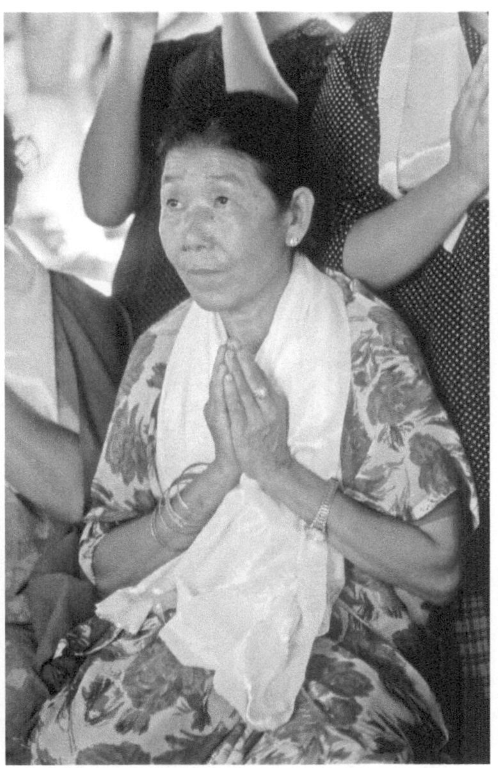

The next morning I awoke on the floor next to Gurudev. I would be leaving that morning for Darjeeling and after that for Delhi and the United States.

Gurudev said, 'How you-me ever apart? From America same sun as India sun. From everywhere sun is same-same. Like time: all time, now time. Remember, God always one.'

I was called into the family's kitchen for breakfast. I sat on a low stool with a plate of food balanced on my knee and a cup of tea in one hand. Shanti heated milk on the wood-fired stove and then she added honey. She poured it into a cup and handed the cup to me. I was holding a cup in each hand and had no hand free with which to eat: I didn't have enough hands. And that is how I will always remember my time there, overflowing with love and kindness.

That night I stayed in my old hotel room overlooking the market in Darjeeling. I left one thing behind in my room the next morning when I left for Delhi and the United States: it was my copy of *The Emperor's New Clothes*.

The author and Gurudev

PART III

A QUESTION OF POLITICS

22

THE UNRESOLVED OMISSION

When I returned to the United States, I went to a cabin in the green hills of Vermont and spent nine months writing the first draft of this book. I wished the book could have ended there. It would have been beautiful to end this book with the birthday, to end on an unsullied positive note, like the clear tone of the sacred conch shell. But that's not how it was going to be.

Something kept tugging at me: Gurudev's involvement with those dark characters, from Ghising on down. The issue was no more settled in me than it was in the book. I realized I had excised the political angle when I told friends stories about Gurudev. The first draft didn't even mention it. There was nothing about bandhs and Ghising and fleeing Darjeeling—none of it.

But it didn't work: these uncomfortable questions always grew back like a weed with strong rhizomes to nag at me. No matter how much I longed for the story to conform to a purely spiritual line, it wouldn't, no more than Darjeeling itself would, despite my naive beginnings there.

I could no longer deny that these same dark politics were right in the middle of the story of Gurudev. So many times when I mentioned Gurudev to people in Darjeeling they said, 'Oh, that Ghising's guru.' How could I *not* mention it? Though I had resisted this being a theme in the book, there it was, a glaringly unresolved omission at the heart of the story. Left unresolved, like a disease left untreated, it could only grow and infect the other parts. It raised doubts in my mind, or rather areas of confusion. Was Gurudev corrupted by his association with these people? Who knows? Was he purposefully engaging them to bring them to his teachings? Perhaps. I might have let it go if it weren't for the heightened responsibility that came with writing a book.

So I returned to Darjeeling. I had to put some rather pointed questions to Gurudev. Without resolving this issue, or at least attempting to deal directly with it, I knew the book would be woefully incomplete. Therefore, when I returned to Darjeeling with the early manuscript of this book, it was to confront the issue, delicately but head on.

I went to Tukvar and was welcomed by the family as warmly as ever. Gurudev, Pema, and the crew were on the road, due back the next day. I took the opportunity of being alone with the family without the focus being on Gurudev to make some gentle inquiries into their feelings about Subash Ghising. Politics had never registered as a topic of conversation there before.

Much as my friend John had warned me, Tukvar was clearly a Ghising stronghold. This came as quite a shock, since beyond the cautious praise everybody had for Ghising before they trusted you enough to overcome their fear and say what they really thought, I'd never actually spoken to anyone with anything favourable to say about the man. The family proudly informed me that Ghising was just finishing the construction of a monastery outside Darjeeling for Gurudev. They said it cost the equivalent of millions of US dollars and that Ghising had solicited funds from the kings of Nepal and Bhutan, from the contractors he granted government contracts to, from shopkeepers, individuals, and from monies channelled through him from the state and Central governments. The family was clearly proud that Gurudev was being given such a well-deserved seat. They also told me that Gurudev was now riding in a new luxury vehicle, also a gift from Subash Ghising. They told me Subash Ghising was a great man, had given all Nepalis in India their identity and was ruling with great wisdom and compassion. It seemed relations couldn't have been closer.

I cautiously countered their enthusiasm by telling them that most people I met were actually afraid of Subash Ghising, and that the prevailing opinion amongst almost everyone I spoke with was that Ghising was corrupt and used violence to maintain power. That, I opined, was why there was no viable opposition—because everyone was afraid to oppose him for fear of getting killed. They balked at this. 'People who tell you that are working for the state of West Bengal,' they told me, 'or else they have been duped by Ghising's opponents.'

One of Gurudev's close male relatives went on to make a statement that still rings in my ears:

'I'd kill for Gurudev. Why not?'

He was speaking of a recent incident in which someone—he must have been deranged—had come with a big knife to kill Gurudev. When Gurudev apparently intuited this man's intentions before he'd even brandished the knife, Gurudev bared his chest and said, 'OK, do it now, kill me.' The man had been so unnerved that he ran away. Pema happened not to be present at the time, but when he returned he took it upon himself—as Gurudev's chief protector—to avenge the would-be attacker and took off to track the man down, intent on who-knows-what. Everyone was happy Pema didn't find him.

They gave me my old room in the original family house. Gurudev had permanently moved across the dirt track to the substantial new concrete house, which had grown since I'd been there. Maybe it was because with distance my eye had grown critical, but when Gurudev returned the next day my enthusiasm for his routine just wasn't there. When he broke off a branch of a common flowering herb and explained to me its medicinal qualities, for probably the tenth time, the magic I'd felt the first time he'd done so was missing. He had a new crop of attendants, boys he'd picked up somewhere, none of whom I knew. They were young—eighteen or nineteen—and were a rough lot. One could tell they were new in their role as attendants of the living god and had the zealousness of new converts. It seemed they were being trained by Pema.

Gurudev had always appreciated the spirit of my approach: while everybody else bowed, prostrated, followed blindly, submitted, believed, and saw unending miraculous manifestations of the divine, I challenged him. He said it was a good thing, that I was 'testing the purity of his gold', as he once put it. And that's who I am, how I've always been when in the presence of someone considered by others to be wise: there he is, the Doubting Thomas, lugging in his anvil and placing the words of wisdom on it. There he is pounding his heavy hammer on those golden utterances to see if they ring true. Gurudev always understood that my challenges did not put into question my respect for him. Since Gurudev had never spent time with a Westerner it is not surprising that he was examining me with as much interest and astonishment as I examined him. Maybe that's why he liked me being there. He appreciated the spirit of inquiry with which I challenged him, which showed he was more broad-minded than the others. The traditional guru–disciple relationship demands unquestioning faith and devotion. So it's not surprising that many around Gurudev, especially the young lads, took umbrage with anyone standing up to question their guru. As a foreigner I was afforded some leniency. The fact that Gurudev took no offence and even seemed to appreciate my challenges made me a slightly more acceptable aberration in the order of things.

From the moment I'd learned of Gurudev's relationship with Ghising and his party members, I knew that to broach the subject was like stepping on a live wire, and it had to be approached with the utmost decorum and diplomacy. That's why I had never dared bring it up and had left it unresolved.

I wanted to catch Gurudev alone, where we'd both be free from others' reactions, where he could confide his true motives, especially if they were different from what he expressed publicly. Unfortunately, the opportunity didn't arise. I spent a few days with Gurudev in Tukvar. Though consciously trying to position myself so that I could be alone with him, circumstances always conspired to thwart it. The few times we were alone in his room it was only momentarily; long before I dared open my mouth the door always opened to the next group of visitors.

When the day came for Gurudev and his crew to return to the road and the next series of events staged in his honour, I declined the offer to accompany them. They did, though, make room for me in the vehicle to give me a ride up the hill to Darjeeling. The vehicle, a recent gift from Subash Ghising, was so new that it still had the clear plastic covers on the seats. It had that new-car smell and it was huge and luxurious. Despite the vehicle's smooth suspension and plush seats, I felt extremely uncomfortable.

The strangest and most disquieting thing about riding in that vehicle was that as we came into Darjeeling no one seemed to pay any mind that Gurudev was sitting in the front seat. In the past, people would notice, they'd approach his window excited at their good fortune, palms pressed, all smiles when we were stopped in traffic. Even just driving by, they'd see him and press their palms with heads bowed. Now the only ones who seemed to notice us were the Darjeeling Traffic Police, who aggressively cleared the traffic before us, pressed their palms, and bowed their heads at our passing, almost as if it were now official policy. Perhaps the others didn't expect to see Gurudev, known for his simplicity, in such a fancy vehicle.

I stayed some weeks in Darjeeling at my old hotel, holed up in my room with the balcony overlooking the heart of the market. I was still working on this book's first draft—adding the political elements to the story, details on the bandhs, my fleeing, and so on—as well as getting a feel for current conditions in Darjeeling. Ghising had recovered, though many believed that while his skull had stopped the shrapnel from entering his brain, the assassination attempt had both added elements of paranoia to his personality and made him prone to spiritual flights of fancy. There were wild stories circulating about him, in which he claimed that Sai Baba was appearing before him, instructing him on how to govern and hold on to power.

I lined up a Nepali friend who spoke perfect English to come with me to see Gurudev and to act as interpreter. I would request a private interview along with my interpreter so I was certain to attain clarity on the issues. I called the family to make sure Gurudev was there. The trip turned out to be one continuous source of frustration. I hired a van and we got to Tukvar before noon. A group that had come all the way from Nepal had spent the night. They were in his room all morning, and just when they were called out to take their lunch and I thought my opportunity had come, another group of people arrived. It was the family of a teenaged girl who was possessed by a demon. They had also brought the village priest and a few sadhus. Each sadhu wore a loincloth and sported dreadlocks. The girl's hair was dishevelled and matted, flying loose around her head. Her clothes were filthy and torn and she was held by two strong men who kept a firm grip on her at all times. She would alternately flail her arms and shake her head, blathering gibberish in some unrecognizable language, then fall into a catatonic state. The whole time, even when she was raving, her eyes were completely blank, staring straight ahead with no show of consciousness whatsoever. It was both uncanny and unsettling, and it took the afternoon for Gurudev to bring her back, which he did, with the aid of clouds of medicinal incense and a ritual to entice the demon out of her. She left Gurudev's room late that afternoon looking like the normal schoolgirl that she undoubtedly had been before the demon (or was it madness, or epilepsy?) overcame her. She took her leave, shyly thanking Gurudev and accepting from him a bunch of bananas as a parting gift. While it was fascinating to be present at such a spectacle, it didn't exactly afford me any time alone with Gurudev, and we left with our mission unfulfilled.

I made one more attempt to bring my friend to Tukvar to interpret. This time I called to make sure Gurudev was there, but when we arrived they told me he was in Sikkim and had been there for some days. I was certain they had told me he was there when I called, and I left confused and ticked off that I had wasted both my friend's time and the money for the vehicle.

One thing transpired while I was there: they told me Ghising was going to inaugurate Gurudev's monastery outside Darjeeling on the way to Ghoom in about a week's time and that I was invited to come with them. I'd be able to meet Ghising, they told me. Making up a lie on the spot, I said I would be in Sikkim at the time, and was sorry that I wouldn't be able to attend. Previously I had hoped to meet Ghising, maybe even in Gurudev's presence, and see their interactions at close hand, but I didn't want to be present at this public event when all the press would be sure to be there and the cameras rolling. Things had heated up in the Hills, I was a foreigner, and it just wouldn't be wise to be seen publicly with the 'Supremo', as they called him.

While in Darjeeling, it was difficult for me to tell people of my association with Gurudev because of his connection with Ghising. Almost invariably when I mentioned Gurudev to non-devotees, they would dismiss him as Ghising's guru. They'd seen them together too many times, either in person, in the newspapers, or on the local cable TV station at the inauguration of any number of Ghising's projects. Their names were intertwined. I started broaching the subject with people who knew Gurudev and considered themselves devotees, and I found they were usually confused. They wondered, as I did, how he could have relations with such men.

To avoid the occasion, I actually did go to Sikkim at the time of the monastery's inauguration. Too many people in Darjeeling knew my connection to Gurudev and that I was writing a book about him. It would have seemed too odd if I was in town and didn't attend.

From Gangtok I read in the newspapers that the town of Darjeeling had been closed down as they paraded Gurudev through the streets in a fifteen-foot-high wooden chariot overtopped with a parasol. Thousands thronged the procession chanting 'Hare Rama, Hare Krishna' as they wheeled this Tibetan lama, worshipped by Hindus as an incarnation of Krishna, through the city and the five kilometres up the ridge to the monastery. Subash Ghising himself performed the purification ceremony for the chariot before Gurudev climbed into it, and all the councillors of the Darjeeling Gorkha Hill Council were there, as well as other government officials. Schools were off that day so the young scholars and their teachers could attend. Representatives of various ethnic and religious groups dressed in their traditional costumes added colour to the unprecedented procession. A constant stream of flowers and flower petals rained down upon the chariot. Subash Ghising had gone ahead to await Gurudev's arrival at the monastery. Then he personally enthroned him on the huge throne overtopped by a multi-headed cobra.

Lavish quarters for Gurudev, his attendants, and family had been built. Gurudev slept there that night, and though Ghising must have assumed Gurudev would then take up residence at the monastery and hold court there, Gurudev left in the morning and, as I was to find out later, he never once returned.

I visited the monastery later, which was built overlooking a theme park tourist attraction run by the Darjeeling Gorkha Hill Council, prominently featuring Mickey Mouse, Donald Duck, and other perennial Disney characters, which added another surreal dimension to Gurudev's very unusual monastery and temple.

To the right of the temple door was a huge wall painting of Gurudev sitting in the lotus posture floating on a cloud. To the left was a painting of Krishna, and around the sides the walls were painted with Jesus with a flock of sheep, and Mahavira, the founder of the Jain religion. And as if this wasn't strange enough in a Tibetan Buddhist monastery, inside the main temple, where normally there would be brightly coloured

Gurudev floating on a cloud, painted on the external wall of his monastery

depictions of various Tibetan Buddhist deities, the walls were bare concrete. At the far side of the temple room was a raised platform covered in plain yellow tiles (the type usually found in bathrooms) and Gurudev's throne in the centre of it with the huge metal multi-headed cobra rising behind.

According to the watchman who let me in and kept a keen eye on me, Gurudev not only had never set foot inside the monastery after its inauguration, but he had ordered that none of the traditional paintings depicting the various deities of the Tibetan Buddhist pantheon should adorn the temple walls. 'What would a Hindu or a Christian feel walking in here?' Gurudev had asked. 'This temple must be for everyone, and for no particular denomination or creed.' So the walls of Ghising's greatest present for Gurudev remained bare and the temple stood empty of its master, his disciples, and any real signs of life.

Gurudev's throne at the monastery

23

BLACK MONEY

I was in Gangtok some time later when I heard Gurudev was staying at a devotee's house below the city. I dropped what I was doing and went down there and as always I was immediately part of the entourage—even though I didn't really want to be. I didn't feel comfortable riding in Ghising's new gift to Gurudev, and his new attendants were almost militant in the execution of their duties. I knew none of them from before, and even Pema wasn't there. I did not feel at home. What I wanted was to have some time alone with Gurudev in order to ask him what exactly he was doing associating with Ghising and his political cronies. And actually it was better to do this in Sikkim than in Darjeeling, since the influence, effect, and corruption of Ghising and his associates stopped at the border.

I spent a few days hoping for a break in the schedule, a moment free, such as there used to be, when I could be alone with Gurudev. I even managed to line up various people to translate for me so that I could record Gurudev's answers with precision should the opportunity arise. But it never did. Then one morning I heard that the next day Gurudev and his entourage would be returning to Darjeeling. I became desperate. I had to finish the book, and to do that I had to at least give Gurudev the opportunity to provide answers to the questions that were proving beyond my comprehension. At the time I even became convinced that Gurudev somehow knew exactly what I wanted from him and was deliberately providing me no opportunity.

It was the afternoon before his departure. Gurudev was holding court in the master bedroom of his wealthy sponsor's house below Gangtok. Though the house was crowded because of his presence, a moment came when there were only a handful of us sitting on the floor around the bed: the sponsor, a few members of his family, and some of the attendants. I was sitting next to the attendant with the best command of English. My desperation that Gurudev would leave the next day without my putting my questions to him was acute. This might be my last opportunity.

So with a pounding heart, I asked the attendant if he would interpret something for me. He agreed, and I said to him, 'Please ask Gurudev this: What is your relation with Subash Ghising?'

The attendant, a boy from a tea garden in Darjeeling, laughed nervously at my request. But I insisted. 'It's my question, not yours. Please ask him *for* me.'

He did.

'The foreigner is asking what your relationship is with Subash Ghising.'

The buzz in the room suddenly stopped. You could have heard a petal from one of the flowers piled on Gurudev's table glide through the air and hit the floor.

'He is a devotee,' Gurudev replied, 'like many. That is all.'

'But isn't it true that he is your main sponsor?'

'Sometimes Subash Ghising is my sponsor,' he replied. 'Not always.'

I screwed up my courage to say what I thought. I could feel my blood pounding through my ears. 'Everybody knows that Subash Ghising is a dangerous man,' I said. 'Some even say he uses violence to stay in power. Most people I speak with say they are afraid of Subash Ghising and wish he were gone. Yet when I ask them why they don't say something, the most common answer is that they don't want to become six inches shorter. You are from Darjeeling. You must know what that means. They are talking of a gang of goons coming with *kukris* and beheading them. This is no imagination on their part. This is no idle threat. This is very real, and everyone in the Darjeeling Hills knows it.'

My interpreter proved quite good, and interpreted what I said, sentence by sentence.

I continued: 'You know, Gurudev, that I have the highest respect for you and your teachings. The one thing I cannot understand is your relationship with Subash Ghising and his deputies. It confuses many of your devotees as well. So please tell us, how can you deal with such men?'

Everyone in the room started speaking at once, but Gurudev put up his hand to silence them. 'Each person is different,' he said. 'Some are deaf; some are mute. You might think one is good, the other bad. The mother has equal love for each of her children, the same love for the one that is good and the one that is bad, a thief or a good man. So it is that everyone is equal to God. That kind of love is God's love. Equal love for all.

'I must give love to all people and guide them in the right direction. If I call Ghising a bad man and have no relations with him, how can I influence him? And with a man like Ghising, it does not always work. Ghising was attacked some time back. I went to see him in his hospital bed in Siliguri. Ghising said he wanted to call a bandh. I know how much suffering bandhs cause ordinary people. So I told him not to call this bandh. But he did not listen. What to do?'

I looked around, and the room was suddenly full of people. They had heard what was going on, and they came to see. It was a far cry from the private discussion I had envisaged, but it was too late to put the cork back in the bottle. Pema came in. He stood protectively at the foot of Gurudev's bed.

'I cannot make anyone do anything,' Gurudev continued. 'After I told Ghising not to call the bandh, he said if he didn't achieve Gorkhaland he would start a Third World War. I told him if he did that I could not protect him. Ghising is like bin Laden, like George Bush. Dangerous—same-same.

'Each of us has two qualities within—the good qualities and the bad qualities. If the inside is good—good. If outside is good, and inside not good—not good. George Bush—white outside, black inside.' He laughed.

'We are used to saying there are good and bad people. But if we make an operation on ourselves, we'll find our stomachs very dirty: there is dirtiness within us all.'

He made his finger like a flying insect. 'It is like the bee. If we do good to the bee it will give us honey. If we do bad to the bee, it will sting us. It is like the poisonous snake. Isn't the poison also used as the medicine?'

'But Gurudev,' I said, 'how about your new vehicle? Isn't it a gift from Subash Ghising?'

'Yes, it is.'

'How can you accept a gift from such a man and then enjoy it? Everybody knows Ghising is the head of the Hill Council. He gets a salary from the government. He is a public servant. He cannot possibly earn enough clean money to buy his guru such a nice vehicle. How much does such a vehicle cost?'

The driver had come into the room. Gurudev asked him, and Pema put in his idea and it was agreed among the men in the room—who, now that I looked at them, were looking quite distressed at the direction the conversation was taking—that such a vehicle costs about nine lakh rupees (900,000 rupees, or about US $20,000).

'OK,' I said. 'Let's say someone steals a TV and gives it to you as a gift. If you know the TV was stolen and still you accept the gift, in most countries you can also be found guilty of theft—you can be thrown in jail. Now, you know Ghising cannot possibly afford through legal means to buy you such a vehicle. Therefore it must be black money that bought that vehicle. You accepted it, and now you ride in that vehicle, enjoying the comfort. Please, Gurudev, tell me, how can you justify this?'

I felt emboldened to continue on my reckless course by knowing I was asking about Gurudev's relationship with Ghising not only for myself, but for all those devotees who were made uncomfortable by it, but could never ask. And Gurudev's relationship with Subash Ghising confused many. Once I had been riding with a carload of devotees, following Gurudev's vehicle to the next event. Somehow, the subject of Subash Ghising came up. I think there had been the threat of a bandh. It was clear none of them were in favour of Ghising or his underlings. So I asked them what they made of Gurudev's relations with these people. 'None of us can understand it,' came the reply. 'We all wonder, but how can we ever ask?'

I am sure no one had ever questioned him about it, not so directly. The room was buzzing again.

Gurudev put up a hand again to silence the crowd, which was growing by the minute as word spread about what was happening.

'As you know,' Gurudev said, 'this is not the first vehicle I have accepted from Ghising. The first was a Marshal and I used it for quite some time. But I returned that vehicle. I returned it when Ghising acted with particular violence, as I told him I would. This is how I engage Ghising. Ghising felt guilty that I had returned his vehicle in that way. So he presented me with this new one, even better. I accepted it, but only under one condition: I told him that if he does anything violent I will return the vehicle, publicly. I gave back that first car. He knows I will do it again. He will have to think of that before he commits violence again. Maybe it will stop him. Maybe not. This is my way to try to stop him from creating violence in the Hills. It is a balance. For peace.'

I pressed on. 'But the fact remains that in the meantime you are enjoying his gift. You accepted a gift of stolen money. Where did the money come from for the vehicle?'

Pema spoke up in defence of Gurudev, his voice tense. 'It is from the Tourist Department. It is not Gurudev's vehicle. He cannot sell the car. It is only to ride in. It is a government vehicle. You can see the papers. We don't *own* the vehicle. It is on loan. The minute they say they want the vehicle back, we must give it back. You see, it is part of his monastery, the one Ghising built for Gurudev. The monastery is also under the Tourism Department.'

'Is this true?' I asked Gurudev. 'This vehicle was bought from Tourist Department funds?'

'Yes, it was.'

'How is *that* right?' I exclaimed.

My heart was really pounding now. Probably I should have taken a breath.

'The Tourism Department,' I said, 'is set up to use taxpayer money to help local businesses attract tourists and to help their business. Look, I'm the only tourist here! This is taking money for one thing and using it for something else. How could this possibly be a legal use of Tourism Department funds?'

'If I don't engage these people,' Gurudev said, 'how can I influence them? I accept his gift in order to engage him. Look, George Bush is searching for bin Laden. If he would search for bin Laden with love and with peace he would get him. But he has made a war, so he has not caught him. It is just like that. We have to catch that man with love and peace. If I push Ghising away, if I reject his gift with negative judgement, it would be an act of violence, and then he would repeat that violence. Instead, I love him. And through that I try to transform him, for the good of all.

'If you want to control someone, even a member of your family, maybe a son or a daughter, if you scold them, if you beat them, if you treat them like an animal, then *definitely* one day that person will attack you.

'There is a very bad situation for Nepali people in Bhutan. The Bhutanese king has been making problems for them. He has kicked many out, and others have had to flee. There are now about 100,000 refugees in Nepal, living in United Nations camps. I go to these refugees in their camps, and they are angry. I tell them not to try to attack the king of Bhutan or say anything against him. I tell them to love him. If you do so, I tell them, one day you will *definitely* be able to go back to your homes. The king will change; through love and affection and through peace the situation will transform.

'Many times I go to tea gardens. Often I am invited to the manager's house, or to the tea garden owner's. They lay out a large table and offer me all manner of sweets and food. But I take only one piece, a single bite, and I tell them why. "You are offering me this wonderful food," I tell them. "I will take it as prasad, as an offering. The big offering to me will be when you look well after your workers, when you give them fair wages, when you provide them with good roads, water, and doctors. Then your actions will be in accord with the dharma—when you do good for others."'

Gurudev's fist came down on his open palm. 'Sometimes to do good you must smash a diamond. And to prevent something bad, you cannot give even one penny.' He snapped his fingers. 'You see, sometimes you have to accept the gift, other times you cannot—for the same effect. A knife in the hands of a thief can kill a hundred people. The same knife in a surgeon's hands will save a hundred lives. Only the way of thinking is different. The knife is the same. Money also can be used for good or to harm others. And money is just like blood. It must flow freely. Never hold on to too much of it and block it. Free it. Let it circulate. It has to circulate, it has to move.'

Gurudev pointed to various parts of his body. 'This part America. This part India, this part Pakistan. The body is like the world, and money is like the blood. If the blood stops in one part of the world, it will affect the entire world, won't it?'

Gurudev was silent for some moments. 'I can only do my work according to my ability. Within that limit, I always try to help those in need. Suppose there is a car going to Siliguri, and you want to go there. And suppose that car is full. If you get in that car it will be beyond its capacity. It could tip over into the river. The car can take only up to its capacity. In the same way I can do only to my capacity. Often Ghising doesn't do as I advise. I never get angry. Still I give him my love.'

There was a hush in the room.

'Subash Ghising is like a broken-down engine,' he continued. 'Doesn't the mechanic have to go to the engine?'

Recently I had stumbled upon a story from the Bible that seemed pertinent, and I told it to him. I had read it in *The Times of India*. It was from the Book of Matthew. Jesus was seen having dinner with some tax collectors. Tax collectors were a particularly corrupt lot in Jesus's day, members of the community who extracted money from people to give to the occupying Roman Empire after keeping a hefty slice for themselves. They were considered the worst kind of traitors, inflicting pain on their neighbours for personal gain. Afterwards, people complained to Jesus's disciples, wondering what kind of master he could be, accepting a meal from such bad characters. When Jesus heard of this, he gave them a spiritual lesson: he said it is not the healthy who have need of a physician, but those who are sick. Jesus came, he said, to help those in need.

'If you know this so well,' Gurudev said when I was finished telling him the story, 'how can you ask me about my going to Subash Ghising? You should know why. We should never condemn, but always extend our hand.'

For so long it had hurt my heart to question Gurudev's motives. Now, it seemed, I'd tested him and once again he'd come out shining. There was a palpable release of tension in the room. Gurudev held out his hand. I jumped up and we shook hands.

'If we discuss like this,' he said, 'we will all gain knowledge. No knowledge without college! These are very important questions—very important for your book.'

And with that the meeting broke up and we cleared the room so that Gurudev could rest.

24

FLOWERS AND CHOCOLATE

'Mr Thomas, I would like to have a word with you.' The room had just been cleared, and I was being led outside by an important Sikkimese devotee of Gurudev's, a well-dressed and cultivated man. We sat on two chairs in the house's courtyard, and he leaned towards me.

'You are quite new over here, I would say, and I would like to give you advice from the core of my heart.' He rocked his head in the Indian fashion and looked with compassion deep into my eyes. 'Please believe me that it is from the very core of my heart that I am giving you this sincere advice.'

He glanced around furtively, and I noticed we were being watched by just about everyone who had been in the room. Gurudev's new attendants were gathered around Pema, and they were in heated discussion, eyeing me. The look in their eyes was like ice.

He leaned towards me and continued almost in a whisper: 'When you are in Darjeeling, when you are over there, and you ask this type of question in front of the people, it could be very dangerous for you. You see, everybody knows Ghising's rowdies. He is a politician and everybody has fear of him. He could send in his spies, and this could put you in danger. It is for this reason that I am giving you this most sincere advice.'

I leaned towards him now and replied in a hoarse whisper, 'Yes, I am quite aware of this. In fact I've been awaiting the opportunity to ask Gurudev these questions for over two months now. I wanted to speak to him alone, but I never got the opportunity. When I heard that he'd be returning to Darjeeling tomorrow I became desperate. I have to finish my book, and to do that I needed to hear his side of the Ghising story. That is why I finally asked him, even though others were present. And I must say I was happy with his response. It was what I thought he'd say, and what I was hoping, but I *had* to hear it from him. I was fully mindful of the dangers—you should have heard my heart pounding—but I was desperate, and I figured better here than in Darjeeling.'

'You are quite right, Mr Thomas, better here than in Darjeeling,' he said. Then he continued in a whisper both softer and more intense, 'But even here there may be spies; his people may be listening. What you said about Ghising could be very dangerous. Everybody knows, but nobody says. These are politicians, and I *hate* politics like anything. They use fear to control the people, not love like Gurudev. Their politics is the politics of fear. And they can go to any extent.'

He pointed to a large flowerpot in the corner with the withered stem of last year's flower poking out of it. 'One thing as per my experience: let us take the bad things, like the dirt in that pot, which is useless and only a nuisance. If you dig around in it, it will only come back in your face.'

He looked deep into my eyes. 'I just thought I'd give you a friendly advice. I hope you don't mind what I am telling you. It is sincere advice. So please be careful.'

'Of course,' I said. 'I will be extremely careful.'

❖ ❖

I woke up and glanced at my watch. It was 3:35 a.m. I was sleeping on the floor next to Dawa. He had arrived in the early evening, after my rather pointed discussion with Gurudev, and I was very glad to see him. I trusted Dawa. I knew him from the first moment I stepped into Gurudev's movie, and there was something clean about him, inside. He combined intelligence and innocence, and we had developed a true friendship over time.

I was especially glad to see him because of the behaviour of the other attendants since my talk with Gurudev. Call it paranoia, call it noticing the obvious, but I swear these guys had eyed me all evening with such a cold glint in their eyes that if Gurudev wasn't in the vicinity they would have come after me. They were too young and impetuous to understand Gurudev's answer to my questions. All they had registered was that I had publicly questioned not only the guru, but the political leader as well—and all in one breath.

We were sleeping in the room next to Gurudev's. There was a glass panel over the door to Gurudev's room and I could see that the light was on. I could hear agitated voices—those of the young attendants. I could also hear Gurudev. He was obviously trying to calm them down. I sat up and cocked an ear. They were speaking rapidly in Nepali and I could make out only a few words. '... Thomas ... Subash Ghising ... black money ... vehicle ... Thomas ... Subash Ghising...'

I poked Dawa awake. 'Dawa,' I whispered. 'Listen! What are they saying?'

Dawa sat up, instantly alert. He stared at the door, and a serious look crossed his face. 'Oh,' he said, and listened some more. 'Oh ma-ma, oh my, oh ...'

'What, Dawa, what? What are they saying?' He put his hand up to quiet me so that he could listen more. 'I think you better not go back to Darjeeling for some time. It might be dangerous for you.'

'What do you mean, dangerous?'

'The boys are angry,' Dawa said in a measured tone as if making a summary, 'and though Gurudev is trying to calm them down, word of what you said, what you did, might get back to Darjeeling.'

'And then?'

'They can be quite violent over there. It isn't like here in Sikkim.

'Yes, Dawa. I *know*. My God! What have I done?'

'It isn't that bad,' Dawa whispered. 'If you wait some time, you'll probably be all right.'

'Probably?'

The light in the other room went out. Dawa went back to sleep. I lay the rest of the night not daring to close my eyes, my body tensed, fearful of the door opening and of a glint of steel.

In the morning I woke Dawa up. 'Dawa, I want to speak with Gurudev about what happened last night and I want you to interpret. I feel I made a tremendous error, asking my questions in public.' I was exhausted, tense, and frightened.

'No. I don't think this would be good. It isn't that serious.'

'But Dawa, you said it would be dangerous for me to return to Darjeeling.'

'Yes, I think it would be. You should not go back there.'

'How can you then say it isn't serious? I must speak with Gurudev about this so that I know. And I want you to interpret.'

'I don't think this would be good. It would only get the boys more angry.'

'I want the conversation in private, just Gurudev, you, and me in the room.'

'No. Please, Thomas, this would not be good.'

'Dawa, is this because you don't want to get involved? I'm

thinking I have to flee the eastern Himalayas because there could be fucking murderers after me—so I take this very seriously. I've got to speak with him.'

'I don't think—'

'You're afraid because of your position?'

'No, it's not that—'

'Then what?'

'Sometimes people want to speak with Gurudev privately, and this is never granted—'

'I don't care.'

I grabbed Dawa by the arm and dragged him into Gurudev's room. The boys stiffened and flanked Gurudev's bed.

'Gurudev,' I said, 'I want to speak with you and have Dawa interpret and have no one else in the room.' The boys glared at me. Cold shivers rode up my spine.

Gurudev asked me, 'On what topic?'

'I don't want to say with others in the room. It is private. It's as simple as that.'

Gurudev motioned for the boys to leave. They stiffened, and didn't budge. Never had I seen anyone defy his order. They wanted to protect him, from me. Gurudev snapped at them. 'Now go!'

Reluctantly they moved to the door, eyeing me.

I bolted the door from the inside.

'Gurudev,' I said, 'I'm afraid that what I said yesterday has caused troubles. I've been wanting to ask the questions I asked yesterday and I always imagined it like this, with one person interpreting and no one else in the room, and I think I made a mistake by doing it in front of the boys. Now I feel in danger. I've been warned not to return to Darjeeling. What can I do?'

Gurudev spoke, and Dawa interpreted: 'What he is saying is that you spoke yesterday from your heart. You said that though he is a very revered guru, a master, whom others take as a living god, you were questioning his association with corrupt politicians.'

'Yes, that is what I was asking about. But what I'm afraid of is that I was so bold as to speak openly what most people feel about Ghising but never say publicly. And now I'm afraid.'

'He is saying,' Dawa interpreted, 'that he explained to Pema that it is all right, that you were right to ask your questions. Yet whatever is in your heart, you shouldn't necessarily speak of it to each and every one. For instance, he is saying someone might ask you about George Bush, or bin Laden. You might think they are bad people. Of course they are. But there are millions who are in favour of Bush, and sometimes you must be careful.'

'But that is the mistake I made,' I said. 'The people around Gurudev are in favour of Ghising. I realize that now, and in front of them I said bad things about him.'

Dawa interpreted my words.

'Gurudev is saying that you are not the first one to say bad things about Subash Ghising. There are people who are *staunchly* opposed to Ghising, and Gurudev still goes to their villages, to their homes, and he is always trying to make peace between them and Ghising. In the present political situation, for instance, there is a lot of tension between Ghising and the chief minister of Sikkim, Pawan Chamling. This is because when there are strikes in Darjeeling, the road to Sikkim is always cut. Gurudev also goes to Chamling. He tries to act as a bridge between them.'

After Dawa interpreted this, Gurudev spoke quite some time. Dawa listened carefully. I could tell they were talking about Pema.

'He is saying that Pema has two qualities: compassion and a hot temper. Even when Gurudev is ordering Pema what to do,

Pema is not following that order. Gurudev is saying you should do one thing: you should buy some sweets, a yellow *khata*, and a bunch of flowers. Give these to Pema and shake hands.'

'OK,' I said, 'I will do this. But I also want to make clear to Gurudev that my questions yesterday were asked out of full respect. Gurudev once said it can take a disciple up to seven years to test the teacher and seven years for the teacher to test the disciple. And I feel that I am still in that testing phase.'

'You have not completed seven years, so you are not perfect. He is saying like that.'

In my mind, *he* was the one being tested, but I let it slide.

A fist pounded on the door. It was Pema, demanding to come in. Gurudev motioned to Dawa to unlock the door. Then Gurudev told me in a whisper not to forget the sweets and flowers.

Pema and Gurudev

❖ ❖

Dawa and I walked up the road to the market. Dawa was also on a mission for Gurudev. One of the many unusual things Gurudev gave out was underwear. Men's underwear. Dawa was earnestly trying to fulfil his master's instructions to buy ten pairs of black Jockey underwear. And it wasn't easy on a Sunday morning in Sikkim. Nor was it easy to find cut flowers of a suitable quality to sooth Pema's hot temper. The only flowers I could find were wilted. I grew desperate. We found a sweet shop and I bought a box of the finest balls and squares of honey-drenched Indian sweets and chocolates available, gift-wrapped and tied with a big red bow. This should do its part to keep my head attached to my neck, I thought to myself as I left the little shop, but the flowers continued to prove elusive. It simply wouldn't do to present wilted flowers on such an important occasion. And Dawa was having his own little crisis: not many clothing shops were open at that hour, and while some of them had men's underwear, only a few had the higher-quality Jockey, and none of them had the particular cut Dawa's master had sent him to purchase. Gurudev would be leaving for Darjeeling at midday, so we didn't have much time.

I gladly laid out twice as much as I should have for a bunch of cut lilies whose stems were already beginning to grow tired, and after Dawa found his underwear—only half of them in black and the rest in dark blue—we headed back to the house.

Gurudev was already getting ready to leave. Pema was loading the vehicle. I waited until I caught Pema alone in a room.

'Pema,' I said, 'I have something for you.' Swallowing both my pride and my sense of justice, I handed him the box of sweets and the bunch of flowers. I took out the yellow ceremonial scarf I had folded in the prescribed way and put it around his neck with a little silent prayer that it might protect *my* neck.

'I know you were angry at what I said yesterday,' I said in as meek a tone as I could muster. 'Please believe me that I didn't mean to offend. I am a foreigner, and sometimes foreigners act in insensitive ways. I never meant to cause any harm. And now I know I shouldn't have spoken how I did. It was very impolite. It upset you and I know it. Please forgive what I said and accept these gifts as a little token of my apology.'

Pema laughed nervously. 'You needn't have done this,' he said.

'I did.' My hand instinctively went to my neck. 'I'm sorry and I want you to know I'm sorry, so we can be friends again.'

'Don't worry,' he said. 'You are not in danger.'

Who had mentioned danger?

Soon after that, they placed Gurudev in his seat in the now-disputed vehicle, the road crew got in after him, and amid clouds of incense and the sounds of horns and cymbals such as I was well used to at Gurudev's departure, they went south out of the city and back to Darjeeling.

That was the last I would see of Gurudev for over two years.

25

BOOK, WHAT BOOK?

I stayed on in Sikkim for some time, and while there an old woman told me a story of how when she was young she'd followed a charismatic Tibetan lama on an expedition with over 300 people high into the snows and ice of Mount Kanchenjunga in order to find a hidden valley of immortality, a magical place of wonder fabled in both Tibetan and local tradition. I started tracking down other people who had been on this remarkable journey and began my research for what would become my book *A Step Away from Paradise.* I visited places important for the book and interviewed people who had been on this improbable expedition. Though this was important work, I was really stalling my return to Darjeeling, fearful of what awaited me there. Sikkim is a restricted zone because of its proximity to Tibet, and foreigners are allowed a maximum of a two-month visit. I stayed out my two months and with some trepidation took a share jeep to Darjeeling.

I was alternately fearing this return and feeling silly for that fear. How could I take myself so seriously as to think my verbal transgression against Ghising great enough to merit anyone doing me harm?

The police and other authorities routinely turned a blind eye to killings amongst local Nepalis. A notable example was when a man was literally hacked to pieces with *kukris* at the taxi stand. I heard the news as it spread across town. It was a busy market day and the murder took place at 10 a.m. not more than twenty steps from the police station and within sight not only of the two guards at the station door, but hundreds of citizens. The police fled, and not a single civilian witness came forward. In Darjeeling, one of the ways power is expressed is by killing in broad daylight in front of as many witnesses as possible. The more brazen the attack, the greater the fear instilled in the witnesses and therefore the greater the impunity. This demonstrates the unfortunate relationship between fear and power in the Darjeeling Hills. Thus the saying in Darjeeling that if you stick your head up, if you speak out against the rulers, you will become six inches shorter. And they aren't talking about the bottom six inches. Beheadings were a surprisingly common form of political expression during the violence in the late 1980s. There were heads impaled on stakes in those difficult times, heads of journalists, school directors, and others who had tried to expose what was happening. It is not unheard of today.

I used to go photographing quite a bit in the main bazaar in Darjeeling. There was a public toilet I sometimes used behind the vegetable market, not out of choice but out of necessity. It was a filthy place, thick with the almost unbearably pungent stench of urine. One morning the news spread through town that a man's head had been found in this public toilet. The body was later found a few alleys away. This particular incident was apparently not political but the result of a drunken dispute between porters.

The longer I stayed in Darjeeling the more aware I became of this dark underbelly, so chillingly base in its raw violence. One could feel the city go into shock after each of these murders, the roll shutters slamming down like a wave across the city as word spread and the city closed down. A bandh would be called, by whom I never knew, but I think it was by common agreement. Children would be sent home from school, and shops would be closed. All transportation except by foot would be forbidden. Always, it seemed Darjeeling was enshrouded in thick depressing fog when I heard such news. I had only to look at the face of the unsuspecting and naive Western tourist at such a time, blundering through the city having no idea what was going on, to recall my own first impressions of Darjeeling as a peaceful and harmonious place. Behind Darjeeling's exotic and peaceful exterior, attractive to the foreign tourist, there was tremendous darkness lurking, so primitive in its expression.

I comforted myself with the fact that if an American tourist were harmed, the embassy would become involved and an investigation would be demanded from on high. It would be a big event, splashed across national newspapers. Unusual pressure would be applied to catch the perpetrator. Surely, anyone contemplating such a deed would be deterred, knowing it would be different from an act of violence between locals and that there would be no impunity. That is, unless the perpetrator was exactly as impetuous and base as he'd have to be to contemplate the deed in the first place. And that is what I feared. It could even be one of Gurudev's own followers, deluded no doubt, wanting to right the double wrong I'd committed against the leader *and* the guru.

My fear was alloyed with a healthy dose of awareness of the degenerative effects of paranoia. It was with a slightly bemused inward smile that I observed the machinations of my mind, and tried not to take my fears too seriously. Surely, the biggest danger I faced was letting what was happening between my own ears spin out of control.

Darjeeling had been relatively strike free, so the place was swirling with tourists and steeped in normalcy. I checked into my regular hotel, and even got my old room back with the balcony overlooking the heart of the city. On the first evening I walked over to the Chowrasta, and a local Nepali man I'd never seen before, middle-aged, wearing a striped blazer and sunglasses despite the hour, addressed me by name and sent me on an irrevocable course of fear and paranoia. Once one finds the slightest external confirmation of one's fears, the line is easily blurred between one's paranoia—whose references are interior—and an objective condition of danger. One loses all sense of proportion.

'Mr Thomas,' he said, 'how is your book coming along?'

This question within an hour of my return from a man I did not know, who not only recognized me but also knew my name—and knew that I was writing a book—made me sputter.

'W-What book?'

'About Gurudev.'

My response to his question came with lightning speed and with a force of conviction that surprised me. Yet the moment I spoke, I knew it was true.

'Oh, that?' I said nonchalantly and with great candour, 'I've decided not to write that book. There will be no book. I'm working on something else now.'

The man studied me closely for a moment, then he turned and walked back to the small group of men with whom he'd been standing. He told them the news. Their stares were brazen and unwavering.

That was the moment I abandoned this book.

I had only two other choices. One was to airbrush out the political angle of the story, make it exclusively a dharma book, a religious book about the teacher and his teachings. But since I wanted the truth of my experiences to survive the contradictions, I knew this was not a viable option. My other choice was to publish it in all its details and risk my rather fond attachment of my head to my body. Since I'm more cautious than that, I could only write the book if I left the area and was willing to close the possibility of returning.

Despite its darker aspects, I'd grown rather attached to the Darjeeling and Sikkim area—something about it fascinated me—and I couldn't see sacrificing my future there. So the only choice left was to abandon the book. Luckily, I had stumbled upon the story that was to become *A Step Away from Paradise*, so I was not without direction or purpose for remaining in the area. I had friends there now, and the rich mix of peoples—which, it was true, sometimes erupted into violence—made an interesting dynamic.

That I was wise to abandon the book was confirmed in the next few days when I was approached two more times by men I did not know who addressed me by name and asked me about the progress of the 'Gurudev book'.

These incidents struck me as most unfortunate. Each time, I was just beginning to lose my fear. It seemed whenever I convinced myself I needn't worry, there was a clue that hinted otherwise. These men weren't aggressive; they were merely inquiring, and seemed satisfied by my answer. Yet the fact that so many people suddenly knew of the book and felt compelled to ask me about its progress struck me as most ominous. Cautious though I was of falling prey to irrational fear, it frankly got the better of me. I hoped my response that I'd abandoned the book in favour of another project was spread amongst those who might want to do me harm. I started keeping track of who was walking behind me, and for a while I stopped going out at night.

Time passed. I received no further inquiries, and thankfully the whole issue began to fade. Then one day as I walked out of my hotel I noticed an old beat-up blue car parked across the street with a cracked windshield. But it wasn't the crack that caught my attention: along the top of the windshield were stuck plastic letters that spelled out the name 'Gurudev', though the 'e' was missing. As I walked by it, I noticed sitting in the driver's seat a man I recognized from Tukvar. He was a short, stout man, perhaps in his mid-thirties, who used to show up sometimes in the middle of the morning to see Gurudev. I'd often had the feeling he'd been drinking, a feeling that was confirmed early one morning when I took a walk through the village and saw him with a group of young toughs passing around a bottle. I don't think I had ever spoken a word with him—in fact I had avoided him because of the dark atmosphere he exuded—but I recognized him sure enough, sitting in his old car across from the entrance to my hotel.

My troubles began when I returned to my hotel about two hours later and he was still there. It's amazing how quickly the fear I'd let dissipate came rushing back on me and hit me like a wave, constricting my breath.

'Oh, my god!' I thought to myself. 'They know where I am.'

Late that afternoon I was meeting a friend for a cup of tea on Nehru Road. The old blue car was gone. He must have been waiting for someone. I don't think he had even noticed me. Again, it was just my paranoia. I found it interesting to watch myself and experience the power of negative suggestion. Isn't it amazing how quickly the mind can weave a mere coincidence into the most sinister scenario?

I must admit that the next morning I couldn't help myself from looking for the car as I stepped out of the hotel's front door. He was back, parked about ten paces to the right of where he'd been, but again within clear sight of the entrance to my hotel. Why?

I turned left and moved quickly away, feeling his eyes burrow holes in the back of my head. When I turned around as nonchalantly as I could, he appeared to be reading a newspaper. He was also speaking now on his mobile phone.

It made no sense.

Why would he be staking out the front of my hotel? To learn my routine? But why? Surely, if they wanted to get me they just could. They wouldn't need to go to such extremes. And I wouldn't have attributed to them such long-term planning. Yet what other explanation could there be? There was a school a short way up the road. It was highly unlikely, but maybe he had a child who attended that school. Maybe he was just waiting to pick up his kid. Why did it necessarily have anything to do with me? Was I *that* important? I had a large umbrella with a curved handle like a walking stick. I started taking it with me, even on sunny days.

Over the course of the next ten days or so, the old blue car was parked there most of the time when I entered or left the hotel. At one point I considered approaching his open window, saying hi to him, and innocently asking him what brought him to the neighbourhood. But I couldn't muster the courage.

All this time I was of exactly two minds. My transgressions against Ghising were now over two months old, had occurred in Sikkim, and it all seemed too remote and far away to motivate anyone to plot anything against me. This was my voice of reason, cautioning me continually against the insidious danger of falling unnecessarily into fear. Though this voice was never completely silenced, it became overwhelmed by a very real fear that arose in me as a result of the man's presence outside my hotel. Nothing really made any sense.

I began to suspect I was being followed. Maybe he was staked out at the entrance to the hotel so he could follow me or perhaps contact others by mobile phone about the direction I was taking.

One day when he was parked out there I turned left when I exited the hotel and instead of following the road left again down to the bottom of Nehru Road, I dodged right onto a smaller road that narrowed to an alley and followed the top of the ridge to the Chowrasta, along which no car could follow. When I got to the other side of the alley—a walk of less than ten minutes—to where another road met the alley just before the pony stand and the Chowrasta, I was met with a dumbfounding sight. Parked at the head of this other road, facing the little alley along which I walked, was the old blue car with the plastic letters on the windshield spelling out 'GURUD V', with the 'e' missing. How could there even have been time for him to drive the circuitous route necessary for a car that would allow him to reach that spot before I did? He must have set off the very moment I turned the corner. But why? This time, and for the first time, he was looking up. He watched me pass with a look that could easily be interpreted as either blank, devoid of all recognition—or else as an ice-cold stare.

When I entered the Chowrasta I had the first of two tremendous strokes of good luck. I ran into a friend who lived in a flat off Nehru Road. He told me he and his wife were heading to the United States, and he offered to let me stay in their flat. The next day I made five or six trips to their flat, each time filling my daypack with my belongings so that to anyone watching it wouldn't look like I was abandoning the hotel. Of course, just as if to pull my leg and convince me of my paranoia, the blue car was conspicuously missing.

My second stroke of luck, and what has turned out to be the greatest good fortune of my life, was that I went that night to Sonam's Kitchen for dinner. Sonam is a wonderfully spirited Nepali woman who runs a small restaurant at which I sometimes ate. For a long time she had been telling me I should meet Barbara, a German woman living in Kalimpong who ran an NGO there for the study of traditional medicine, and organized sponsorship for a whole slew of children to go to school. One afternoon some weeks before, I was walking by Sonam's Kitchen when Sonam ran out and told me Barbara had come in from Kalimpong for the day, was eating lunch, and that I should go in and meet her. I was on my way back to my hotel, having spent the morning having tea with some friends and tea had morphed into lunch. I felt I'd wasted the morning, and was eager to get back to my room to write. So I declined Sonam's invitation.

As I said, Sonam's Kitchen was small, consisting of three or four tables, and guests often shared tables with total strangers. My luck that night was that I happened to sit next to a woman with long blond hair who, it turned out, was the famous Barbara from Kalimpong. To make a long story short, she invited me to come to Kalimpong and stay at her NGO, the International Trust for Traditional Medicine, which was housed in a village on the outskirts of Kalimpong in a large and rambling British-era house with guest rooms for foreign researchers. I was only too happy to have an excuse to leave Darjeeling for Kalimpong, a three-hour drive away. I went, and Barbara and I ended up falling in love. I moved in, and we ran the centre together. Later, we got married. I was sure to tell no one there (apart from Barbara) of my connection to Gurudev. The Gurudev manuscript, while not forgotten, was buried away in a folder on my hard drive.

Tea garden between Darjeeling and Kalimpong

26

THE IDOL OF INDIA

And so it was that the book you are now reading became an unfinished manuscript on my laptop's hard drive, and so it remained for a number of years. If a digital file could gather dust, it would have had a thick coating—probably of 0s and 1s—growing on it, disturbed only occasionally when I'd open the file and randomly leaf through it, wistful of how it seemed that the best stories could never be told. Occasionally I'd see a small procession of vehicles plying the roads of Kalimpong with a jeep at its head, and though my heart would race thinking it could be Gurudev, it always turned out to be someone high up in the army, another lama, or else a politician.

It was about two years later that Barbara and I were in Darjeeling for a few days. I hadn't seen Gurudev in all that time, and Barbara had never met him. We hired a vehicle and driver who would wait for us, and we drove down the steep switchback road through the tea gardens to Tukvar. It took a bit of courage on my part, but after all I had Barbara as my bodyguard. My feelings were just about as mixed as they'd been when I'd last seen him, though with time the contradictions tended to resolve themselves into a growing fondness—as is often the case with distance.

When we arrived, there was a buzz of excitement in the family: the prodigal son had returned, with his new bride. The women seemed genuinely happy that I'd come. And though the men were cordial, their manner was stiff, as if they were smiling because they had to. Shortly after we arrived—we were still standing outside—I went to an open spigot to wash my hands, and when I returned to the front steps one of the men I had been particularly close to was there. He came to shake hands, and I hesitated a moment because my hands were wet. He pulled away, all too ready to take my action as a snub.

'Thomas!' Gurudev exclaimed when we entered his room. He was truly happy to see me. Of all the people in Gurudev's scene, I knew that he was never bothered by my behaviour. He said the first thing that was on his mind. 'I always thought,' he said, "Why did Thomas speak so badly about Subash Ghising? Why? Now I know. Thomas was correct." I have taken that vehicle you were asking about and I returned it to Ghising.' He picked up a large bunch of bananas, broke off a few, and handed them to me with a huge smile.

Barbara had of course heard my story with Gurudev and seemed quite taken by him. Since she speaks Tibetan, they could easily converse. For me, it was another story. I was struck by how nothing in his routine had changed. It was as if I'd walked out the day before. He even showed me the same medicinal herbs as when we first met. I longed to feel the love I'd felt in his presence in the past, that beacon of light, but in reality I felt a bit bored by his routine, by his shtick, and wanted to leave. It was almost as if he were bored with it himself and I was picking up on that. Maybe I was bored because of my familiarity with the routine, even the little shock I felt to be walking into his room after two years only to find the same scene repeated. Something about his being in the eye of the hurricane, whipping the winds himself at every stage, bored me. It fell flat; the spark was gone. It was as if he were a flattened version of his old self—or at least that was my perception.

I knew well Gurudev's skill in controlling every aspect of his environment, including the actions and reactions of those around him. Was he trying to bore me into leaving so that I'd never have the urge to come back? Did he want to get rid of these prying eyes? If so, he succeeded. We left after what turned out to be a short and rather formal visit.

It must have been about two years later. Barbara and I had been going back and forth between Kalimpong and Oxford, where she was pursuing a doctorate in social anthropology. That year we were away from September through late winter. And when we returned, as our vehicle left the plains and started into the mountains towards Kalimpong, we could see that something was underfoot. The place was in ferment. Everywhere political banners were stretched across the road. There were convoys of flatbed trucks, jeeps, and vans full of people waving flags and shouting slogans. And the flags were everywhere, raised high on slender lengths of bamboo, in some villages in front of every house and every shop and stall. It was a flag we'd never seen before, comprised of green, white, and yellow stripes. It was the flag of a newly formed party that was challenging Ghising, and the story of its sudden rise to power was as astounding as it was surreal.

It all started with the reality television show *Indian Idol*, the hugely popular, nationally broadcast talent show sponsored by Sony. That year, one of the contestants was Prashant Tamang, a twenty-four-year-old Nepali from Darjeeling with a beautiful singing voice whose day job was as a constable for the Kolkata Police.

Bimal Gurung, Ghising's deputy from Tukvar whose event for Gurudev I had attended, the one often spoken of as the most feared man in the Hills, realized the potential of a Tamang win. Nepalis feel perennially marginalized and sidelined by Indian society. This feeling is largely behind their bid for Gorkhaland. If only one of their own could win the biggest talent show on the subcontinent! What Bimal Gurung realized when he backed Prashant Tamang to become Indian Idol was the tremendous swell of pride that would be felt by the Nepalis in India if Tamang won. What Gurung also realized was that if he could spearhead the successful bid, he could harness this pride for his own political ends. He could rise up and seize power.

The winner of *Indian Idol* was determined by the viewers of the show, who 'voted' for their candidate. Votes were cast by sending text messages on mobile phones. The contestant with the largest number of messages sent on his or her behalf was declared Indian Idol, instantly becoming a superstar throughout the Indian subcontinent. Bimal Gurung spearheaded a campaign across the Hills, setting up banks of people with mobile phones sending first hundreds and then thousands and ultimately hundreds of thousands and millions and finally tens of millions of text messages on behalf of their brother, their bhai, Prashant Tamang. Money for the text messages was donated, cajoled, and even extorted by Gurung's gangs from shopkeepers, contractors, schools, businesses, and individuals throughout the Hills. Rallies were held, schoolchildren were brought in. The fire spread to Sikkim and Nepal and to Nepalis across India who all felt the delicious swell of pride at one of their own stepping so gallantly onto the national stage. Even the Kolkata Police, for whom Prashant worked, raised funds and sent messages.

Seventy million text messages were sent on Prashant's behalf, more than had ever been cast in the history of *Indian Idol*, and he won. Euphoria spread across the Hills. People partied through the night and the next day was declared a holiday and schools were closed. Nepali pride had probably never been so high.

But it wasn't to last long.

A few derogatory sentences spoken against Nepalis the next day by a radio DJ in Delhi sent the Nepalis of Darjeeling from euphoria to fury. In India, Nepalis often hold lowly jobs, most stereotypically as gardeners and night guards; they are routinely discriminated against because of it. The DJ asked, what are we to do now that this Nepali guy has become Indian Idol? If all Nepali guardsmen became Indian Idols, who will guard our private property?

You could call the Nepalis of Darjeeling touchy, for this was all it took.

Even though no one in Darjeeling heard these comments (they were broadcast in Delhi, over 1,000 km away), by the next day news of it—and outrage—spread throughout the Hills. The Prashant Fan Club, which was headed by Bimal Gurung, declared a bandh. Effigies of the DJ were burned in the streets. And down in Siliguri, 5,000 supporters of Prashant Tamang marched to the courthouse to lodge an official complaint against the DJ. A skirmish broke out between the Nepali supporters of Prashant Tamang and Bengali shop owners, which turned into an all-out communal riot. About 800 Nepalis, including 50 schoolchildren, took refuge in the courthouse grounds and were followed by a rain of stones and bricks. Riot police moved in, but when teargas proved ineffective against the rioters, the police fled.

Harnessing the potent mix of pride and outrage flowing freely in the Hills, Bimal Gurung seized the moment and rose up against his political mentor, Subash Ghising. Ghising had not backed Prashant Tamang, and this proved to be his undoing. Accusing Ghising of selling out the call for Gorkhaland, Gurung announced the formation of his own party and vowed to overthrow Ghising with a renewed call for separate statehood. He made this announcement within a week of Prashant's win, and he did so before a crowd of 20,000 people in the heart of the Darjeeling market.

Most surreal was when I read in a Kolkata newspaper that Gurung had started coming every morning to Tukvar to get Gurudev's blessing and that many said the new party flag was Gurudev's creation, was blessed by him, and that the colours had mystical significance. Many people throughout the Hills attributed the genesis of Gurung's master plan, the spark that caught fire across the Hills, to Gurudev. I'd been to events Gurung had sponsored for Gurudev and knew they were from neighbouring villages in the same tea garden and that they both belonged to the Gurungs, one of the ethnic groups of Nepal. Later, when this most feared man in the Hills started spouting Gandhian non-violent rhetoric, the clear hand of Gurudev was apparent.

It was Gurung's struggle for power that we were witnessing upon our return to Kalimpong, some four months after Prashant's win. Gurung's party was sweeping across the Hills like a tsunami, taking whole villages at a time. You could literally see the green flags of Ghising's party fly over a particular village one day only to be replaced by the tricolour flag of the new party the next. Pitched battles were fought. Many of Ghising's councillors switched sides. Some didn't, and houses were burned, people fled. Huge rallies were held. When Ghising wasn't calling a bandh to stop the uprising, Bimal was, to prove his muscle.

Life for us in Kalimpong was becoming increasingly untenable. Barbara's NGO was set up as a base and research centre for foreign scholars and researchers. More than once we had to evacuate our guests in the middle of the night in defiance of a bandh. We had to advise people who were scheduled to come not to do so. Since the centre was dependent on the money researchers paid for staying there, money to pay the rent quickly ran out. We had already sent out an urgent appeal to former guests and supporters to help keep the centre alive. Their generous support helped for a while. We couldn't ask again.

All of this coincided with a very close brush with all-out violence in our village. One of Ghising's closest allies, the local councillor, lived just above us. Our village had officially turned to the new party, and people started circling the man's house and threatening to burn it down and kill him if he didn't switch sides and back Gurung. He refused. The few remaining Ghising loyalists in the village barricaded themselves inside this man's house and vowed to fight to the end.

The final straw came one morning when we heard that Gurung was calling for a forty-day bandh starting the next day to press for Ghising's ouster. Forty days with everything closed, no transportation, and not only no food in the market, but no market. Foremost in everyone's mind was the forty-day bandh in the late 1980s, when many were brought to the edge of starvation. Gurung's announcement of a forty-day bandh was an obvious echo back to this most horrific of bandhs. In people's stories of the struggle, it was always this bandh that marked the point of crisis, the darkest passage in a long, dark saga. Since everything would be closed for the duration of the bandh, people had to stock up for the announced forty days before it started. People were frantic, and many didn't have the money to buy what they'd need. So they resorted to selling off their family jewels to buy provisions.

It took us about ten minutes upon hearing of the bandh to realize what we had to do. It was a momentous decision made in a flash. No matter which way things went, there was no foreseeable end to the struggle and we realized it would be impossible to bring the centre through the political storm. This was an especially difficult realization for Barbara, since it was her vision and dream that brought the centre into being over twelve years before. She had created a vibrant community, a place that had meant a lot to a lot of people and now—like that—we realized it was through. We gave our landlord the requisite two months' notice, paid off the rest of the rent, and locked the building up tight. Then we fled to Sikkim.

As we drove through the city on our way down to the Teesta River and north to Sikkim, the air was electric with ferment. The streets of Kalimpong were full of groups marching under the new tricolour flag—men, women, and children full of anger and hope and uncertainty. We were overtaken by a huge crowd parading an effigy of Subash Ghising through the streets to a mock cremation. A few weeks before, this would have been unthinkable. No one would have even dared speak publicly against Ghising then. We were witnessing the release of years of pent-up rage.

Sikkim, as usual, was a peaceful oasis, a good place to ride out a bandh. We'd still have to return to Kalimpong in order to dissolve the centre and ship our belongings 1,200 km away to the western Himalayas, where we hoped to shift our base. But for now we were safe.

In a senseless reversal, which was to become characteristic of his tenure in power, Gurung called off his forty-day bandh after only a few days. When we heard the news we were happy that the people of Darjeeling wouldn't have to face starvation as in the forty-day bandh of the 1980s. Yet how sad for those poor folks who had sold off everything to buy sacks of rice and dal to make it through.

We stayed on in Sikkim a few weeks, travelling to the west to meet some of the people important for the book I was then working on, *A Step Away from Paradise*. We kept our ears open to what was happening in Darjeeling and read the newspaper whenever we could. People were now openly accusing Ghising of colluding with the government. They said he had sold out his call for separate statehood in favour of the status quo of the Hill Council of which he was the supreme leader. With the escalating threat to his regime, Ghising left the Hills to confer with government officials. And once Ghising was gone, Gurung blocked his return. Gurung's men, armed with sticks and knives, set up roadblocks and checkpoints on all roads leading into the Hills to bar his entry. Men, women, and even schoolchildren went on hunger strike to press for Ghising's resignation. As pressure mounted, hope was in the air that the tyrant would finally topple. Few voiced concerns that the new leader, Bimal Gurung, was the most feared of Ghising's underlings, renowned for the band of toughs under his command.

Finally, Ghising threw in the towel. He tendered his resignation to the government and ended his long years of iron-fisted rule. And with his ouster, control of the Hills was effectively handed over to his former deputy, the fourth-class dropout Bimal Gurung. Gurung's association with Gurudev seemed to be bearing some limited fruit. Though following in the footsteps of his predecessor by continuing to use fear as a political tool, he was at least making speeches espousing Gandhian non-violence, no doubt under Gurudev's tutelage. In such an area of darkness, this was a ray of hope. Unfortunately, Gurung didn't seem to understand the connection between rhetoric and deed. As he consolidated his reign, there were articles in the Kolkata and local newspapers about Gurudev's connection with Bimal Gurung, drawing the obvious parallels between Gurudev's relationship with the two leaders.

An article that came out in the *Himalayan Beacon* said:

> Political analysts believe that Gurudev's influence was not on religious and cultural affairs only. Subash Ghising took his advice even on issues concerning governance, which at times resulted in bizarre incidents.
>
> 'Subash Ghising is said to have thrown pebbles in the direction suggested by Gurudev at Tiger Hill at the foundation-laying ceremony for a helicopter strip there. The pebbles, which had been blessed by Gurudev, were to specify the location where the helicopter strip was to be built,' says Prof. Sharma, a prominent academician from Darjeeling now working at a prestigious college in Kolkata.
>
> 'I was present there and it was obviously comical when the chairman threw the pebbles and tried to convince the engineers that the helicopter strip was to be built at the place the pebbles fell. Of course, he could not understand the fact that a great deal of scientific study had to be carried on out for such an endeavour. Ghising further broke into an ugly outrage when the engineers tried to point out the selected site for the helicopter strip. To an extent, Karma Wangchuk Tulku [Gurudev] played into Ghising's paranoia and as a result extended that paranoia to extreme psychological levels where Ghising was ultimately led to believe that it was his destiny to become the 21st Century Prithivi Narayan Shah for Gorkhas in the Hills. Subash Ghising's ultimate removal after a coup d'état was a reckoning, but the end of Gurudev's influence over politics in the Hills still may not be that forthcoming.'
>
> Eccentric, revered and respected by a great multitude of the Hill population, Monk Karma Wangchuk Tulku Rinpoche may not be accepted by the elite and the learned as an individual who should be given the title of the Gurudev of all Gorkhas; his followers, who include a majority of the Hill people, may, however, have something else to say.

'I admire him greatly,' says Bimal Gurung, president, Gorkha Janmukti Morcha. 'He has had a great deal of influence in my life. When we formed Gorkha Janmukti Morcha and took out our party flag for the first time, it did not come from nowhere, everything was blessed by him,' the Gorkha Janmukti Morcha president adds.

A picture of Gurudev hangs at the office of the Gorkha Janmutki Morcha President, showing visitors to the office how much the Gurudev is respected.

'Whenever he enters the office he lights incenses before the photo of Gurudev and pays obeisance,' a close confidant says.

Truly, in present day politics in the Hills and beyond, it is common to worship Bimal Gurung but very uncommon to be worshipped by him. Monk Karma Wangchuk Tulku Rinpoche Gurudev is just one such individual.

After a few weeks in western Sikkim, we had to return to Kalimpong to dissolve the centre. It would be a tearful departure since the centre had been an integral part of the village for over a decade. But first we had to get from western Sikkim to Kalimpong. We decided to go via Darjeeling town. That way we could say goodbye to friends there. So we bought seats on a share jeep to Darjeeling. Our route took us south to the Rangeet River. We crossed the bridge from Sikkim into Darjeeling district, and proceeded up the steep switchback road toward the city of Darjeeling, perched at the top of the ridge. This route brought us up through the Tukvar Tea Estate and Gurudev's village. Quite spontaneously we had the jeep stop in the village, and we asked someone if Gurudev was there. I wanted to say goodbye. We were told he was there, and though I knew that hardly any vehicles plied the road between Tukvar and Darjeeling, especially in the afternoon, and though I knew the road was too steep to walk up with our luggage, we got down. Despite having spent so many nights in

Tukvar, there was no way I wanted to do so now. It was better not to be there when Bimal Gurung showed up in the morning for Gurudev's blessing.

The new concrete house of Gurudev's family, across the dirt track from the first house I'd stayed in, had grown by a storey or two. It was by now the largest house in the village with the exception of the tea garden manager's. It was both the family house and the place where Gurudev could hold court in a bigger way. There were rooms where devotees from afar could sleep, rooms for people to wait for their audience with Gurudev. Nothing was where it used to be. The kitchen at the back of the house was now a dormitory for women. Concrete staircases, still unfinished, spiralled to a concrete-slab roof covered with potted plants. People were bustling about, groups in small rooms with gifts and offerings, awaiting their turn to see Gurudev. Though we were treated cordially there was a palpable tension at our presence, as when you have the feeling you've been talked about in your absence and a verdict handed down. We had to wait to see Gurudev, and as we were brought by his room on the way to the roof for tea, somebody hurried ahead of us and closed the door. They obviously didn't want us to see who Gurudev was talking with and to overhear what they were saying. It felt strange.

After tea we were brought back downstairs just as Pema was leading four men out of Gurudev's room after a private audience. We shared a moment with these men as we fumbled to take off our shoes and they started putting on theirs, which had been piled outside the door. It was difficult to look any of these men in the face, for they averted our gaze and exuded an atmosphere of nefarious plotting and violent intrigue. They were dark and greasy, the type of thugs you saw stumbling from the sleaziest watering hole selling hooch behind the meat market in Darjeeling. Padding out in their socks, which

I couldn't help but notice were full of holes, they almost looked vulnerable, especially as they fumbled to get their shoes on over their heels.

If Gurudev were giving them advice on curbing the violence they exuded I would have heartily commended him as a tantric master taking on the darkest of forces, transforming the basest of lead. Most lamas sit in their monasteries and work on conquering their inner demons, instructing believers to do the same. These demons—representing the lowest level of human emotion such as lust and greed—are depicted in Tibetan Buddhism as a vast array of wrathful deities and demons, which are considered elements of the practitioner's own mind, to be conquered by elaborate visualizations and meditations. They are ultimately seen as having no intrinsic existence; they are but illusions whose hold on one is to be conquered. But what of the master who takes his practice out of the monastery—who even refuses his place at his own monastery—to seek out those with power, those whose base nature, whose violence, greed, lust, and aggression cause suffering to whole communities? By engaging them, by attempting to transform their nature with the perennial wisdom teachings, the transformation of a few individuals would potentially alleviate the suffering of thousands. Was this what Gurudev was doing behind closed doors? The question pulled at me as I fumbled with my shoes and, at the same time, it struck me that I would never know. I was there to say goodbye.

We entered Gurudev's room. And there he was, as always, sitting cross-legged on his bed, buckets of flowers on one side and mounds of fruit on the other. Attentive only to what was before him, he was buoyant in his simple adherence to the present moment. It struck me as powerfully as the first time I met him. What a contrast to the plots and intrigues surrounding him, to the very atmosphere left behind by those four men.

We presented him flowers we had plucked outside the house. He gave us each an apple and indicated for us to sit on a long bench that ran along the right-hand side of the room beneath the windows.

I wanted to tell him that we were leaving the area, that we'd come to say goodbye—and that we wouldn't be coming back. I had said goodbye to him before, when leaving the area for Delhi and to travel to the West. I'd felt his blessing carrying me forward, and especially at the beginning I'd felt the tremendous mystery and wonder evoked by his presence, the love that was all the greater by being entirely impersonal, love before it divided into love *for* anything in particular. It was like a beacon of light, shining on whatever stood before it. I had basked in that light and felt graced by the opportunity to experience it, fully aware of the preciousness of the gift.

Perhaps it was inevitable that things changed. Never was it my intention to sit under someone else's tree. It is not in my temperament. It was by chance that I wandered into Gurudev's life and the circus surrounding him. I had started immediately on the inside, accepted into Gurudev's world like a member of the family who happened to have been born on another continent. It was like that from the moment I appeared. My entry was spontaneous and marked by a quality of innocence. Goodbyes, weighed down by experience, are often more deliberate.

Once everything was open. Now the atmosphere was swimming with secrets. It was in the air. Though I longed for what was lost, all I wanted was to get it over with and get out of there. I was worried about getting up the hill.

While once it was an asset that I was writing a book about Gurudev—it opened doors and got people to talk—now, even though I had abandoned the book, doors were closing because of it; being a writer meant I had prying eyes, and for whatever reason there were things they didn't want me to see, conversations I was not to overhear. This was both obvious and painful to realize. The women in the family had told us that what the newspapers said was true, that Bimal Gurung was coming every morning for Gurudev's blessing. So Gurudev had his role in the new regime, which, despite its Gandhian non-violent rhetoric, was turning out every bit as violent as the one Gurung replaced. It was because of this we were uprooting ourselves and permanently leaving the area.

We hadn't got much further than telling Gurudev that we had just come from Sikkim and were on our way up to Darjeeling when the door opened and a group of people, Sikkimese village folk by the look of them, flooded in with sacks of rice from their fields. Gurudev immediately started having them fill a mound of small plastic bags, which somehow magically appeared so that the rice could be given out to many people. They were in the middle of this when Pema came in. He had a few private words with Gurudev, then told everybody that we'd have to clear the room. Since I wanted to tell Gurudev why we'd come so that we could get up the hill to Darjeeling, we lingered as the others left; but the moment wasn't right to say goodbye, not with Pema trying to clear the room. We were the last ones out. As we were putting on our shoes outside the door, the rough men we'd seen before were taking their shoes off again and going in. They must have had further business with him. We were brought upstairs and the women of the family made us more tea. Apart from Gurudev, they were the only ones who acted naturally towards us. Not having been privy to whatever discussions had undoubtedly occurred, their feelings towards me hadn't changed. They gathered around to speak with us, happy we had come, and delighted to touch Barbara's golden hair.

We were only halfway through our tea when Gurudev emerged from his room. We were brought down and followed him to his vehicle where the driver was waiting. Other attendants were there and they put Gurudev in the front seat and told us to get in behind him. Gurudev knew we were on our way up to Darjeeling. He was surely aware how difficult it was to catch a ride. We thought maybe Gurudev had anticipated our problem and would give us a lift. We enquired, but no, they were going back down the way we'd just come, towards the Rangeet River and the Sikkim border. We'd just come five hours on that narrow, jostling road and the last thing we wanted was to go back that way. They insisted, and we found ourselves playing well our role in the Master Director's movie by submitting to his will and squeezing in with eight or ten others. And thus it was we found ourselves setting off down the switchback road we'd just come up from the Sikkim border.

It was an incredibly tedious trip, packed in like that, the handle for the window biting my ribs with every bump in the road. We stopped what seemed like every five minutes—at this person's house and that, sometimes to pick up a potted plant and take it to someone in the next village, sometimes just stopping in the middle of the tea bushes, getting out for no apparent reason, then getting back in and continuing on our way. At one point we put a load of wood on the roof racks, tied it down, and delivered it to the next village. As always with Gurudev, there were multiple storylines, plots, and subplots being played out. It was as if he were a master at three-dimensional chess, an adept at picking the pieces, choosing their places on the board, and moving them himself. Since every move affected every other piece, to foresee effects required tremendous insight.

There was no doubt his taking a potted plant from one village and giving it to someone in another was working out a story between the people involved and between them and him. And there were many such stories going—one with each of us. And as always, he called all the shots; only he knew the desired outcome. One could only assume that he was so good at his role as Master Director that one's reaction was also in the script.

I had the feeling Gurudev was bringing us in the most tedious manner down the road we'd just come up in order to bore us to tears, frustrate us, and get rid of us once and for all. While I don't think his feelings towards me had changed, he was deeply into work that my witnessing and questioning could only hamper. This, of course, was pure conjecture, and if it were true would be entirely unnecessary, since if he'd just stop directing and manipulating every moment he'd find these prying eyes were going anyway. Who could blame him for not wanting me around, especially not when he had dealings with thugs the likes of which we saw at his house. I had proven myself only too willing to ask uncomfortable questions; I could only get in his way. It took us two hours to reach the bridge that marked the border with Sikkim. Gurudev told us to walk onto the bridge and look at the river while he sat in the vehicle reading a newspaper. People started coming to his window and he spoke with them. We found out later Bimal Gurung's party had held a large rally next to the bridge the following day.

Maybe a half-hour went by, and then we returned slowly to Tukvar.

The thugs were still there. They went back into a private audience with Gurudev and we were given a meal upstairs on the roof. Then it was arranged that since there was no other vehicle going up to Darjeeling, these men would give us a ride.

As we took our leave, we finally told Gurudev and the family we were leaving the area for good and that this was goodbye. It was a strange moment. The male members of the family showed no emotion, but one could sense they were glad. They were charged with protecting Gurudev from all harm and I was now suspect. I could only get in the way. The women of the family would have rushed up to press my hands and give an emotional farewell if they could, but the circumstance dictated they hold back. And Gurudev, the man at the centre, was happy—as always—not because we were leaving but because he exuded the happiness he always did, regardless of circumstance.

As we were moving towards these men's vehicle, one of the male members of Gurudev's family quietly warned them that we knew some Nepali, so they should not talk in front of us about what had transpired with Gurudev. We understood enough to comprehend the warning. On the way up, we tried asking them where they lived and what they did for a living, things like that to figure out who they were. All we could get from them was that they were businessmen. Everything about them smelled of darkness and thuggery.

It was just getting dark when they dropped us off at the taxi stand in the middle of the Darjeeling market. As we started walking up the narrow alley that passed behind the meat market and rose towards the Chowrasta, a thick fog, so characteristic of the city and my memory of it, engulfed us.

EPILOGUE

2013

Five years have now passed since we left Darjeeling. I've never seen Gurudev again. Occasionally we check online for the news from Darjeeling, and every time we are glad we left. Bimal Gurung is still in power and though at the moment things seem quiet, it seems but a lull in a programme of endless strikes and acts of political violence. Madan Tamang, a major opposition leader, was hacked to death in broad daylight in the middle of Darjeeling. A small army of police guards reportedly fled at the arrival of the *kukri*- and sword-wielding mob. This happened at the bottom of Nehru Road, right in front of a Tibetan restaurant I used to frequent. He was once Barbara's landlord and I knew him as well: a very intelligent and reasonable man. Gurung calls endless strikes, which he calls off, then re-imposes at will with no apparent logic. He has organized a youth brigade reminiscent of the Hitler Youth, the Nazi's notorious paramilitary youth group. Gurung's youth brigade was recently called up to act as a 'morality police force' to enforce a ban on holding hands in public. I kid you not.

The people continue to suffer under Gurung's rule as they had under Ghising's. I wonder about Gurudev's continuing role, but I'll never know. We're still in touch with people in our village so we hear first-hand the endlessly crippling effects of politics in the Hills.

Now that Ghising has gone from power and we are living in another part of the Himalayas, it has been possible for me to finish this book. We are continually surprised by how smoothly things work here and how peaceful a place can be. I hope I don't offend anyone by writing my experiences as honestly as I have.

When I think of Gurudev now, I miss the close relationship I was once honoured to have with him. I wonder how I could have done things differently; I imagine other possible scenarios. But in the end, the time itself in which we enjoyed our closeness has passed, and there is no turning back.

I've never been able to completely put my mind around Gurudev's dealings with the Hills' most unsavoury characters. It is too much of a stretch for me to take in in one breath such lightness and such incredible darkness. Since I've never seen Gurudev act in any way other than from the highest order of love, it has never worked for me to attribute impure motives to his actions.

I would like to oblige the reader with a conclusion, a set point of view about Gurudev. We expect our writers to offer us conclusions about the world they describe in their books. Perhaps this is because we expect the same of ourselves in our own lives. We try to draw conclusions about the world around us, and when we've succeeded we feel more secure in it. From the beginning, I strove for a single point of view from which to perceive and understand Gurudev, but always in vain. Now I have given up the folly of the search.

There are rituals in the Tibetan Buddhist tradition in which the lamas lure demons into the temple with offerings of liquor and incense. It is beautiful that they don't cast them out, as other religions do, but invite them in and entice them with vices. Once inside, the lamas open the ancient scriptures and give them teachings on love and compassion.

I think it is in that spirit that Gurudev does his work.

Gurudev, spinning the world

ACKNOWLEDGEMENTS

Since being in Gurudev's presence often gave me a glimpse of a realm beyond personal motivation and causality, I will begin by giving thanks to the happy coincidence that led to my first meeting with him on that cloud-enshrouded hillside in Sikkim. Unbidden, unplanned, unimagined or sought after, it planted the seed that gave rise to this book.

That said, first and foremost I would like to thank Gurudev for providing me with the rare gift of a front-row seat in what often seemed the greatest show on earth, which encompassed openness and candour as well as intrigue and shadows, both equality and hierarchy, unity of vision and total contradiction, as well as a deep sense of the absurd—usually followed by bright flashes of wisdom. It is a gift I can never repay. To Gurudev's family I give thanks for their generous hospitality, lively discussions, and for putting up with my inquisitive questioning with such grace. Thanks to Pema for accepting my apologies with my meagre gift of wilted flowers.

I thank the people of Darjeeling and Sikkim for opening their homes and hearts to me and for entrusting me with their stories. In return I offer this book, an outsider's glimpse of their beautiful and tumultuous land. Thanks to those who found themselves in the position of impromptu translator; without them everything would have been that much more mysterious. Special thanks here go to Dawa, who not only translated for me on innumerable occasions, but became a trusted friend and confidant.

In the preparation of this book I benefited from the insightful comments of a number of perceptive readers, including Anna Hopewell, Mark Canner, Ray Lowe, Steve Brock, Liz Nicholas, and Zazi Porcsalmy. I thank Jeffrey Heiman for his wise literary and aesthetic counsel throughout the years.

To my editor at HarperCollins India, Rukmini Chawla Kumar, whose careful read resulted in a cleaner and tighter manuscript, I offer my sincere thanks and respect.

On matters of the history of Darjeeling and Sikkim, I had the help of Dr. Saul Mullard and Niraj Lama. That said, all errors in this regard are my own.

And saving the best for last, I thank my wife, companion, editor, mirror, advisor, and sometimes bodyguard, Barbara.

PHOTO CREDITS

All photographs in this book were taken by the author except for the following:

- The childhood photos of Gurudev on pages 38 and 161, which are reproduced with the permission of Gurudev's family
- The photos of the author with Gurudev on pages 36 and 228 were taken with the author's camera by someone who happened to be there
- The photos on pages 165 and 188 were taken by Barun Roy of the *Himalayan Beacon* and are used with his permission
- The map is modified from the Internet version of *The World Factbook*, published by the United States government and found on Wikipedia (public domain)

ABOUT THE AUTHOR

Writer and photographer Thomas K. Shor was born in Boston, USA, and studied comparative religion and literature in Vermont. With an ear for unusual stories, the fortune to attract them and an eye for detail, he has travelled the planet's mountainous realms—from the Mayan Highlands of southern Mexico in the midst of insurrection to the mountains of Greece and, more recently to the Indian Himalayas—to collect, illustrate and write stories with a uniquely personal character, often having the flavor of fable.

Shor has lectured widely on his writings and has had solo exhibits of his photographs in Europe and in India. He can often be found in the most obscure locales, immersed in a compelling story touching upon fundamental human themes.

Visit him at:
www.ThomasShor.com

ALSO BY THOMAS K. SHOR

A STEP AWAY FROM PARADISE

THE TRUE STORY OF A TIBETAN LAMA'S
JOURNEY TO A LAND OF IMMORTALITY

Penguin Books, 2011
City Lion Press, 2017

IN THE EARLY 1960s, a Tibetan lama, a charismatic and learned visionary mystic named Tulshuk Lingpa, led over 300 followers into the high glaciers of the Himalayas in order to 'open the way' to a hidden land of immortality fabled in Tibetan tradition dating back at least to the 12th century.

Fifty years later, Thomas K. Shor tracks down the surviving members of this visionary expedition and entwines their remarkable stories of faith and adventure with his own quest to discover the reality of this land known as Beyul. What emerges is a breathtaking story alive with possibility, bringing the reader as close to the Hidden Land as a book possibly can. As the astounding account unfolds, the reader is sure to repeat the question constantly raised by the author in his interviews: And then what happened?

A STEP AWAY FROM PARADISE tells the story of Lama Tulshuk Lingpa's life and his unlikely expedition to a land beyond cares while reflecting on what this means for the rest of us. It draws on both research and extensive interviews with his surviving disciples and family members. The book is richly illustrated with portraits of those who went with Tulshuk Lingpa and the places he traveled to. The book also delves into the tradition within Tibetan Buddhism of Shambhala and the hidden valleys, which mirror legends around the world of utopias and lands of milk and honey, thus showing that the quest for the hidden land is a universal urge of humanity.

FROM THE FOREWORD BY JETSUNMA TENZIN PALMO

A STEP AWAY FROM PARADISE is a riveting tale of adventure, intrigue and Devotion. [It] deals with an aspect of Tibetan Buddhism that is in some ways more honest to the real spirit of Tibet than all the usual books on Tibetan doctrine and will, I am sure, be of interest to a wide audience. It is a fascinating account of a little-known charismatic figure that will challenge even the most skeptical mind and provide a fresh perspective on what we normally regard as 'reality.'

Like no other book I have ever read, A STEP AWAY FROM PARADISE is both unique and intriguing. Highly recommended.

INTO THE HANDS OF THE UNKNOWN

AN INDIAN SOJOURN WITH
A HARVARD RENUNCIANT

Escape Media Publishers, 2003
Pilgrim Publishers, 2006
City Lion Press, 2019

"I think you should come with me to India."

Thus begins the story of the author at the age of 21, when he happened to sit next to Ed Spencer, a brilliant 70-year-old ex-Harvard professor turned wandering holy man, who makes this offer within an hour of their meeting on a Greek ferry.

Though unsure whether the old man is some kind of a bum or a realized being or both, he agrees to go with this enigmatic stranger whose credo is: "Take the money out of your pocket and put yourself in the hands of the Unknown."

When they arrive at the border and Ed passes the money exchange with hardly a glance, Shor begins to understand the gulf that separates the old man from the rest of humanity.

The ensuing journey takes us on an epic trip by foot into the heart of South India and then to the Himalayas where the author makes his first contact with the Tibetan people.

Into the Hands of the Unknown has been revised and has a new Postscript describing Shor's subsequent encounters with Ed Spencer. The book was originally published as Part II of *Windblown Clouds*

FROM THE REVIEW BY THE RENOWNED BRITISH POET KATHLEEN RAINE

In Thomas Shor's narrative the absorbing writing is the least of his gifts: he creates the imaginative adventure of his life as he lives it.

Thomas Shor's life is a continual unfolding of those inner and outer worlds which his sense of wonder discovers continually. His story reminds us that we are, or could be, travelers in a world of marvels, of love, and encounters with men and women themselves on pilgrimages of the imagination. Did not the Emperor Haroun al-Rashid for a thousand and one nights hear in the city of Baghdad endless stories that make up the one story of the world? Once involved in Thomas Shor's adventure of life, one hopes only for more.

~Kathleen Raine (D.Litt., Cambridge; Commander of the Ordre des Arts et des Lettres, France; Commander of the British Empire; Winner—Queen's Gold Medal for Poetry, England, etc.)

THE MONK AND THE SLY CHICKPEA

TRAVELS ON CORFU

Escape Media Publishers, 2003
City Lion Press, 2019

THE MONK AND THE SLY CHICKPEA tells the story of a journey the author took in 1981 as a young man to the Greek island of Corfu. His journey starts in an idyllic coastal village in a house surrounded by lush fruit and olive trees. While many a young man's journey to Greece would feature a coastal village and even a strip of white beach, Shor's journey led him, with a certain inevitability, to the island's highest mountain, the wind-swept and craggy Mount Pantokrator, and to the ancient stone monastery that crowns its peak. It was there that he lived with the monastery's sole inhabitant of over forty years, the fiery-eyed Greek Orthodox monk Evthókimos Koskinás, a man of both the mountain and of God. From that stormy peak, often pounded by bolder-splitting lightning, sharing meals of chickpeas seasoned with the mountain's wild herbs drenched in olive oil, Shor comes to some startlingly profound insights for a young man of twenty-two.

THE MONK AND THE SLY CHICKPEA, which is revised and has a new Postscript describing the author's return to Corfu and his encounters with the monk after twenty years, was originally published as Part I of the book WINDBLOWN CLOUDS by Escape Media Publishers, USA, in 2003.

FROM THE REVIEW BY THE RENOWNED BRITISH POET KATHLEEN RAINE

In Thomas Shor's narrative the absorbing writing is the least of his gifts: he creates the imaginative adventure of his life as he lives it. He plunges into the story almost by accident, leaving a steamer bound for Athens by mistake at Corfu. But in Thomas Shor's life there are no mistakes, only opportunities, and before long we find him sharing the life of the last surviving monk at a monastery high on Mount Pantokrator, his meals of chick peas, garlic and olive oil, his toils, and the dense fogs and storms of the highest mountain on Corfu. The old monk wants him to become his successor, but life runs on, leading perhaps inevitably to the Indian subcontinent.

Thomas Shor's life is a continual unfolding of those inner and outer worlds which his sense of wonder discovers continually. His story reminds us that we are, or could be, travelers in a world of marvels, of love, and encounters with men and women themselves on pilgrimages of the imagination. Did not the Emperor Haroun al-Rashid for a thousand and one nights hear in the city of Baghdad endless stories that make up the one story of the world? Once involved in Thomas Shor's adventure of life, one hopes only for more.

~Kathleen Raine (D.Litt., Cambridge; Commander of the Ordre des Arts et des Lettres, France; Commander of the British Empire; Winner—Queen's Gold Medal for Poetry, England, etc.)

LEOPARD IN THE CITY

AN URBAN FABLE

City Lion Press, 2019

A Leopard is Loose in the City!

LEOPARD IN THE CITY tells the tale of a leopard, a real leopard of the jungle, who suddenly finds himself in the center of a huge European city.

If seen, even by a single human being, he knows his fate would be sealed—either with a bullet through his heart or the sting of a tranquilizer gun, followed by a lifetime behind bars at the city zoo.

And who's to say which would be worse? In the zoo he would live out his days being gawked at as an anomaly, the famous mystery leopard from who-knows-where, the wild beast everybody read about in the newspapers, the one who disrupted life in the city and then was caught.

What he really needs is a miracle.

In order to avoid detection, he only moves about in the shadows deep in the night. Finding no edge to the city, no place where the city ends and the jungle begins, he sets himself the task of learning the ways of human beings. By understanding them he hopes to discover a loophole, a way out.

Befriended by a house cat, he comes to understand that long before human beings domesticated cats and dogs, they domesticated themselves: they tamed their own wild natures. It was by harnessing themselves that they were then able to harness nature's laws, which led ultimately to the engineering of skyscrapers and the angled grid of streets which appear to have no end, and through which the leopard is now forced to navigate.

Should he give up the dream of escape and follow the path of domestication as laid out by house cats, whose ancestors sacrificed their wild natures for security? Is it true, as house cats would have it, that the way to freedom is to submit willingly to domestication? Does way to salvation really lie in captivity? Does freedom come from in accepting subjugation? Is safety truly found not in liberty, but in the confinement, in the comfortable fate of a house cat living a privileged life of leisure with a secure place by the fire?

SCULPTURE GARDEN OF THE GODS

ANIMATED LANDSCAPE PHOTOGRAPHY FROM THE GREEK ISLAND OF IKARIA

City Lion Press, 2018

The Greek island of Ikaria has gained notoriety lately for being a so-called "Blue Zone," one of the select places on the planet where people live the longest. This otherwise obscure island was also known to the Ancients as the birthplace of the Greek god of ecstasy and wine, Dionysus, who was born upon the rocky ridge of mountain that runs down the center of the island.

SCULPTURE GARDEN OF THE GODS, a book of black and white photographs and prose, is the fruit of the author's three winters upon this mountain—often blown by hurricane-force winds and engulfed in thick fog.

Shor weaves the poetic force of his eye with that of his pen to take us on a journey to this otherworldly landscape, where lashing winds sculpt solid granite into forms that look like living beings with an uncanny regularity.

It is a place of mystery and beauty, where the most enduring is dissolved by the most fleeting, where wisps of fog blown by a gale can cause an entire mountain-side to disappear in an instant.

GANGES LAMENT

BLACK & WHITE PHOTOGRAPHIC PORTRAITS FROM THE SACRED INDIAN CITY OF VARANASI

City Lion Press, 2018

THESE INTIMATE PORTRAITS from the alleys close to the Ganges River were taken in winter when the river mist rose into the alleys, often persisting throughout the day. These alleys are among the oldest continuously inhabited places on the planet.

Varanasi is known as the City of Learning and Burning, referring both to the city's numerous schools, universities, ashrams, and pundits, as well as the many funeral pyres where faithful Hindus burn their dead by the river. Life and death are often juxtaposed in this chaotic and ancient city.

While the photographs portray people from all walks of life—and from differing faiths, ages, and social standing—they are mostly of people that others tend to consider outcasts and shy away from: the poor, street-dwellers, beggars, rickshaw pullers, widows discarded by their families, mourners with their shaved heads.

www.ingramcontent.com/pod-product-compliance
Ingram Content Group UK Ltd.
Pitfield, Milton Keynes, MK11 3LW, UK
UKHW041634190726
13854UKWH00006B/2484